CRISIS DREAMING

CRISIS DREAMING

Using Your Dreams to Solve Your Problems

**Rosalind Cartwright, Ph.D.
and Lynne Lamberg, M.A.**

HarperCollins*Publishers*

To all those who shared their dreams

"Personal Constructs" test which appears on pages 48–50 adapted from Kelly, George. *The Psychology of Personal Construct* Vol. 1. Adapted by permission of the publisher, Routledge.

"Depression Symptom Checklist" which appears on page 281 and "Post-traumatic Stress Disorder Symptom Checklist" which appears on page 282 adapted from American Psychiatric Association. *Diagnostic and Statistical Manual of Mental Disorders*, Third Edition, Revised, Washington, DC, American Psychiatric Association, 1987. Used by permission.

HarperCollins books may be purchased for educational, business, or sales promotional use. For information, please call or write: Special Markets Department, HarperCollins Publishers, Inc., 10 East 53rd Street, New York, NY 10022. Telephone (212) 207-7528; Fax: (212) 207-7222.

FIRST EDITION

Designed by Alma Orenstein

Library of Congress Cataloging-in-Publication Data

Cartwright, Rosalind Dymond.
    Crisis dreaming : using your dreams to solve your problems / Rosalind
    Cartwright, Lynn Lamberg. — 1st ed.
        p. cm.
    Includes bibliographical references and index.
    ISBN 0-06-016761-0
    1. Dreams—Therapeutic use. 2. Psychic trauma. I. Lamberg, Lynn.
    II. Title.
RC489.D74C37   1992
616.89'14—dc20   91-58344

92 93 94 95 96 ❖/RRD 10 9 8 7 6 5 4 3 2 1

Contents

87369

Acknowledgments

MANY MORE PEOPLE help bring a book to publication than those whose names appear on its cover. Our special thanks to our editor Carol Cohen; her probing questions and skillful editing made the book richer and more readable, and she showed enormous tolerance for the idiosyncrasies of not merely one but two authors. We thank our agent Sandra Dijkstra for her advice and encouragement throughout the writing and editing process. We are grateful to Mary Lou Robbins for typing and retyping the manuscript without complaint. We also are grateful to our families and friends for their support and understanding when we were frustrated or preoccupied.

R.D.C. and L.L.

Rosalind Cartwright's
Preface

*H*OW WAS IT THAT IN MID-LIFE I became a dream researcher? It was an answer to my own life crisis. My husband had just walked out, leaving me with two small children and a heap of trouble. I was devastated, depressed, and sleeping badly, if at all. When I did sleep, the nights were filled with anxiety-ridden dreams. Well, I thought, since I can't sleep anyway, I might as well do something productive with my time. I hired a baby-sitter to spend the nights, and I opened a sleep laboratory to find out what happens when sleep is working well and why it goes wrong.

Right from the start, I felt at home watching the polygraph pens write out the sleepers' patterns of brain waves, waiting for the dream indicators to begin, counting the minutes before waking them by calling their name over the intercom and asking them the classic question, "What was going through your mind, just before I woke you?" I found I understood dreams as if they were my mother tongue. I did, in fact, learn to understand dreams from my mother. She was a poet who drew heavily on her dreamlife for the imagery of her work. Sitting alone in the lab at night, I felt close to her in a new way. I also had a new sense of purpose, a mission to explore this rich resource. Besides, it had a welcome side-effect: When I got home in the early morning, I was so dead tired I could at last sleep deeply.

That was more than 25 years ago, and dreams have intrigued me ever since. The more I listened to the dreams of people who were going through bad times of their own, the more convinced I became that dreams are a display of how we view our troubles and that they are tests of ways to cope with difficulties; however, these perceptions and experiments do not always work. Sometimes dreams let us down, get stuck, seem to need a push. Is there some way to repair our dreams so that they can get back to work? That was the question that led me to do the study that is the basis of this book.

I did not become a sleep researcher out of the blue. I was a research psychologist, trained at the University of Toronto from 1941 to 1946 and then at Cornell from 1946 to 1949, after which I went to work at the University of Chicago for the distinguished psychotherapist Carl Rogers. He had developed an innovative type of psychotherapy that concentrated on helping troubled people to get in touch with their feelings, to learn to recognize and accept their emotions as part of themselves. He and I began an investigation to find out whether this psychotherapy really helped people change their minds, their hearts, and their behaviors. Our research laid the basis for my interest in how people can best learn to master the unrealistic fears that hold them back and the blue moods that leave them without hope. Working with people while they were awake was frequently slow going. They often didn't want to face the feelings that were undermining them. With tremulous voices, they would say, "I'm not scared. Who says I'm scared?" However, they could recognize a dream that demonstrated their fears and uncertainties in a way that was clear and undeniable.

Maybe they can learn about themselves more quickly from their dreams, I thought. But most people have very little recall of their dreams. As I pondered that problem, just next door, beginning in the early 1950s, Nathaniel Kleitman and his students were doing basic research on sleep that would open the way to catching dreams as they happen during sleep. A few years later, when my marriage was over and my own sleep deserted me, it was time to make the leap. I had a lot of help from my friend Allan Rechtschaffen, by then head of the sleep research laboratory at the University of Chicago. In the early 1960s, he taught me not the ropes but the wires: the basic know-how necessary to equip and run a sleep laboratory of my own at the University of Illinois. This started me off on a life-long hunt, chasing our ephemeral dreams to understand how they fit into our waking lives, what they do for us, and how to make them work better when they work against us.

In 1977, after many years and many studies, when I became director of the Sleep Disorders Service at Rush-Presbyterian-St. Luke's Medical Center in Chicago, I finally returned to confront what had brought me into the field of dreams: the study of dreams of people in crisis, to look into the difference between the night-life of those who are handling the disruption of their lives with equanimity and those who were, as I was, thrown for a loss.

Doing this work required two things: money and people willing to share their dreams. The money came from the National Institute of Mental Health. They have funded this work continuously since 1977, and I am very grateful. The people came in response to ads offering a small fee for three nights of sleep, first during a time of crisis and then one year later. To them, gratitude is not enough. They touched me deeply. Their dreams spoke from their hearts and will touch yours, I'm sure.

To bring this work into book form, to tell the story of what we found, I needed a writer who knew the field of sleep and dream research. Lynne Lamberg, who had followed my work and reported it in magazine articles, was a natural collaborator. Because the book reports my research and work with patients, we use the word "I" frequently. The writing, though, is really "we." Thanks, Lynne.

I hope this book will be a help to you in getting acquainted with your inner voices. We are by nature makers of dreams: wondrous, creative, underground commentaries on the texts of our waking lives.

Lynne Lamberg's Preface

ERE IT NOT FOR A DREAM, I might not have worked on this book. It came while I was considering Rosalind Cartwright's invitation to collaborate on a book focusing on her study of dreaming during divorce. My dream had nothing to do with the book, or so I thought at the time. It concerned my children.

I was on a crowded platform, suspended about 45 feet off the floor, squeezed onto the edge of a sofa, just inches from the edge. I was trying to sew a button on my daughter's coat. The task was difficult because the coat had lots of different-colored buttons, big ones, little ones, each requiring a multicolored thread. My son, a toddler in the dream, 18 in reality, wandered by. I worried that he might fall off the platform, but he kept his balance and stayed a safe distance from the edge.

The dream made me think about my role as a mother. I was facing issues that may arise, as the dream told me, "about age 45." My daughter, a recent college graduate, was about to move to another city to start her first job. The many-buttoned coat reminded me that she soon would be all wrapped up in her exciting new life. She would have fewer threads tying her to home. My son would start college in a few months, yet I still pictured him as my "baby." The dream reassured me that he could maintain his balance if life got shaky.

This dream sharpened my awareness of my children's growing independence. It reminded me that both were embarking on new stages in their lives and that I needed to reconcile myself to letting them go. It prompted some warm talks with my husband about the bittersweet pleasure of our children's increasing maturity. In retrospect, the dream also encouraged me to go ahead with this book by demonstrating what it is that dreams do for us: They serve as colored pens to underline the most important ideas in the texts of our lives. They help bring the subtext into the text, to make us more aware of why we feel and act the way we do.

Like many writers, I keep a journal in which I record thoughts about my life experiences, including dreams. In the past several years, my appreciation for dreams has been nurtured further by New York psychoanalyst Walter Bonime, whom I met over breakfast at a meeting of the Association for the Study of Dreams in 1985. Since then, we have become good friends. In letters and in hundreds of hours of conversation, first at the end of the workday in his Park Avenue office, and more recently in his home or mine, Walter, now in his eighties and still seeing patients, teaching, and writing, has taught me to listen with a more attentive ear to what dreams have to say, to seek out the emotional links between dream life and waking life.

I also am grateful to my husband, Stanford, and children, Niki and Ryan, my mother, Fay Friedman, who died March 28, 1992 after a long illness, and mother-in-law, Margaret Lamberg, many other family members and friends, particularly John Lion, Carol Frank, Doris Diamond, Carole Simon, Toba Cohen, Marty Oberman, and Neil Kavey, for sharing their dreams, insight, and experience as my work on this book progressed.

A dozen years ago, at the start of my research for an earlier book, *The American Medical Association Guide to Better Sleep*, I spent a night wearing electrodes, hooked up to the polysomnograph in the Sleep and Dreams Laboratory of the University of Cincinnati. There, a technician awakened me several times to report dreams. In one of them,

I was giving a party, introducing my friends to a new wine bearing the label University Vineyard. The mood was festive. Everyone loved the wine.

"That's a wonderful dream," psychiatrist Milton Kramer, head of the lab, told me the next morning. "You must find your work very satisfying," he said. "Here you are, a writer, sharing some delightfully intoxicating, heady stuff that you've obtained at a university with your readers, whom you view as your friends."

Dream parties being infrequent, most of a writer's job is hard and solitary work. In the midst of writing and rewriting, I always worry, "Have I made this clear? Concise? Interesting? Will people keep on reading?" At such moments, that dream sometimes comes to mind. I hope you enjoy the new wine from the University Vineyard.

1

How Dreams Work

*L*AURA DREAMED she brought a basket of laundry from the basement to the living room, where her husband was sitting on the couch.

Jim picked up a gold sock and hurled it into a corner of the room. I was shocked and said: "Why did you do that?" He said: "It has a hole in it. I don't want it anymore!"

Al dreamed a crowd of people were trying to fix an unusual railroad switch jammed into buried pipes.

"They hadn't used that switch it seemed like for years and naturally the sand and dust had blowed [sic] into these pipes and it was all rusty."

Tama dreamed her boyfriend proposed marriage. As the teenaged couple walked along the beach to an old house, the idyllic scene suddenly dissolved.

"Characters from a horror movie were there, waiting to axe me. I went over to the beach with my boyfriend. Giant crabs were there, ready to attack."

These dreams do not reflect idle thoughts about home economics, plumbing, or marine life. Rather, they all zero in, with laser-like precision, on current crises in the dreamers' lives, emotional earthquakes that threaten to topple their basic sense of self-identity.

Laura was a 35-year-old mother of four whose husband, Jim, had just left her. Laura's dream summarized her view of herself and her tattered marriage: "Jim broke up the pair of us and threw me away." She thought the two of them were "his favorite pair." Even her use of a basket of laundry, an assortment of family members' clothing, was apt: her own life revolved around family and home. Further, just before the breakup, Laura came home early one day to find Jim dressed in her underwear. This, she told me, was her first clue that he was having problems with his sexual identity and had begun in secret to cross-dress. It's no wonder she dreamed he had discarded her, the sock with the hole.

Al, the man who dreamed about a defective switch and plugged up pipes, was about to undergo major surgery to repair a blocked vein in his leg. A former train engineer, he drew on images from his work identity to express his perception of what was wrong with his leg and his anxieties about how the operation would go. Al spent four nights before his surgery and three nights after it in the sleep laboratory, where psychologist Louis Breger and his colleagues awakened him several times a night to collect his dreams.

Al's other dreams included surgical images, such as cutting up a large piece of meat; repair of other broken objects, such as a stove and a car; and problems with the transport of fluids, such as a half-dried riverbed and a stopped-up septic tank. All these images occurred in dreams before the operation. Not one occurred after its successful completion. He focused on the threat to his body and its functions before his surgery. Afterward, he no longer felt this threat.

In her dream, Tama revealed a normal adolescent's desire

for love and intimacy. But she worried that a calamity would keep her from fulfilling her wish. When Tama was only two years old, a forklift truck overturned on her, crushing her leg and necessitating many operations. When she was nine, surgeons finally had to amputate her leg. Although Tama told child psychiatrist Lenore Terr this dream had nothing to do with her accident, "she actually had been axed," Terr observes. That was how the girl viewed the surgery she had undergone. Furthermore, Terr asks, "what looks more like a forklift truck, after all, than an oversized, shiny, bright orange Alaska king crab?"

A worn-out sock, rusty pipes, giant crabs: dreams are full of these wonderfully fitting images. Although dreams often puzzle us, it's worth the effort to capture and decipher them, for they show us what we otherwise may not see. They help us uncover truths about ourselves that our waking minds may know yet deny or that, awake, we may not be able to articulate clearly. They do so especially in times of intense emotional upheaval, as Laura found when going through a divorce, Al when facing major surgery, and Tama when confronting the fear that her damaged leg would keep her from getting married.

Few of us go through life without encountering such crises. Indeed, times of crisis highlight the important functions that dreams serve in our lives. Events we perceive as both positive and negative, beginnings and endings, pluses and minuses, all place heavy demands on the dream system. When we gain or lose a job, a mate, a home, or when we undergo any major change in our lives, our internal picture of who we are and our sense of security are called into question.

Events such as these represent threats to three big areas of our lives: our physical safety, our psychological integrity, and our social connectedness. The threats may come from the world around us or from within. Both outside events, such as floods and fires, and inside events, such as diseases, may threaten our physical safety. Being fired or failing an exam may cause self-disappointment and threaten our sense of ourselves as smart or capable. The shock of a divorce or the breakup of a friendship may threaten our sense that others find us worthy of love. At such times, our dreams go into high gear. In our dreams, we search through our life story to find memories that can help us cope. We sleep more lightly and awaken more often. Dreams are more apt to stick with us when we're troubled than when life is going well.

The Chinese symbol for crisis includes the characters for both danger and opportunity. The danger we face during a crisis is from the potential shattering of the program on which we run—the present self. The opportunity is in expanding that picture, reshaping how we see ourselves, constructing a new, better-functioning persona.

Dreams during crises show how that equation is working out. Is the danger overwhelming us or are we dealing with the opportunity to assume new roles? Are these roles positive or negative? "Are you a good witch or a bad witch?" the Munchkins asked Dorothy, who, when threatened with the loss of her beloved Toto, dreamed she was blown out of Kansas and into the land of Oz.

THE PRIVATE LANGUAGE OF DREAMS

During the day, we may fool ourselves and others by putting on a good front, by denying the excitement or fear that any major change may bring, but our dreams show what is really going on inside. Night after night, they reflect the ever-changing circumstances of our daily lives. In our dreams, we connect today's experiences to earlier ones that involved similar feelings. We blend past and present. We bring ourselves up to date. Each night, our dreams help us get ready to face tomorrow's demands.

Through the immediacy and clarity of picture images,

dreams perform emotional homework that is as central to the way we master life's lessons as the three R's were to our elementary school days. Our dreams *review* and *revise* our concept of who we are, and they *rehearse* where we are going. Moreover, in times of trouble, if they function as they should, dreams provide a fourth R, a mechanism for *repair*.

Many of us tacitly acknowledge that dreams are useful. When we are trying to solve a problem, unsure of what step to take next, we know it's wise to "sleep on it." Shakespeare described this healing power when he called sleep "nature's soft nurse." Sleep gives us a few hours of time off, but that is only part of its function. It also enhances our ability to put matters into perspective and to think more creatively. We accomplish these mental tasks in dreams, whether we remember them or not. The body rests while we sleep, but the mind continues its work.

If we do remember some of the fantasies that pervade our sleep, we often use words like "weird" or "strange" to describe them. If we happen to recall one that troubles us, we may try to shake off the experience as "only a dream." Dreams often seem alien, tales concocted by some mysterious outside force. In fact, we write the script, set the scene, produce and direct the show, and play the starring role. In our dreams, we may be old, young, of either sex. We even may disguise ourselves as animals. We may live in other times and places, see people we know to be dead, perform feats we know to be impossible.

In our dream world, we speak a private language, known only to ourselves. Indeed, psychoanalyst Erich Fromm calls dreams "the forgotten language." The fact that dreams come to us in pictures rather than words makes it harder for us to grasp their meaning. However, like the hieroglyphs of ancient Egypt, they are easy to translate once we learn the code. The code book is neither mysterious nor inaccessible; it is one our own memory banks create. The images that serve as symbols for what we want to say come from our own past, like the rusty pipes that represent blocked veins in the engineer's dream. In sleep, we draw materials from our waking life to express how we feel. We do not choose the images we use in our dreams consciously, but neither are these images random. Like the discarded sock in Laura's dream, they fit our current situation.

Psychologically, we live in two different worlds. When the alarm clock rings, we leave behind the private world of sleep and reenter the social world. We shower, dress, and tuck ourselves into our public roles to face the daily process of becoming who it is we think we can be, or want, or ought to be. The language of the waking world is literal, and one that we share with others.

In sleep, the process of becoming persists. Matters that we usually keep in the background while awake—our feelings about what's happening in our lives—claim the foreground in sleep. Dreams often reach far into the past to include long-forgotten people and places. Any experience that we ever have had may turn up in our dreams. Our sleeping minds search through our memory banks to find old emotional information that holds relevance to the present. What we find there may aid—or sabotage—our attempts to cope with problems we face today. A small slight, for instance, may remind us of a big insult from the past.

We combine the old and the new in narratives that display how we think about what we feel. We bare our private biases, perceptions, and motivations. We also show our characteristic coping style. Do we flee from danger or confront it, for example? Do we seek closeness or avoid it? If we recall past experiences that enhanced our self-esteem, then our dreams comfort us and tell us that we have overcome adversity before and can do it again. If our early satisfactions were few or absent, indeed if we felt helpless and despairing, then our dreams reflect this gloomy state and reinforce it. Such dreams suggest we likely will have a harder time surmounting the present obstacles.

A PERSONAL EXAMPLE

Here is one of my own dreams to show you how the dream process works:

A young colleague named Michael Young was crossing a busy street on roller skates. On the other side, a young girl, about five years old, told him that he could take off the skates now to get where he was going, Grand Central Station.

"Why Michael Young?" I asked myself. "What is he doing in my dreams? I have very little contact with him or emotional investment in him. Who is he to me that I should dream of him? And what, pray, is he, a dignified man, doing on roller skates?"

I began to think it through, looking for the characteristics that my experience has shown me are the building blocks of dreams, characteristics I call "dream dimensions." These typically reflect the key attributes of the individuals, events, and objects in our dreams. In my dream the main character has the name "Young"; he also is a "young" professional who recently was promoted and awarded a federal grant. So far, I have identified two dimensions that define the main character, young and successful. My experience tells me to think about the opposites of these dimensions, old and unsuccessful, as these also may be important in understanding a dream.

In the dream, what this young, successful person is doing is crossing a street on roller skates to get to a New York City location. Taking "crossing" first, I note that in reality, I see him as a "cross-over" person with appointments in two departments, my own and psychiatry. The setting is New York where my younger daughter lives. Another character in the dream is a young girl. The role of the young girl in this dream is to tell an older successful person that it is safe to proceed. The girl's presence adds a third dimension or set of opposites: male/female.

At that point, I realized that this dream was inspired by an event the day before. As I had pulled into my parking lot, I saw a little girl playing there with a skateboard, trying to master it. I felt anxiety: it was risky for her to play where she could be hit by a car. In my dream, the skateboard is transformed into roller skates that are used to cross a busy street quickly and safely.

In reality, my older daughter, Christine, a young woman professional, was hit by a car and killed crossing a street a few years ago. Her "crossing over" was not successful. She was cut down before getting the grants and promotions that would have been part of her life. This thought adds another dimension: danger/safety.

My anxiety for a young girl with a skateboard exposed to the danger from cars, all experienced in waking, served as triggers for my dream of a young, professional male successfully making it through the same events that led to my daughter's death.

Dreams commonly are thought to provide wish-fulfillment. If the purpose of this dream is to fulfill the wish that Christine had been able to negotiate crossing the road more quickly to avoid the car that killed her, then why not dream directly of her? The answer is that feelings connected with this loss are still so strongly felt that many kinds of daytime experiences connect to the memory network of images related to her. Once aroused, these feelings result in dreams of the safety of my younger child.

Now it was easier to understand why Michael Young appeared in my dream. I believe my choice also was related to another fact about him. He lives near me and on occasion I have given him a ride in my car when he has been waiting for a bus to go to the hospital where we work. I have "saved" him the trouble of negotiating his trip downtown. His appearance thus is connected to my wish to "save" my daughter. The new dream dimension is close/far. A male who lives close to me is saved but my faraway daughter was not. Always look for sets of opposites when searching for the meaning of a dream.

This dream is a good example of how misleading it may be to take the identity of people in a dream at face value. The dream had a clear relation to a conscious waking experience—the little girl in the parking lot. The idea of the girl being hit by a car must have stirred my ongoing feelings concerning my older daughter's death and my sadness over my inability to save her. My dream was an attempt to deal with my continuing anxiety about my remaining younger, faraway daughter by having another young successful professional person safely negotiate his way.

To understand any dream fully, we must know which aspects of our lives evoke strong feelings, the nature of those feelings and their intensity, and the way in which they support or threaten our sense of identity. A large part of my own identity is as a mother. The death of my daughter has left strong, negative feelings, a wound not yet healed. It damaged the security of a part of myself.

Another element of my identity is my work, in which I take pride in my ingenuity in helping others. This aspect of my self-story also is active at night. I design ways to keep others safe. I do not dream of my daughter in trouble. I deflect the danger in the dream to a person of the opposite sex, a capable young man, and I give him a way out. The danger/safety dimension comes up on the positive side. In this dream, parts of my memory system are activated to tell a story that is personally important to me. It reassures me that I would have helped my daughter if I could.

When we find ourselves in the midst of a crisis, dreams seldom prove this comforting. Indeed, dreams sometimes get stuck, like a needle in the groove of a scratched record. We then need to find ways to lift the needle and move on. This book shows you how to work with your own dreams to understand them and fix those that aren't working right.

WHAT DREAMS MEAN

While studies in the sleep laboratory show that dreaming is a normal part of our mind's nightly work, how the mind generates three or four dreams each night remains an area of active research and some controversy. Alan Hobson and Robert McCarley of Harvard University have examined how brain cells turn on and off during waking and in the two types of sleep, which are called REM (rapid eye movement) and non-REM, or NREM, sleep. Hobson and McCarley believe our dream images arise during REM sleep from random bursts from nerve cells in the brainstem, the top of the spinal cord which protrudes into the brain. Like Rorschach inkblots, they say, the images are meaningless in themselves. We experience them as fierce animals or caring friends, bloody massacres or beautiful sunsets, depending on what we need to express.

According to Hobson and McCarley, we add the meaning to these images in order to express whatever story we need to tell ourselves at the time. Dreams thus reflect the higher, or thinking, brain's efforts to make sense out of the haphazard signals generated by the lower brain. We do the best we can with whatever comes along. That's why dream stories are often disjointed and jumbled up.

In dreams we may walk, run, or climb. We may fly, spin, or leap tall buildings at a single bound. Each of these imagined movements, Hobson writes in *The Dreaming Brain*, corresponds to a real message from brain to muscles. Even though the big muscles are paralyzed during dreaming sleep, perhaps to keep us from acting out our dreams, the motor-command sequences, he says, determine the flow of events in a dream. It is only afterward that we fabricate a way to explain the experience, by saying, for example, "And then I fell down the stairs."

When we study dreams of people in the sleep laboratory in the order in which they occur, we find the images much more relevant to the dreamer's life than Hobson and McCarley suggest. The dreams relate clearly to what the dreamer is working on emotionally, and their message is easy to decode. Laura saw Jim, who was a transvestite, throw away half a pair of socks, the one with a hole, just as he discarded her as a sexual partner. In Laura's view, "Jim threw me away just because I am a woman." In one dream, she says it all. Laura knows she has been cast aside and that her married life is over. The image Laura uses may be accidental, but, if so, it is a rather exquisite coincidence.

The same images often reappear in dreams from the beginning to the end of the night. If random signals generate our dreams, what accounts for such consistency? Moreover, some dreaming occurs outside of REM sleep, a fact that makes it hard to tie dreaming to the bursts of activity that occur only within REM sleep. Some people even dream the same dream at different times throughout their lives. Some common examples:

You have to take an exam for which you are not prepared.
Someone is breaking into your house.
You're trapped in a dark cave and can't get out.

How can that happen if the images are random?

Some contemporary theorists go even farther and suggest dreams are made up from daytime experiences not worth saving. "We dream in order to forget," Francis Crick and Graeme Mitchison write. "Attempting to remember one's dreams should perhaps not be encouraged," they say, "because such remembering may help to retain patterns of thought which are best forgotten."

To account for why we spend so much time dreaming but remember so little of what we dream, Crick, who won the Nobel Prize for helping demonstrate the spiral structure of DNA, and Mitchison, a British mathematician, suggest that the mind is like a computer with limited storage space. Since we can't save everything, we need some way to rid ourselves regularly of those accidental or inefficient files we accumulate in our daily lives. The nightly acts of dreaming send charges through the memory networks not to illuminate but to eliminate from the brain information we don't need to remember. Dreaming keeps the computer from getting overloaded, Crick and Mitchison say. Remembering a dream indicates that the brain did not satisfactorily accomplish its nighttime housekeeping chores. Their theory, of course, is speculative, not based on research. Furthermore, there's an important question it neglects: If the brain is ridding itself of an unnecessary load, what determines what is kept?

My experiences in the laboratory with hundreds of dreamers challenge this interpretation. I believe that dreaming is designed not to erase experience but to highlight it, to help us maintain and update our internal emotional picture of ourselves. To continue the computer analogy, we process this material off-line, during sleep, when we can afford to stop attending to the pressing realities of life, such as putting bread on the table and staying out of the way of trucks.

In waking life, our brains receive, organize, store, and rearrange information on many levels simultaneously: the name of the person we are talking to, the curl of his lip, the sound of his voice. We remember the way events unfold, the way the scene looks, the emotions we feel, the visceral sensations we experience, such as chills or sweaty palms. Researchers on memory describe the manner in which we accomplish this mental filing as "parallel processing."

We store pieces of our memories in the many different parts of our memory networks where older, related material already resides. There are many pathways between the various parts of each memory network and between the different networks.

Dreams display our efforts to integrate today's concerns with material already in the memory storage depots. Emotionally hot issues activate a memory network in the first dream of the night and prime that network for further stimulation later. The second dream may trigger the release of older images, feelings, and sensations, from more remote parts of the same memory network. The process continues as sleep proceeds. Because we mix old memory images with more recent ones, we often see conglomerates that incorporate the same or closely related images in a single night.

We may not be conscious of the emotional connections between present and past. Indeed, we at first may lack the words to describe them. But focusing on the feelings or images they evoke can make their connections more apparent. While each dream of a night has meaning when examined by itself, together the night's dreams form an interrelated whole.

One night's dreams from Harold, a participant in my study of dreams during divorce, provide a glimpse of the mind doing its nightshift work. Harold was a freewheeling, rakish, 45-year-old whose wife found him irresponsible. Married eight years and the father of two, he still wanted freedom to come and go as he pleased. His wife wanted him to accept his family obligations. As the conflict sharpened, he began to abuse her physically. She grew frightened, took the children, and went home to her mother.

Harold had left college after two years, then worked in turn as an auto mechanic, truck driver, photographer, and salesman. At the time he volunteered for our study, he was out of a job, broke, and worried. He had just had a big jolt: He had been jailed for failure to keep up his court-ordered child-support payments.

He feared he would not be able to make the payments, and, as a result, would lose the children, whom he missed enormously. Harold's parents had divorced when he was quite young. This experience had left scars. "I know what it is like not to have a dad," he told me. "I committed myself to my children for a lifetime."

His wife's departure had toppled his self-confident image of himself. He had always been the one to leave her behind, traveling, having fun with his friends, sure that he always could return home. He was upset and angry. Here are his dream reports in the sleep laboratory:

Dream 1

I was dreaming about two quarters, just a couple of them sitting there on a red background. (I took some pictures of a souvenir coin on a red background about a year ago for a brochure job.) One coin was kind of old, kind of worn, and had a flying eagle on it. (I had an old coin in my hand the other day, so this was like a recall.)

This dream started with his hottest present concern, lack of money, and set the theme for the night: Harold saw himself as a worn-out, high flyer, down on his luck, and a man who had lost almost everything.

Dream 2

It was kinda funny. One of my friend's kids, a high school kid, and her friends were going out. I must have been trying to give them a hard time, kidding with them, telling them not to go. (We get along pretty good. I'm like her godfather, like Uncle Harold to her.) She wanted to go somewhere with her friends. It must have been in their apartment. (They are getting ready to move, I'm supposed to go over to see them Friday. They are leaving to go to California this weekend. They're like family.) The apartment had white walls and really bright accent colors. Like "Miami Vice" colors.

Here Harold continued to express his losses. He couldn't keep the girl from leaving him. He perceived another break in family ties. The dream dimension of losing/keeping was one that Harold would repeat throughout the night.

The third time we awakened Harold, he could not remember his dream, but on the fourth call, he gave a rich report.

Dream 3

I was trying to put fuel in a truck. Someone was going to flip the hose on top, over the top of the truck, and I said, "No, don't do that." There was a truck driver, somebody I know. I pulled in because I knew him. I saw his truck, but somebody else was driving his truck. This other guy was going to flip the hose over the truck to let me by, like a jump rope, when two people hold the ends and one jumps. I knew he couldn't do it so I told him, "No, no, no." For me to get by, he had to move it or back it up. It was like a barrier. I was saying, "No, no, don't do that!" and I started to get out of the truck. He should have let the hose drop so I could run over it.

The next morning when Harold reviewed his dreams with me, image by image, he readily found their personal meaning. He related his dreams to each other and to his waking life. "In the first dream, it's only two quarters. That's about what I've got in my pocket now, and I have to spend one of them to buy a newspaper to look for a job." The coin image made him think about a photography job he had done the year before, something he would like to be doing now to make some money. The red background, he said, may represent being "in the red." "That's certainly true of me right now," he conceded. The old, worn-out, flying eagle, he added, "may be an image of myself."

In talking about the dream that featured his friend's daughter, he said that he didn't want to lose any more family. Yet he conceded that he felt powerless to keep what he wanted.

"I don't want to go back to driving a truck," Harold said, as he explored his last dream. Although he could make the money he needed that way, he didn't like that way of life. In his dream, he found that other men presented barriers. He couldn't get his hose in the tank. With a loud laugh, he acknowledged that the meaning of this image was perfectly clear. He was cut off from his sexual connection. He saw other men horsing around, playing with the hose, maybe sexually acting out. Again he told someone, "No, you can't do that," but he was impotent, unable to control the other person. This dream added the dimensions, thwarted/effective.

Harold was a man in transition. He was shifting from being the macho "Miami Vice" guy who played around but controlled his wife, even if he had to beat her, to recognizing that this identity no longer worked for him. The images in Harold's dreams repeatedly reflect a single theme, "How can I get more of everything I need?" More money, stronger ties with kids and family, more power. He started with his current child-support problem and, over the course of the night, reviewed the past to see how he got there. He saw himself as losing, not keeping, and as thwarted, not effective. He had not yet reached the stage of revising his self-image or of rehearsing new ways to see himself with more self-esteem.

From first to last, Harold's dreams showed no progress in working things out. However, they did sharpen his picture of the key disturbing issues in his waking life. He had no trouble understanding them. Had he remembered only the last dream of the night, he might have dismissed it as "just a dream about trucks."

It's not practical for most of us to go to a sleep laboratory to get acquainted with our dreams. Fortunately, it's not necessary either. Throughout this book you will learn how to capture, study, and make use of your own dreams at home.

2

How Our Dreams Can Work for Us

*D*REAMS ARE designed to help us maintain our self-identity, our sense of who we are, as our life circumstances change. We need a good self-image to ride successfully the bumps of everyday life. Those whose dreams suggest that all is not well should not be content to shrug them off as unimportant. A bad dream, like an elevated temperature, is a symptom that something is wrong. It is a distress signal, a message from our sleeping mind to our waking mind that is risky to ignore. Dreams serve, psychiatrist Milton Kramer suggests, as an emotional thermostat. His studies show that the mind-set we have during our dreams affects our attitudes and behavior the following day. After a bad dream, we awaken more discouraged than we were at bedtime. After a good one, we feel more optimistic.

Sometimes, when we are in the midst of crisis, our nocturnal review of the day's experiences may be too painful to accept. We may not see a clear way to revise our inner picture to make the needed changes. Our forecast of tomorrow may show nothing to look forward to. At such times, the dream machine goes around in circles. People who get stuck in a bad situation often dream literally of being trapped in some way, in an elevator, for example, or in traffic.

One of my patients dreamed she was driving in a downtown area known, fittingly, as "The Loop." No matter which way she turned, she ran into one-way streets that dumped her back at the very spot she thought she had left. Another woman repeatedly drove up and down and all around a multilevel parking garage without being able to find a place to put her car. At difficult times in my own life, I have dreamed I am driving down a blind alley with no room to turn around.

A diagnosis of a serious illness, an accident, a mugging, or a rape may be followed by intense dreams that repeat the threat over and over. We may interrupt the dream, awakening in a cold sweat in the middle of the night. People who have been caught in the horrors of war, the Holocaust, or a hurricane, flood, or other natural disaster may relive their experiences in excruciating detail in their dreams for many years. Even more extreme are instances where feelings aroused by a crisis prove so overwhelming that the person flees from bed to escape the terror and commits some act of violence while sleepwalking. Repetitive dreams and interrupted dreams represent the breakdown of an overloaded dream system.

The times that try men's (and women's) souls are precisely those when we most need to shift our dreams into action, to turn from simply recognizing the danger to our present self to accepting the opportunity to invent or devise a change and then to rehearse and work on it.

About 15 years ago I was at a pivotal point in my life. I was trying to decide whether to stay in my secure and satisfying job as a professor of psychology at the University of Illinois or to accept an offer to become chairman of the department of psychology at Rush-Presbyterian-St. Luke's Medical Center, the position I now hold.

It was a dark and stormy night. I was up in the air, being blown about, without any power to control my direction. I felt I had to get in out of the wind. I looked down and saw I was above an English moor.

Below there was a tall stone turret with arched openings. I thought if I could work my way on the currents into one of the archways, I would be safe. I did and saw below me a coronation ceremony taking place at the base of this Gothic tower. There was a throne and an archbishop holding a robe open. I floated down into the robe and sat on the throne. At this point, the archbishop placed a crown on my head.

I woke up laughing. I said to myself, "I guess I'm going to accept the chair!" Why the coronation image to express my work dilemma? I had spent my early childhood in Canada during World War II. The two little English princesses, Elizabeth and her sister Margaret-Rose, represented safety and stability in those times of trouble. They broadcast, especially to children, a "good night, sleep well" message that reassured us that the royal household was not worried. If having a throne brought with it this sense of safety, power, and calm, how could I refuse?

The dream's solution to my dilemma about whether I wanted to accept a change in self-image is straightforward and unambivalent. It doesn't deal with the problems that face the person who wields power. However, I saw it as a positive-feeling dream, and it helped make me optimistic about the new job.

People have reported problem-solving dreams like this one since earliest recorded history. They are part of our common cultural heritage. In Greece, pilgrims journeyed to the temples of Aesculapius, the god of healing, where they prayed, offered sacrifices, and attended lectures. In preparation for a night of sleep in a sacred dormitory, where they hoped the god would visit them in a dream to cure them or offer helpful advice, they may have drunk a potion brewed from plants with hallucinogenic properties. In temples in ancient Egypt, dream interpreters known as the "Learned Men of the Magic Library" counseled patients before sending them to a special sleeping room with the suggestion to "incubate" healing dreams. The Hebrew Bible records widespread belief in the meaningfulness of dreams: it contains reports of more than seventy dreams and visions.

From the ancients' view of dreams as messages from a god to the present-day view, as forged by Sigmund Freud, that dreams are messages from within the self, the basic concept remains the same: dreams have something important to tell us about our feelings, about our inner lives, about how we see ourselves.

All of us, even those who claim they never dream, have three, four, even five dreams every night. In the sleep laboratory, we identify each dream as it begins and track how long it lasts by monitoring a sleeper's brainwaves and eye movements. We watch for the time when the pens on our recording device show both a shift from the brainwaves of quiet sleep to those of active sleep (which resemble those we have while awake) as well as rapid eye movements and muscle relaxation. Together, these signs signal "dream in progress." People awakened during REM sleep can report their dreams while they are still fresh.

Our aim is to retrieve all the night's dreams in as pure a form as possible. Since most sleepers have several dreams each night, we also see how the plot of the night's story develops from beginning to end. Once people tell us their dreams during the night, they find it easy to recall them the next morning. When they remember them in their natural order, the meaning begins to become clear. The sequence of dreams, like those of Harold whom we met in Chapter 1, tells an interconnected story.

In the latter half of the nearly three decades I've spent in sleep research, I've focused primarily on the crisis of divorce, not simply to explore how people cope with this common experience in our society, but also because divorce serves as an excellent model for how people adapt to many other life crises. Divorce has much in common with other threats to our self-image. Like bereavement after the death of a spouse, a divorce involves mourning the loss of love and connectedness.

Like the loss of a job or of a home in a flood or fire, it may entail the loss of social, economic, and physical security.

A divorce often involves feelings of self-blame and guilt, similar to those experienced by victims of rape, kidnapping, or other crimes. It may bring recurring intrusive waking thoughts and anxiety-filled dreams that focus on events surrounding the experience, much as Vietnam veterans and Holocaust survivors sometimes continue to reexperience the horrors of war.

Many people in the process of divorce experience the breakup of their marriage as a personal defeat. They don't distinguish between "the marriage failed" and "I failed." They suffer a massive injury to their sense of identity and self-esteem. Depression often follows. Because emotional and physical well-being are so intertwined, the stress of divorce and other crises may undermine their physical as well as mental health. Many can't sleep; some have no energy. Some pick at their food; others eat nonstop. Some develop chest pains, ulcers, headaches, or skin rashes.

Studying the dreams of hundreds of people going through the same major experience shows how dreams function during times of stress and major life changes. It permits researchers to see the differences between those who are coping well, moving on with their lives, and those who are stuck, mired in despair. These findings suggest that how people dream may make a real difference in how quickly, and how well, they repair their self-image and accommodate to their changed circumstances.

WHEN DREAMWORK BREAKS DOWN

Julie, a frail, tentative, wistful 32-year-old woman, who looked and acted more like a teenager, first came to see me on the verge of a major breakdown. In the course of her unhappy marriage to a much older man, she had developed a major health problem, an eating disorder called anorexia nervosa.

As Julie explained it, she was "fed up" with her marriage and "couldn't swallow any more." She ate very little and her weight became dangerously low.

Her husband had abused her not physically but verbally, especially when he was drinking. After one particularly brutal episode, she packed up and ran away from him, her job, and her home in Pennsylvania. She came to Chicago to start over. While painfully thin, timid, and somber, she still showed the spunk to try to reorganize her life. The dreams Julie had on one night in our laboratory provide sharply focused snapshots of the inner turmoil she could address only awkwardly when awake. Here are her dreams:

Dream 1

Some people I was with were trying to talk someone into going on a date. A group of us were trying to set this girl up with this guy. I was on the outside watching. Someone said, "She's free for the evening, why don't you take her to the zoo?" And he stuttered and said, "Well, okay I guess."

Dream 2

I was hitchhiking down the highway stopping and looking into cars like I was looking back on memories or something. I stopped at this one car and it was a boss I had back six years ago who was driving the car. I was on the outside looking in, thinking how much I liked that job and how he was just a really nice man and he was looking back at me and smiling. He said, "When you find a husband it will be the right one. It will be love." I felt like I was ready to start crying and was about to run away from the car. I felt real sad like he was dead. We couldn't talk or hear each other. That's what made me feel he was dead. Last time I really heard from him was the day I got married. He sent a "Best of Luck" telegram. I felt sad that I had disappointed him. I felt I failed him and I couldn't explain because I couldn't talk to him.

In the first of Julie's dreams a group of people pushed a reluctant man into dating a girl and taking her to a strange nighttime destination, the zoo. The first dream set the stage for the second. In the second dream, as in reality, Julie was in transit, but she was going down the highway on foot like a "runaway." The significance of the events in both dreams became clearer the next morning, when Julie reported that the man in her second dream, her former boss, was the one who had introduced her to her husband.

She saw a genial older man she recognized from a happier period in her life, before she was married. She was on the outside looking in. She dreamed of her old boss because she needed to understand how she got into a bad marriage with a man whom she described as "behaving like an ape." She felt ashamed and sad that she had failed the father-like person who expected her to be happy and had had to run away. Her second dream thus continued the story begun in the first and explained her use of the zoo metaphor. "When I went along with dating a big ape, it didn't work out."

The several dreams of a night often are connected this way by a single theme or problem to be solved. Each in turn makes more sense if we know the dreams that precede and follow it. As in many novels, the plot of one night's dreams may develop from chapter to chapter by involving different characters or jumping ahead or back in time. From dream to dream, we look at the same issues from various perspectives, even from opposite points of view. We compare, contrast, and realign the elements. When Julie and I talked these dreams over, she quickly saw that the night's theme was the reason that brought her to my office: "I can't make it on my own, but whom can I trust to understand and help me?" In each of her dreams, she considers this problem in different ways.

Julie had no recall of her third dream; however, in her fourth and last REM period that night, she had a dream that left her feeling anxious and distressed. It focused on her intense feelings of isolation and betrayal, and on her need for help which she was not getting.

Dream 4

I was dreaming about one of my former co-workers, that she was getting ganged up on by her fellow employees. Apparently she was sick and tired of the job, and was wanting to quit. And then it turned into a video of her. Instead of her being there in person, we were all sitting around, watching it. She was crying and perspiring and laughing and obviously kind of losing it, mentally, in front of all of us. I was enraged. I was turning around and yelling at some of the people behind me. Rather than saying, "Look, I think she needs some help," it was like they were getting a kick out of watching this movie. This was supposed to be at work, but it was in my parents' living room.

In commenting on this dream, Julie acknowledged that she was the one who felt ganged up on. Her productivity fell at work when she became ill and was trying to get out of her bad marriage. She assailed her former co-workers whom she felt did not offer her support. She felt they merely pretended to be helpful but actually stood back and watched her self-destruct and even got a kick out of her dilemma. In this last dream she was no longer silent. She screamed in frustration about her co-workers' unfairness.

The setting of this dream linked Julie's present marital troubles with her early home life and reiterated the feeling from her first two dreams of being set up for failure by someone whose judgment she trusted. The key dimensions in Julie's dreams on this night were mistrust/trust, compliance/defiance, outside/inside, shame/pride, and withholding/caring, with the balance falling on the negative side each time. Julie's dreams showed she felt betrayed by those she trusted. She wound up the night denied the help she needed and ashamed of her failure.

Julie's dreams suggested that her identity as an outsider, a waif unable to communicate with older men, may have its roots a long way back in her history. This feeling may relate not only to her old boss but also to her father. That was not immediately apparent to Julie, but it is a familiar axiom of psychotherapy that the past is alive in the present. Patterns of early relationships within the family persist in later life. We find certain people attractive but others unlikable, certain activities pleasurable but others distasteful, in parallel with our early life experiences. When we find the early roots of our current dilemmas, we also may find it easier to untangle our present predicament. We often reveal the emotional connections to these early roots in our dreams.

FROM BAD DREAMS TO GOOD

Julie was the first person I tried to help cope by using a short-term therapy that focused on her dreams. She left her marriage when her husband, a man much older than she, became a dominating, cruel, abusive bully. At the time she entered the divorce study, she suffered from both depression and anorexia nervosa. It would have been unrealistic to hope to cure her eating disorder in just a few weeks. I did hope to help her improve her underlying poor self-image.

In our first session, I explained how we would work on her dreams with that aim in mind, that we would work toward enabling her to stop her bad dreams and change them into good ones. I also pointed out her strengths: Although down on herself, she had had the fortitude to leave a bad marriage, travel a long way from home, and seek help for her problems. Like many people who are depressed, Julie merely listened in silence to these observations. However, the events of the following week showed that the seeds of a new way in which to view herself had begun to sprout.

Learning a little about how dreams work, and thinking about the issues that had been portrayed in her own dreams thrust Julie's dream system into high gear. Julie came to her second session reporting that she had been flooded with bad dreams. She began the hour by saying, "I've had my fill! I woke up from a dream early this morning saying, 'Alright, enough already, I don't want this anymore.' I told myself: 'Get out of this dream! Get out of this dream!' Then suddenly, I was out of it."

I asked her, "Have you done that before?"

"Not that I can remember."

"That's good," I said. "That's the first step. You recognized you were having a bad dream and you stopped it. Now what was the dream about?"

I was up on a roof, a short roof with a steep slant. I was trying to stay away from the edge so I wouldn't slip off. It was snowy and some woman was giving a demonstration on how to make snowballs. I had to melt paraffin wax to make them hold together and hand it to her. She would take the wax down a ladder and show people how to make snowballs that would stick together. She was being real careless with it, sloshing it all over. I kept saying, "This stuff is hot, I mean it's dangerous," while I was handing it to her. I was panicky about being on the edge of the roof. I felt I was going to slip off. I was stuck up there thinking the only way down was to walk backward down the ladder. I didn't dare do that. So I went back to my little corner.

"I have a hunch," I told her, "that I might be the woman in this dream. Maybe you feel I am asking you to do something dangerous, and maybe I'm being a little too casual about things that are too hot for you to handle. You may be wondering if you can trust me not to push you over the edge in some way or get you into hot water or wax?"

"True," Julie acknowledged. "But I wouldn't be sitting here if I didn't find something about you I could trust."

"I will try to be very much aware of your fears," I said. "Now, the slipping and sliding, an out-of-control image—I want you to find a safer way out of that, a way to get down that is not scary. I want you to find an image of safety that would be good for you."

She thought this over and said: "How about a roof closer to the ground, not so high?"

Three weeks later, in our fifth session, Julie reported another scary, up-above and out-of-control dream. However, this time she got down safely, and the dream had a better ending. She introduced it by saying: "Last night I had an interesting dream."

I was in a clothing store, floating above people. It was exciting to be able to look at everybody and see all the clothes, but be out of everyone's reach. I was strapped onto a helium balloon.

Then the dream turned bad. I tried to track down someone who had a jacket I wanted. I went out of the store, but the further I searched, the higher the balloon went and the darker and more dangerous the neighborhood underneath became. I was lost and frightened. It wasn't fun anymore.

I was running out of air and afraid I was going to fall. All of a sudden, I landed in a warehouse where my husband was teaching a karate class. One of his students, a best buddy of his, was standing on the sidelines. I said to him, "You know, my husband is really a dangerous person," and he nodded to me, "Yeah." I was real surprised that he agreed with me, that his loyalty was broken. That was the end of the dream.

"You created an ally! Someone who saw your dangerous husband the way you do, even someone close to him!" I told her.

Julie acknowledged that this was so and that her bad dream had a good ending. She interpreted it as showing that at first she enjoyed being out of other people's reach but then realized that being "above it all" could be lonely and dangerous. She managed to get back to earth safely. Much to her surprise, she found someone who saw her husband as she did. She tentatively had begun to put others in her dream picture on her side. Her dream dimensions were shifting to their positive side: trust rather than mistrust, inside rather than outside, defiance rather than compliance, pride rather than shame, and caring rather than withholding.

We also worked on changing Julie's attitude to food through her dreams. The first food dream she remembered starred her father. In this dream, she was about eight or ten years old, helping her father load a truck.

"When we are done," he said, "let's stop and get some ice cream on our way home." I said, "Okay," but I didn't really want any ice cream. It has too many calories. How was I going to manage not to hurt his feelings because he thought he was giving me a treat, something special just between us?

I decided to eat just a little bit, not enough to drive me crazy because of the calories. I got three scoops in a dish. My dad was off someplace else by then. I ate one scoop and thought, "Well, here I am eating this ice cream to make him happy and he's not even around. I ate it for nothing and now I have to get rid of these calories." I saw this huge sign of all the ice cream flavors, and I found myself getting sexually excited instead of hungry.

"I actually had an orgasm," Julie recalled. "That's how exciting it was."

Julie's dream suggested a reason behind her eating disorder. Somehow she felt that eating pleased her father and led to her growing bigger, more developed, and sexually stimulated by him. Better not to eat! That way she could stay in control. No wonder her loss of appetite and eating disorder emerged when she was trying to break away from her husband, a man who was about her father's age. After this dream report, I gave Julie some homework, suggesting that she try to change her dreams from the past to the present, to remember that she was no longer a child but rather a capable adult who could make her own choices.

At the next session, Julie reported another eating dream. This time she was an adult standing outside her parents' house. She was talking to her sister's friend about the friend's husband, who was overweight.

She was telling me that he is a good provider and she is happy with him. In the next part of the dream, we were inside the house. My sister had a jar of peanut butter. I thought it looked good and stuck my finger in and tasted it and thought, "Wow, this tastes good." I made myself a sandwich of peanut butter and crackers.

With a good husband, Julie was saying in her dream, she would not need to resist food. She could be fat and happy!

Julie's dream therapy stopped after only six sessions because she had to return to Pennsylvania to reestablish residence for the divorce proceedings. Her self-image still needed major repair, although the mending process had begun. Julie had learned to recognize bad dreams and stop them in their tracks. I hoped the dreamwork would continue to help her realize that she did not have to stay aloof from other people to be safe. She could find supportive allies in her battles with her husband. She had more confidence that she could get help or help herself if she were in trouble. She saw that food need not be dangerous, and that it might even be enjoyable.

Julie continued dreamwork on her own. We saw the fruits of her efforts in the dreams she reported a year later when she returned to the sleep laboratory for her dream checkup.

Although many hearings had been conducted by this point, Julie's divorce was still not final. She had refused to sign any financial settlement until her husband had agreed to share the proceeds from the sale of their home. Unfortunately, he already had spent these funds to settle his debts.

The situation seemed to have led to an impasse; however, Julie refused to give in.

Julie had made real strides in learning to take care of herself, and had started to train for a new career in computer programming. She was getting help with her anorexia through psychotherapy. Furthermore, there was a big change in her dreams. While they showed that she still expected to find herself in trouble, she was not running away anymore. Meet the new Julie:

I was on some kind of a slide outside a building. I had all my school stuff, my books and notebooks, and a briefcase. I fell down and lost my footing and all my stuff went sliding off the end of the chute into nowhere, and I thought everything was going to be broken, including my glasses. Somehow I grabbed onto the railing and hung on and saved myself from sliding off the end.

I didn't have all my clothes on either. I was trying to pull my shirt on because all these people were watching me and nobody was offering to help. I was buttoning up and thinking all my things are ruined.

Finally I got myself together and eased myself over the edge into a room where there were rows of tiny blue chairs for kids, but the sign said it was a police headquarters. I thought it was comical that it was like a nursery school with tiny chairs lined up. I went through the door to get out. A policeman was there. I had to go by him to pick up my briefcase and glasses that were stacked neatly on a table, like someone found them and laid them there for me. But I had to go by the policeman to get them.

I felt scared and I made a joke about how many children did he arrest in a day? But he didn't crack a smile. When he didn't laugh, I went past him, picked up my things and went on my way out of there.

The Julie of this dream had the resilience to recover from her fall and from the social embarrassment of being seen in public without all her clothes on. The picture language of dreams is beautifully economical, often condensing many meanings into a single image. Seeing herself undressed may have represented to Julie exposing herself in therapy, in the dream laboratory, at the several divorce hearings that had left her financially stripped, or all three. Despite all this embarrassment, Julie collected what was hers and went on.

The policeman may represent Julie's new therapist whom she granted the power to punish her for her youthful mistakes. What was new to Julie was that she was able to joke about it. Her major dream dimensions were more firmly on the positive side. She had more trust in herself. If outside, she could go inside if she wished to do so. If caught in a shameful situation, she could overcome it. She was no longer reviewing the past and expressing anger and shame about her marital mess. Rather, she was revising her sense of her ability to cope with the present. When she fell, she got up. She did not let an older male-authority figure intimidate her. She put on her clothes and walked by the policeman and out the door to move on with her life.

3

A New Dream Therapy

ORKING WITH JULIE, as well as others who were in the process of divorce, convinced me that dreams offer a shortcut to understanding and overcoming the emotional stumbling blocks of people in crisis. As a result, I began to refine the treatment approach Julie and I started together, developing a therapy that focuses on dreams. Useful in many situations, the crisis dreaming method aims to change negative, hurtful dreams to positive, healing ones. It enables people to stop bad dreams while they are in progress and rewrite the scripts. In this way, we can redirect dreaming to perform its proper function: to update our inner narrative, our sense of identity—first by recognizing those aspects of our present crisis that are negative and demoralizing, and next by finding images of strength already filed in our memory banks. We then can activate these images to change our waking attitudes. In so doing, we can adapt faster and more fully to the emotional hurricanes we all encounter.

The crisis dreaming method has value in good times as well as bad: It shows how we can use dreams not only to understand ourselves better but also to foster desired changes in our waking lives.

The technique is one you can undertake alone or with a

therapist. If you are working on your own, you will find examples of how the method works and step-by-step instructions throughout this book. If you are suffering from depression and seek help from a therapist, focusing on dreams can be a practical and speedy alternative to other types of psychotherapy. It's also useful as an addition to, or, in consultation with your therapist, as a substitute for, antidepressant medications.

People with life-threatening illnesses and victims of rape, child abuse, and other demoralizing assaults that have robbed them of their self-esteem have used the crisis dreaming method to restore their self-confidence and reactivate their personal growth. Their stories (with names and other identifying characteristics disguised) form the core of this book.

Some of us negotiate our way through stormy times more adroitly than others. Four factors seem to explain why some people are more successful: They have good friends, good genes, a good self-image, and good dreams.

Good friends provide us with a sense of continuity in our identity. Friends expect us to act as we always have acted, to behave "in character." Their steadiness helps stabilize us, even if inside we feel ourselves to be strangers in a strange land. Julie fled from home and job, leaving behind the few friends she had. Most were her husband's friends anyway, and she felt she couldn't count on their support. She was very much alone in her time of crisis.

Good genes give us the biological stamina to weather periods of major upset without succumbing to illness. You cannot, of course, control your biologic inheritance, but you can be sensitive to your family's characteristic responses to illness. Stress exacerbates some illnesses that run in families, including headaches, stomach upsets, and depression. You may be able to intervene actively to minimize trouble if such early warning symptoms appear. Julie inherited her mother's vulnerability to depression. Julie's mother had been too absorbed in her own problems to provide the necessary support to Julie, and Julie rejected her as a role model. Julie's father kept his distance from his wife and their children. As she grew up, Julie tried but failed to achieve closeness with him. She repeated this pattern in her marriage. She coped by turning to older men for support. She wanted to marry a man like her father but do a better job than her mother had done. Unfortunately, she chose the wrong man.

A *good self-image* provides the confidence that new demands can be met. If we have trust in ourselves and know how to reach out for help when we need it, we are better equipped to handle new crises as they come along. But Julie saw herself as a "runaway failure."

Good dreams aren't on most lists of "the right stuff" for coping with crises, although they should be. A good dream system enables us to reorganize our sense of ourselves internally, to make the necessary transformations in point of view when circumstances change, to create a new, self-respecting version of who we are. Luckily, Julie had the potential to be a good dreamer.

The crisis dreaming method addresses malfunctioning dreams directly to try to change those that reveal a continuing, underlying, poor identity pattern. People in crisis often turn for help to a physician, psychotherapist, or other counselor. Yet few of these professionals look into their patients' dream lives to find the inner scripts that may be responsible for their patients' sense of despair. Some who do ask about dreams are handicapped by the poverty of their patients' recall. They must work with whatever fragments of dreams their patients happen to remember and are willing to discuss. That's like trying to reconstruct the plot of a 500-page novel from just one page.

These therapists rarely hear about the dream that came before or after the one the patient remembers or chooses to discuss. Often, a therapist assumes a dream is important because the patient remembers it. Its meaning comes not from the context of that night but from the associations the patient makes while awake, letting his or her mind float freely around the dream story.

There is, however, a better way. In the sleep laboratory, we have developed techniques to capture dreams that anyone can use. Once you discover the trend of what is happening from dream to dream, you can identify more easily those that are unproductive or even self-destructive, and you can start to work on dream repair that very night.

If you currently are wrestling with a major life crisis, the first step is to pay more attention to your dreams. This book provides you with guidelines for sharpening your skills in capturing your dreams and exploring them. Learning how others have dealt with pivotal events in their lives by transforming their dreams will give you new perspectives on issues that may now be troubling you.

You may be skeptical. The conventional wisdom is that most of us recover from a crisis by changing our waking lives, not our dreams. Can it work the other way around? Those who have tried the crisis dreaming method answer this question with an enthusiastic "Yes!" Many of those with whom I have worked tell me that dreams provided them with both the insight on how the present connects to the past and the impetus to change the program of the self to create a better fit with their present lives. They have found that changing the endings of their dreams can be a giant step toward those goals. This concept shocks traditional psychoanalysts. It challenges the basic idea of the nature of the relationship between the waking mind and dreams, which Freud introduced nearly 100 years ago.

WHAT FREUD DIDN'T KNOW ABOUT DREAMS

The Interpretation of Dreams, originally published in 1900, did not bring Sigmund Freud instant recognition. In the first six years, only 351 copies were sold. Like many writers, Freud carped about the reviews. "The few notices of it that have appeared in scientific periodicals show so much lack of understanding and so much misunderstanding that my only reply to the critics would be to suggest their reading the book again— or perhaps, indeed, merely to suggest their reading it," he tartly noted in the second edition, published in 1909.

Despite its inauspicious debut, *The Interpretation of Dreams* vastly altered the understanding not only of dreams but of human nature as well. Dreams, Freud says, show us what lies behind the masks we present to the waking world. Generally considered Freud's finest work, the book provides an overview of mental functioning, and it introduces psychoanalysis, the talking cure, as a global tool for exploring how the mind works.

Nearly a century later, Freud's views are widely, although not universally, accepted. Most therapists who propose other approaches explain the ways in which their theories contrast with those of Freud, who charted a new course for both psychiatry and popular culture. Try to imagine Woody Allen or Tennessee Williams or even *The Simpsons* without contributions from Freud.

Freud's work became the touchstone for dream psychology. Fifty years before the first sleep laboratory studies proved him right, Freud pictured the mind as always active, both awake and asleep. He saw it organized as a pyramid, with thoughts coming from three different levels in various states of consciousness.

The top level, the *conscious* mind, operates in the here and now. It contains what we see, hear, feel, smell, and taste, plus what we remember from the past and can imagine about the future. In this part of the mind, we can choose to turn our attention this way and that, inward to mull over some problem or outward to listen to conversation. In our conscious thinking, we form our picture of reality. We acknowledge that what goes through our minds are our own thoughts and feelings.

The middle layer on Freud's pyramid is the *preconscious* mind. It houses thoughts and memories not presently in use. They are, however, at the edge of our awareness. With a little effort, we can bring them into focus.

The deepest layer is the *unconscious* mind. This area holds the dark, primitive parts of ourselves, both our never-gratified childish wishes and the dangers and punishments we fear might befall us for having them. We may deny having feelings of anger, hate, jealousy, or spite, for example, and because we have banished them from our conscious minds, we cannot control them at will. Nonetheless, Freud says, they lurk in the basement of our minds and influence our behavior. In sleep, they rise to the top of the pyramid. Released from waking constraints, they supply the fire to forge our dreams.

We neither acknowledge having these feelings nor think about them consciously, Freud says, because they arose so long ago in our developmental history that we have forgotten them. Here lie the old rivalries, as the Smothers Brothers capture in their routine, "Mother always liked you best." Moreover, if we tried to act on our impulses, they would get us into trouble. "I would like to murder you," a child might think about the new baby in the house. "But if I did, Mother wouldn't like me."

We learn early to keep the peace by putting these impulses out of our minds. And there they stay, at least until we sleep, when they come out of hiding to parade through our dreams. During sleep, we need not obey the laws of reality, nor heed our promises to be good. We get to dream our deepest wishes, to recollect this forgotten part of ourselves.

Freud used the term "wish" as we ordinarily use it, to mean desires and aspirations, both those we acknowledge and those we don't. Because dreams seem real to us while they are in progress, Freud says, we feel the pleasure of having our forbidden wishes satisfied. Dreams are our safety valve. Our uncon-

scious cons us in dreams, lulls us with the imaginary fulfillment of our most strongly felt longings.

If dreams are such a safe expression of our inner selves,
why don't we have more explicit fantasies? If dreams forced us
to confront our hidden wishes head on, Freud says, they
would scare us awake. That's why we code our desires into
symbols that stand for the real thing and why we condense
sequences of thoughts into visual metaphors. Sometimes we
transfer our feelings to another character, an animal, or an
object in our dreams. We may even disguise a feeling by
dreaming about its opposite. A dream that wakes us is a dream
that failed. It did not hide our unacceptable thoughts well
enough. It did not protect our waking self-image and our
sleep.

How then can we account for anxious dreams and nightmares, particularly those that put us in the same terrible situation night after night? Freud's answer was that not all dreams
succeed. We try in these dreams to rewrite early scripts, to
master situations in which we originally were helpless.

Dreams, Freud says, in one of his best-known aphorisms,
serve as "the royal road to a knowledge of the unconscious
activities of the mind." Understanding dreams links the conscious to the unconscious. Dreams light up the way our minds
work. They may lead us to the reasons behind persistent life
dilemmas that we do not recognize and that we cannot talk
about directly.

"The psychoanalyst, like the archaeologist in his excava-
tions," Freud says, "must uncover layer after layer of the
patient's psyche before coming to the deepest, most valuable
treasures." Dreams provide shards of memory that show us
where to search as we seek to unearth the ancient mental history that helps perpetuate our present emotional problems.

Freud saw this exploration as hard work. He distinguished
the manifest, or explicit, dream story from its latent, or
implicit, meanings. He thought the dream story, the narrative

that we view in our dreams, served as a curtain behind which forbidden wishes, urges, and fantasies hid.

To discover a dream's true meaning, Freud explains, we must decode the symbols in the manifest dream by examining the thoughts, memories, and feelings they stir up. Thus, a man who dreamed, "I am riding in my car but another man is driving," might be saying, "Someone else—my father, my analyst—is running my life," and further, "I would like to kill my father, get him out of the way, so I could be in the driver's seat, that is, marry my mother." Freud might say the dream *conceals* this basic conflict. Our more contemporary view is that the dream *reveals* it.

Freud taught us that the reasons for our behavior may be quite complex and that thoughts and feelings from our earliest years are still alive in the present, even if unrecognized. Nonetheless, Freud's picture of the mind as a small, rational area sitting atop a swamp bubbling with primitive impulses of sex and violence offends us today. The scientist asks, "Where's the proof?" And the rest of us find it hard to believe that we cannot do better than that in understanding ourselves and controlling our behaviors.

In today's society, far more open than that of Freud's Vienna a century ago, is it still so hard to face sexual and aggressive feelings that we must express them only in our dreams? Isn't it more likely that our dreams are unclear to us only because we don't understand their picture language? Perhaps our difficulty merely reflects differences in the way memory links our thoughts together in wakefulness and in sleep. Perhaps if we could capture more of our dreams as they unfold, if we acquired some fluency in their language, we might not find them hard to figure out at all. Julie and Harold quickly made this discovery for themselves.

A dream starts before nightfall, Freud says, when some feeling or thought remains active in the corner of the mind's eye as we fall asleep. When sleep begins, this day residue crosses paths with some unconscious wish that is seeking expression. If similarities exist, the wish and the day residue combine, much as in a chemical process, and a dream crystallizes. In this way, my concern about a young girl in danger of being hit by a car connected with my unconscious wish that I could have saved my daughter, and prompted my dream of a young man crossing a busy street on rollerskates.

Since the day thought and the strongly emotional wish undergo transformations in the merger process, we may find it hard to recognize the meaning of the new images and feelings. We wake up with the sense of having had the strangest dream. We may be able to trace part of the dream back to a recognizable source, the part that leads to the trivial conscious thought. But we will miss the point of the dream unless we also uncover the unconscious elements it expresses.

We can imagine Freud warning his patients: "Your best efforts to understand dreams on your own will yield little, merely the trifling day thoughts, not the really important inspiration, the unconscious wishes. For that, you need in-depth, long-term, one-on-one psychoanalytic work."

In Julie's first dream in the sleep laboratory, a group of people push a reluctant man into taking a woman to the zoo in the evening, an inappropriate time. Julie might recall a conversation about blind dates the previous day. But without figuring out why the dream involved this poor choice of activities, she won't see the parallels with her own unsuitable mating to an older man, nor will she see how her marriage choice reflected her unconscious wishes to please her father, still a potent influence in her life. Freud encouraged his patients to associate freely about their dreams, to say whatever came to mind; in this way, they would uncover their dreams' underlying significance via the dreams' links to the past.

My dream about a young person safely negotiating a busy street shows where Freud's contribution to our understanding of dreams still holds up. The dream demonstrates how a daytime reminder can stir up an underlying wish that remains active years later. However, this inspection also shows where Freud's view is not valid. The dream is not too difficult to decode without the help of an analyst, and its meaning does not shock or embarrass me.

Psychoanalysis had its heyday in the early part of this century. By the 1940s, dream interpretation fell out of fashion in psychiatry. Psychologist Erik Erikson blamed the disregard of dreams on the lengthy business of psychoanalytic treatment, often involving five-day-per-week sessions for several years with, he felt, an endless morass of dream associations that took patient and therapist farther and farther away from present reality. Researchers interested in the unconscious began to employ other means to get there. They used techniques such as hypnosis and projective tests that were faster routes to the inner world. They viewed dreams as too ephemeral for serious study.

Then, in the 1950s, the development of potent new medications made it possible to treat thousands of patients hampered by depression and anxiety even more quickly. This advance fostered an emphasis on biologic psychiatry that continues today, as is reflected in the widely held concept that using medications to relieve symptoms is much more practical than employing dreams. The use of medications, along with new behavioral treatments, made the pursuit of dreams, in some therapists' eyes, too indirect, too long, and too cumbersome a route to mental health.

Furthermore, the economy today is tighter. Government agencies and health insurance companies impose more restrictions on the use of mental health services. Short-term therapy often focuses more on symptom relief than on redefining identity. Dreams usually get short shrift. Moreover, the next generation of therapists is receiving little formal education on how to work with dreams.

However, interest in dreams is not dead—it's merely resting. Freud heard what we now know to be only a tiny fraction of all the dreams his patients experienced; until recently, all therapists faced the same dilemma. Freud recognized the difficulty poor memory for dreams presents, but he had no way to cope with it. Modern-day dream therapists do. They can make use of techniques developed in the sleep laboratory. These same techniques can be used at home.

UNDERSTANDING DREAM DIMENSIONS

Key questions to ask yourself about any dream you recall are: "Why this dream?" and "Why dream this dream now?" For that, you need to look for the underlying themes that bind together your dreams and waking life, the emotional issues that prompt your sleeping self to declare: "This is what I am feeling. This is what day-to-day events remind me of. This is what it is about my present self that needs more attention."

We build our dream stories to express these underlying themes using various dream dimensions, distinctions that we make to define and categorize our experiences. Dimensions, which reflect opposing states or qualities, constitute our own unique and habitual way of organizing the world we live in. We start in infancy to make big evaluative discriminations: This feels good; that feels bad. This is warm; that is cold. By the time we reach adulthood, we have added many such distinctions. In dreams, the specific images, along with their opposites, show how we see people and events and express our innermost evaluations of them and feelings about them. Our sense of who we are rests on where we are on the spectrum of categories revealed by our most important dream dimensions.

The idea of our using a system of opposites in our dreams is one I have adapted from the work of the noted anthropologist, Claude Levi-Strauss, who used this approach to analyze the characteristic ways of thinking and myth-making in tribal cultures. He suggested that the mind works on problems by dividing key issues into pairs and then by juggling these elements, this way and that, patiently rearranging and recombining them, until they fit the needs of the person telling the story.

Studies of waking memory show that we mentally file new information with bits of similar information as well as with their opposites; that is, we sort a new fact not only by what it is but also by what it is not. Thus, it's no surprise that we dream about winning the lottery when we're worried about not being able to pay the bills, or about striking out at bat at age 10 just after receiving a big promotion. The following list comprises some of the most common dimensions we see in dreams in our laboratory:

- Safety versus danger
- Helplessness versus competence
- Pride versus shame
- Activity versus passivity
- Closeness versus distance
- Independence versus dependence
- Trust versus mistrust
- Male versus female
- Authenticity versus pretense
- Defiance versus compliance
- Old versus young

While each dream in a series may have several dimensions, the same few dimensions usually are expressed repeatedly in a single night. Some parts of a dream may reflect the positive pole, and others the negative side. A dream expressing feelings of danger, for example, may precede or follow one expressing feelings of safety. Honing in on any one concept that a dream presents and stepping back to ask, "What is its opposite?" may open our eyes to important issues we wouldn't otherwise see.

In Julie's first dreams in the laboratory, she watched others arrange a date, walked down the highway looking into cars, and saw a former co-worker being mistreated by her fellow employees. She repeatedly was on the outside looking in. The key dimensions in her early dreams were mistrust/trust, defiance/compliance, outside/inside, shame/pride, and withholding/caring. As Julie gained control over her life, her dream dimensions remained the same, but she transformed them to their positive side.

Here is another example of how we use dimensions to build our dreams: Bob is a young man who was trying to break off a relationship with his girlfriend, Gloria, without hurting her or feeling guilty about disappointing her. He reported this dream:

There was a mad dog in the backyard. I didn't really see it, but I knew it was there and was a threat. So I poisoned it. I knew it was dead because I saw an old woman standing over the body. She looked like my grandmother. Then I was in my apartment, and it seemed the dog or a wolf was now in there, too. It was a hovering menace behind a door. Then I saw myself in the wolf's skin. I just pulled it over me.

"What do you make of the mad dog?" I asked Bob.

"Gloria sometimes calls me the Bad Boyfriend," he said. "She sometimes chides me when I forget to phone her by saying, 'Bad dog.' I guess the mad dog/bad dog is part of me that is a threat to other people."

"And its opposite?"

"I need to get rid of that bad dog image she has of me. It makes me uncomfortable. I'm not really like that. I'm really a good friend, helpful, dependable. But just now, I don't want to get closer."

The main dream dimensions Bob has identified so far are hurtful/helpful, bad/good.

"Why do you suppose you saw your grandmother in this dream?" I asked.

Bob hesitated only a moment before starting to talk about his father, now dead, an out-of-control alcoholic who left the family when Bob was in his early teens. Bob and his mother then lived with his father's mother.

"My grandmother is still alive. I'm sorry I rejected my father so completely before he died. I never wanted to visit him. I suppose in some ways I must be like him, but I don't want to be." The appearance of his grandmother in the dream is related to the disappearance of Bob's bad father and to his question, "Am I bad, too?"

Other important elements of Bob's relationships were closeness/distance, and accepting/rejecting. Bob felt that he was being distant, rejecting, and hurtful to Gloria, just as his father was to him. He wanted to get rid of the relationship that brought out these traits in him. In the dream, he poisoned the bad dog, but it came back to haunt him.

"You can't get rid of the part of you that is like your father that easily," I remarked. "What's the opposite here?"

Bob laughed. "I am!" he said. "I am a sheep in wolf's clothing."

His dream image resolved his discomfort with seeing his resemblance to his father. It enabled him to reassure himself, "I'm really good underneath. My bad dog behavior is superficial. I'm not evil pretending to be good, but good appearing to be bad, only because this relationship with Gloria is not right."

⇨ SELF-HELP: Keeping a dream diary

To use our dreams, we first have to recall them. That requires some system for record-keeping. In the 1890s, psychologist Mary Calkins of Wellesley College collected several hundred of her own dreams in just a few months with a few basic tools: paper, pencil, candles, and matches.

Such materials still suffice, although modern gadgets such

as flashlight pens and clipboards with small battery-operated lights attached may make the job easier. If you don't have to worry about disturbing a sleeping partner and prefer talking to writing, use a tape recorder. If you use one that is voice-activated, you won't have to turn on the light. Keep your recording tools at your bedside.

Write down or tape-record all that you remember, the more details, the better. Seemingly trivial aspects of a dream may turn out to be meaningful later. Images or events that seem bizarre or out of context may prove significant in relation to what came before or after, or to a dream you had yesterday or will have tomorrow.

Making a record is important. The exercise of putting thoughts down on paper or tape is especially helpful for those who are not used to recognizing inner emotional responses while going through the day's routine. The process reinforces the habit of getting in touch with your inner mental life. The act of recording a dream often will help you recover parts of it that initially seemed elusive. Make a sketch if that helps you to visualize the dream better.

It would be ideal to record dreams as often as you remember them and to make diary-keeping a habit, like brushing your teeth each morning. However, most of us lead busy lives. If weekday responsibilities interfere with dream-recording, try to allot some time on weekends.

Record the dream before you shower and have breakfast. Dreams that are vivid when you awaken seldom stay as memorable as the day progresses. Tell the dream to someone if you can. Repeating a dream—like telling a joke—will help you remember it better.

⇨ **SELF-HELP: Discovering your dream dimensions**

By the time you have recorded approximately 10 dreams in your dream diary, you should start to see patterns emerging in the dream dimensions you frequently use. Paying attention to your dream dimensions will help make you more aware of the ways you habitually characterize life experiences. Because our self-identity evolves out of how we see ourselves through the eyes of other people, it is especially useful to discover how our dreams reflect our feelings about others and about their reactions to us. Try the following techniques as a way to start this assessment process:

◆ Review your notes about your dreams. If you have not already done so in your journal, jot down in the margins hunches about what was going on in your waking life that may have triggered a particular dream.

◆ Underline the adjectives you use to describe other people and yourself in relation to them. Use a different color ink to make the words stand out. Some examples from several dreams include:

He was a *huge* man, really grossly *obese*.
He was *old*, wearing *white*, with a *scraggly* beard that was also *white*.
I was *angry* with my mother for being so *critical*.

◆ On a separate page, write the adjectives you use frequently (e.g., more than three times in 10 dreams).

◆ After each adjective, write another that has the opposite meaning. For the examples above, the dimensions would be huge/tiny, obese/slender, old/young, white/black, scraggly/kempt, angry/loving, critical/complimentary.

◆ Look for these dimensions in future dreams.

⇨ SELF-TEST: Assessing relationships

Psychologist George Kelly developed a test to help discover what he called our personal constructs: the distinctions we make about people who are emotionally important in our lives. The *Personal Constructs* test shows how we compare and contrast these "significant others." We have adapted it to help you begin to find out how you think about yourself in relation to these people. While Kelly did not design this test for analyzing dreams, it is a good way to discover emotional landmarks as you undertake this task. Set aside about an hour to complete the test.

PART 1. PEOPLE IN MY LIFE

List names or initials associated with these descriptions:

1. My mother (or person most like a mother to me) _____

2. My father (or person most like a father to me) _____

3. My brother nearest my age (or person most like a brother to me) _____

4. My sister nearest my age (or person most like a sister to me) _____

5. My closest girl/boyfriend immediately before I started going with my spouse or present significant other _____

6. My wife/husband or closest present girl/boyfriend _____

7. A boss or other supervisor, under whom I served in a period of great stress _____

8. A person who for some reason appears to dislike me _____

9. A person I have met recently I would like to get to know better _____

10. The person I would most like to help or feel most sorry for _____

11. The smartest individual I know personally _____

12. The most successful individual I know personally

_____

13. The most interesting individual I know personally

_____

PART 2. COMPARING AND CONTRASTING

Look at your list of 13 people. In each group of three listed
below by their numbers, think of an important way that only
two of these three are *alike*, with a characteristic that the third
person does not have. After you have decided what that
important difference is—young/old, warm/cold, smart/
dumb, whatever strikes you as apt—write the similar characteristic in the first column and the opposite characteristic in the
second. Circle the numbers of the two people who are alike.

A personal example: When I compared and contrasted 2,
7, and 8, I discovered that I could describe both my father and
Carl Rogers, my early colleague, as remote, whereas I would
identify the other person in this group, someone who appears
to dislike me, as extremely intrusive. I discovered by doing this
that I can tolerate remoteness but not intrusiveness: this tells
me about a dimension important to me and which side is positive and which negative.

	Characteristic of Two	Opposite of One
Characteristic		
8,9,10	_____	_____
3,12,13	_____	_____
4,9,11	_____	_____

2,7,8   _____   _____

7,9,1   _____   _____

1,4,5   _____   _____

6,10,12   _____   _____

1,2,6   _____   _____

2,3,5   _____   _____

PART 3. HOW YOU THINK ABOUT YOURSELF

Write down each of the positive characteristics in the list you made for others (e.g., "helpful") and then rate yourself on these same characteristics, using a scale of 1–5. (Use additional paper if necessary. We provide only five spaces because you probably had some duplicates.)

	Not Like Me			Very Like Me	
Characteristics					
1. _____	1	2	3	4	5
2. _____	1	2	3	4	5
3. _____	1	2	3	4	5
4. _____	1	2	3	4	5
5. _____	1	2	3	4	5

(Adapted from George Kelly's *Psychology of Personal Constructs*)

Completing this test should sharpen your sense of how to look for opposites in dreams recorded in your dream diary.

While this test focuses on interpersonal relationships, it gives you a good idea of how the search for dream dimensions works. You need to be alert to many types of dimensions expressed in dreams. Watch, for example, for those that involve setting, such as light/dark and open/confined, and those that call attention to the passage of time, such as spring/fall and new/old. The more dream dimensions you can identify, the fuller your understanding of a dream's many possible meanings is likely to be.

4

Chasing Dreams

KNOWLEDGE of how to tell when dreams are in progress was discovered almost by accident. In the early 1950s, physiologist Nathaniel Kleitman of the University of Chicago was trying to catalogue differences during sleeping and waking in heart rate, breathing, types of body movements, and other activities. Kleitman asked a graduate student, Eugene Aserinsky, to monitor the eye movements in infants. While it's easy to see eyes moving beneath closed lids during sleep, watching wiggly babies is an arduous chore. Aserinsky found an older subject, his own eight-year-old son. To make his task even simpler, he taped electrodes beside his son's eyes and attached them to a recording device.

To his astonishment, he saw that while his son slept there were several episodes a night of very fast eye activity. He and Kleitman, now honored as the father of modern sleep research, found that during these periods, when eyes darted to and fro much as in waking, the heart beat faster and breathing quickened. The researchers wondered if these rapid eye movements—or REMs as they dubbed them—signified that people were watching their dream stories unfold. A second-year medical student who then joined the project, William Dement, was assigned the task of awakening sleepers at different times during the night.

The researchers found that awakening sleepers during episodes of REM sleep almost always yielded reports of visual dreams. By contrast, awakening sleepers when their eyes were still, during non-REM (or NREM) sleep periods, seldom did. The researchers soon learned that REM sleep alternates with NREM sleep approximately every 90 minutes. We spend nearly two hours in REM sleep every night, from infancy through old age.

Not only do we dream a lot, our need to dream may be as basic as our need for food and water. If we don't get our usual quota of dream time, we make up for it when we next sleep. Indeed, when we did research trying to eliminate REM sleep by awakening sleepers every time they entered that state, we found that within three nights we had to awaken some subjects as many as 30 times a night.

Before the discovery of REM sleep, most scientists believed that sleep is a quiet time, both physically and mentally. The finding that sleep had within it both quiet and active states electrified investigators. "This was the breakthrough," says Dement, now director of the sleep center at Stanford University and one of the field's foremost researchers. "It changed sleep research from a relatively pedestrian inquiry into an intensely exciting endeavor pursued with great determination in laboratories and clinics all over the world."

In their eagerness to discover how dreams are constructed and how they relate to our waking life, researchers engaged in a wide variety of inventive experiments. They tried to stimulate sleepers with lights flashed over their taped-open eyes, water sprinkled on their faces, and sounds piped into their bedrooms. They served pepperoni pizza and banana cream pie at bedtime.

In some early studies in our own laboratory, we tried to determine if experiencing highly emotional stimuli before sleep would affect dreams. We showed pornographic films borrowed from the Kinsey Institute to groups of heterosexual and homosexual young men. However, none of these attempts had much impact. The sleepers' dream machines chugged along, churning out dreams based on their own day-to-day lives. If our stimuli showed up at all in dreams, they merged into the ongoing stories, the ones the dreamers constructed themselves.

"We all know what dreams are like," writes psychiatrist Frederick Snyder. "We know that they are vague, irrational, disjointed, incoherent, bizarre, absurd, nonsensical and extravagant—a kind of temporary madness reflecting an alien, archaic world beyond the laws of time or space or logic or morality. In the case of our own dreams," he adds, "we might privately suspect that they are often expressions of unsuspected brilliance, wit, poetry and intuition."

It turns out that such a private suspicion fits very few dreams. We remember our bizarre dreams better precisely because they are bizarre. Despite their reputation as abstract Fellini-like productions, most of our dreams prove to be rather mundane. Indeed, most dreams pale beside the fantastic flights of ideas we can experience while awake. Writers, poets, artists, and musicians often deliberately seek to portray the weird, the preposterous, or the absurd. Under the influence of drugs, when suffering from fever, or in states of profound sleep deprivation, we may see and hear things that aren't there. In ordinary waking life, the mind may wander in ways not intended.

In a landmark early sleep laboratory study at the National Institute of Mental Health, Snyder collected 635 laboratory dreams from 250 healthy, normal volunteers.

"The most striking feature is the pervasiveness of the self, the all-important 'I'," Snyder writes. We appear in 95 percent of our dreams and play a distinct role in the action. Indeed, we almost always assign ourselves the starring role. In perhaps one dream in 20, we aren't conscious of taking part in the dream but simply observe the action. We may not recognize until later that we are there in some symbolic form, a massive stone wall, for example, or a car that won't start.

We are almost never alone. The cast includes both recognized and unrecognized persons. Although we think of dreams as primarily visual, what we most commonly do in our dreams, Snyder reports, is sit and talk. Dreams usually take place in familiar settings, or, even if not, in ordinary surroundings. Only rarely do we conjure up exotic or fantastic, out-of-this-world locations. Dreams, in fact, he says, are "a remarkably faithful replica of waking life."

Dreams contain unpleasant emotions twice as often as pleasant ones, with fear and anxiety most prominent, followed by anger. The most common of the pleasant feelings reported is friendliness. Snyder and his colleagues rated only one dream in five reported in their study as "interesting"—that is, a good story. Some people, not surprisingly, had more interesting dreams than others.

MODERN DREAM COLLECTING

Today, we still use the same methods established by the early researchers to collect dreams in the laboratory. The subjects arrive around 9 P.M., pajamas and toothbrushes in hand. We show them to a private bedroom and try to make them comfortable and relaxed. When they are ready for bed, the technician tapes tiny electrodes at several places on the scalp, beside each eye, behind the ears, and under the chin. These electrodes pick up small electrical signals and transmit them via thin wires to another room. There, polygraph devices amplify the signals and trace brain waves, muscle changes, and eye movements across a moving paper chart throughout the night. Each night the sleeper generates a paper trail more than a half-mile long.

Before turning out the light, we tell sleepers in dream studies that we will awaken them several times. "When you hear your name called, just tell whatever has been going through your mind at the time," the technician says. "You may be dreaming, or thinking, or not aware of anything at all. Whatever you can report is fine. We will ask you a series of questions each time before you go back to sleep. Okay? Goodnight."

The technician monitors the recording chart and watches the sleeper on a video monitor. Each time the brain waves speed up, the eyes begin to move rapidly, and the muscle tone of the chin drops, we know that a dream is hatching. Some people think that dreams burst forth, fully formed, in seconds. They don't. They last from about 10 minutes at the beginning of the night to as long as 45 minutes just before we wake up. We get a quick preview of coming attractions and later a full-length feature.

The first dream usually states the theme for those that follow, drawing on a recent experience, usually one involving some feelings of anxiety or uncertainty. The next harks back to a similar earlier experience, and the rest integrate the old and new, jumping ahead to the future, often winding up back in the present. Dream stories also become "crazier" in each succeeding REM sleep period, more complex in their story structure, with stronger emotions and older images that are more and more remote from present reality. It is from the last one, the one that is often the most fantastic, that we usually awaken at home. Thus, we fool ourselves into thinking that all dreams are like this one, the grand finale. In the laboratory, it becomes apparent that this is not so.

In waking sleepers, we try to come as close as possible to the end of each REM episode to permit them to experience most of the dream. It is risky to wait until brainwaves show the dream is over; once sleepers shift out of REM sleep, they have a hard time remembering even the most vivid of dreams. To capture a dream in the laboratory, we must interrupt the show while the film is still running. True, this means we miss the ending, but we do catch most of the plot. By following this procedure, we collect most of the several dreams of a night.

In cadence with the natural lengthening of REM sleep episodes across the night, the technician waits five minutes longer each time to awaken the sleeper for a report. For the first REM period, the call comes after five minutes; for the second, after 10 minutes; and so on through the night.

Between dreams, our minds don't simply go blank. However, if awakened during NREM sleep, we're more apt to say we've been thinking rather than dreaming. Our REM sleep dream reports are more visual and story-like. They capture our attention by involving us in the action, as in this example:

I was in a toy car racing along a highway, but it seemed to be on tracks so that I couldn't steer it. It felt dangerous because I was surrounded by wall-to-wall trucks. I was on my way to California.

NREM sleep reports usually lack both the imagery and the immediate sense of being there that characterizes REM reports. They are more like our everyday thoughts:

I was thinking about going to California and wondering whether my little old car could make it.

Indeed, NREM sleep thoughts often are so logical that we don't believe we are asleep at all; instead, we believe that we're merely lying in bed, thinking things over. Some people who report that they suffer severe insomnia really are sleeping lightly and doing a lot of NREM pondering.

REM dreams may contain several episodes. It may take hundreds of words for the dreamer to narrate one dream completely. By contrast, a NREM thought often requires only a single phrase or sentence. Some people, of course, are better visualizers than others. Some individuals report images when awakened from all stages of sleep. Others report more thoughts than images even during REM sleep.

Learning about dreams by collecting them in the laboratory has some disadvantages. Something about the situation discourages dramatic reports. Sleeping in a strange place, wearing electrodes, knowing that you are being watched with a camera, being awakened unexpectedly and intermittently—such environmental influences are bound to color dream reports. Dream stories prove less sexual and aggressive, less concerned with either success or misfortune, than those the same people report having in the privacy of their own bedrooms. They often deal with the laboratory itself—certainly an unusual topic for a home dream. Being summoned from sleep to tell a dream over an intercom to a technician you've just met is not like telling it to your therapist or even to family members at the breakfast table. In the laboratory, people often tell us that they hope they do not shock us or embarrass themselves by what they dream.

Nonetheless, when researchers compared home and laboratory dreams collected under the same circumstances, they found the two quite similar. In one study, people set an alarm clock to wake them at 6:30 A.M. They then dictated a report of their dreams into a tape recorder. Whether they did this at home or in the lab, their dreams proved equally vivid, though images dreamed in the lab were still less aggressive than those dreamed at home.

Judges given the task of sorting out the dreams of any one person from a series of nights can tell reliably which dreams occurred on the same night. They also can distinguish the dreams of one person from the dreams of others. Our dreams are as individual as our fingerprints.

Dream studies conducted in sleep laboratories support many of Freud's theories, yet allow us to go beyond them. Freud was right about the mind's working on many levels simultaneously. Awake, we usually stick to the business of living. We scan reality and respond to it. As we fall asleep, the conscious channel of the mind becomes like background noise, a sort of steady hum we usually can ignore until morning. Sometimes we sleep with one ear open to hear the baby's cry, but mostly we pay little heed to the outside world.

Once we settle into sleep, the second level of the mind, the one that attends to our ongoing emotional concerns, seizes the spotlight of our awareness. Emotions that we may not identify in waking life carry over into sleep. When REM sleep arrives, these emotions trigger memories of times when we experienced similar feelings. We weave past and present into the story—like hallucinations of dreams, drawing from a vast storehouse of images filed in our memory networks. Feelings serve as the thread that links one dream image to the next and all the dreams of a night to one another.

Suppose, for example, that in the back of my mind I am worrying about aging and the coming hardships of winter. I also have a long-standing fear of looking ridiculous. Before I go to bed I hear a weather report predicting snow. If I were awakened during the first NREM period and asked what was going through my mind, I might say,

I was wondering if I could learn to ski at my age.

Then I enter the first REM period with its more excited brain state. Memories surface that connect emotionally with my underlying waking concerns. These come from the level that Freud called the unconscious. A dream jells:

I was skiing, wearing only my pink silk panties. Everyone was laughing.

The identity message of this dream says, "It's embarrassing to be seen when I'm not at my best." I also answer the question I posed in my first NREM period by telling myself, "Perhaps I could learn to ski if I could stop worrying about looking foolish."

Two Boston psychoanalysts, Ramon Greenberg and Chester Pearlman, recorded in a sleep laboratory the dreams of a man undergoing psychoanalysis. They found that his dreams often reflected the major emotional concerns he'd voiced during the preceding analytic hours. Moreover, the dreams often showed attempts to resolve these concerns. On those occasions when, in fact, the man did resolve one of these issues in his dreams, his analyst's report showed that his waking emotional equilibrium also improved.

Greenberg and Pearlman then decided to see how faithfully their own dreams reflected the important issues in their waking lives. Although neither was able to spend time in a sleep laboratory, they both decided to keep two journals: one to write down the day's events, and the other to record their dreams during their summer vacations. One of them soon found he was waking up three to five times a night with a remembered dream, a pattern consistent with the normal frequency of REM periods.

Their first dreams involved both their guilt about leaving their patients over the vacation period and their efforts to learn more about dreaming. These themes surfaced in dreams of searching detectives, binoculars, keys, and taking things apart. Their dreams also incorporated feelings about parents who came to visit during the vacation and about a child going off to college, subjects of books they were reading, and problems of becoming accepted by the group at a camp one of them attended. At the end of the vacation, their dreams looked forward, addressing concerns about going back to work.

Sometimes the dreams portrayed actual situations and conveyed a picture of thoughts in which they were absorbed. The father of one of the analysts had died at the beginning of the summer. The analyst's preoccupation with grief and attempts to cope with it pervaded both his waking hours and his dreams.

OBSTACLES TO REMEMBERING DREAMS

Most of us ignore our dream life. We have learned not to concern ourselves with it. Our action-oriented culture discourages paying attention to dreams. They are so impractical! The idea that we forget our dreams because they dredge up desires we're not prepared to face in our waking lives may be intriguing, but we don't need such complex reasons to account for the usual poverty of the morning catch. There are many practical reasons for our poor recall. Among them:

Emotional state at bedtime

When at peace with ourselves and the waking world, we tend to sleep soundly, dream regularly, but remember few of these dreams. When we are worried, have a bad conscience, or are excited by any strong feeling before sleep, we sleep more lightly. Intense emotions and light sleep are definite aids to dream memory. When we sleep fitfully, we may awaken before a dream is over, making us more apt to remember it. Up to a point, stress increases dream recall.

Sometimes, however, dreams that wake us prove so disturbing that we'd prefer to forget them and promptly do so. As we'll discuss in Chapter 11, Holocaust survivors may erase dream content not only from their memory when they awaken in the morning but even from REM sleep. People who have sleep terror attacks or sleepwalking episodes in times of stress may abort a dream altogether and have no memory of what they did instead.

How long we sleep

Long sleepers remember dreams better than short sleepers because they spend more time in dreaming sleep. They simply have more dreams to remember. Furthermore, because the proportion of time spent in REM sleep increases across the night, the longer you sleep the more likely you are to awaken from—or soon after—a REM period.

The style of the dream

Sometimes, while still asleep, you may recognize that something strange is going on and realize that you're dreaming. The more absurd or bizarre the fantasy, the more likely it is to catch and hold your attention. Odd dreams are easier to recall than routine ones.

The strange aspects of a dream often are the key to its meaning. A woman in the process of divorcing told me this dream:

I opened the door to my apartment, saw my ex-brother-in-law in the hall, and invited him in. But he refused to come in. I was disappointed.

This woman had always liked her brother-in-law and missed him when she and her husband broke up. Her dream was short and easy to recall, but one detail bothered her. She could not understand why the door to her apartment opened the wrong way, out into the hall, instead of inward to her apartment. It was only as she tried to explain the image that its meaning struck her. "In relation to that family," she realized, "I am on the wrong side now, an outsider."

In some dreams, the plot is tightly woven into a story. In others, the drama shifts from scene to scene with little connection between scenes. Sleep memory, like waking memory, depends on how connected the dream is. A good story is easier to remember than a grocery list. If the several dreams on any given night don't seem related to each other, they will be harder to keep straight hours later when we awaken.

Some dreamers pack a lot of content into just a few minutes of REM time and tell complicated dreams with many scenes. Others say, after the same amount of REM sleep, "I can't remember a thing. You woke me just as the dream was starting."

The degree of drama

Some dreams contain strongly charged feelings such as anxiety, anger, terror, joy, or sexual excitation. In others, the feelings are neutral or bland. Strong emotions prove more memorable.

Sensory texture

Dreams may embody many kinds of sensations. We may see, hear, taste, touch. Some dreams involve strange physical experiences, like legs that feel too heavy to run or attempts to cry out without being able to make a sound.

A dream may not be visual at all. A dream such as "I was hiding in the dark under the porch and heard my mother calling me" concerns what the dreamer was thinking and hearing while she was hiding. The richer the dream is in sensory texture, the more likely that we can hold on to it.

Readiness to face the issues in the dreams

Some people are eager to learn what their inner voices are saying. Others prefer to turn a deaf ear. It's easy to guess which ones are better dream recallers.

Motivation to recall dreams

If our dreams frighten us or enlighten us, we are more likely to remember them. Artists and writers looking to their dreams for ideas remember their dreams better than people who think dreams serve no useful purpose. The surrealist poet Saint-Pol-Roux posted a sign on his bedroom door, saying "Do not disturb. Poet at work." People in therapy and members of dream groups remember dreams better than those who have no outlet for sharing. The desire to please someone who has asked us about our dreams stimulates dream recall.

⇨ SELF-HELP: Tips and tricks for remembering dreams better

Keep a journal of waking events and concerns in tandem with your dream diary

Spend a few minutes jotting down whatever is on your mind each day, preferably at bedtime. Writers often say that they write to find out what they are thinking about. Putting words on paper has the almost magical quality of leading you from one thought to another. If you make it a habit to review your day just before going to sleep and to note the events or thoughts that stirred up the most intense feelings, you also are priming your dream system with raw materials for the night ahead. It's like a television "promo" that whets your interest in a later feature film.

Freud focused on "day residue," not "yesterday residue," as a prime ingredient in dreams; however, laboratory experience tells us that daytime events may take a week or more to appear in our dreams. With a journal of both daytime and nighttime experiences, you can look back to find the source of a dream. You have to learn from experience how much to write.

As we get better at understanding our dreams, we often can make do with fewer and fewer notes. We learn economy— what we need to include, what we can omit. However, the more you write, the more you have to draw on later when trying to see how a dream connects to your daily life. When you get to the event that triggered the dream, you may feel a sudden flash of recognition.

Remind yourself of your intention to keep track of your dreams as you drift off to sleep

In the same way in which you have better recall of directions to an unfamiliar location if you drive there than if you simply go along for the ride, putting yourself in the driver's seat for the trip down Freud's royal road will help you better remember where you go in your dreams. People who agree to sleep in the laboratory to have their dreams monitored know we will ask them for a report each time we awaken them. This waking expectation helps them get ready to tell what was happening when we call.

Program yourself to wake up after each REM period

It's not hard to master the technique. In one study in our laboratory, we asked sleepers to choose their own time to be awakened for a dream report by pressing a switch taped to their hand. We told them we would call them only when they made a fist to show they were aware that they were dreaming. We asked them to test the switch before they fell asleep to help them set their minds to the task.

All 10 people who tried the switch were able to signal to us correctly at least once the very first night. Most often they pressed the switch near the end of a REM period. Some waited until the REM period was over, saying, "I wanted to see how my dream turned out before you called me." Some didn't even recall pressing the switch. On being awakened, they asked, "How did you know when to wake me?"

You may find it surprising that people can split their attention in this way, but it's easy to do if you set your mind to it and it's worth the effort, at least occasionally. Attempting it on a regular basis might backfire: you'd lose too much sleep.

When you wake up—during the night or in the morning— lie still while you go over the dream

Prolonging the muscle paralysis typical of the REM state helps bring back what was going through your mind at that time. When we awaken people in the laboratory, they often begin by saying, "Gee, I don't know ... wait a minute ... I think ... oh yes ... I was ..." and so on. After shifting out of sleep, it's hard to shift back into it enough to search for and recapture the retreating dream. You're more likely to recall a dream if you awaken spontaneously and permit yourself to hover for a while between sleeping and waking than if you awaken to the sound of an alarm or music, which competes with the dream for your attention. A voice-activated tape recorder will let you describe your dream without moving.

Translate the pictures into words before you open your eyes

If you awaken during the night, fixing a key word or image in your mind often will help you reclaim the dream in the morning. Making up a title first is often a potent aid to dream recall. If you make the title a summary sentence—*My husband runs away with Sophia Loren, The radiation-lady tries to capture me, John brings me raspberry truffles*—you'll find the rest of the dream easier to remember.

To jog your memory, pretend you're a detective interviewing an eyewitness. What's the last thing you remember? Before that? Going backward can help you reconstruct a dream more easily.

If all you remember is a fragment but you want to try to recover the dream, think of that fragment as you fall asleep on the following night

Often the details of the rest of the dream will come back more fully in the first few minutes of sleep than it did when you woke up in the morning. Thinking about the fragment seems to jog the network of memories from which it came and makes the dream active again.

Try to recapture the feelings evoked in the dream

Focusing on the feelings prompted by a dream often will bring the story back, the way the ringing of one bell resonates with sounds of others.

If you have trouble catching dreams, try sleeping late on weekends

The longer you sleep, the longer your REM periods and the longer and more complex your dreams. When you linger in bed until you are slept out, you're more likely to awaken from REM sleep than from NREM sleep. As a result, you raise your odds of having a memorable dream.

Try interrupting your sleep at different times during the night

Some people ask a night-owl friend to help them. They call this friend on a bedside phone just as they turn out the lights. The friend then waits for an hour and a half and calls back to ask what they can remember of their trip to dreamland. Catching the first dream identifies the theme of the night and fosters the memory of later dreams.

By getting up early on weekdays, many of us forfeit the last and longest dream of the night. As an aid to capturing dreams, one man sets his alarm clock for 4 A.M., jots down the plot line of the dream, and returns to sleep.

Try new technology

An automated recording system for home use is a high-tech aid to dream recall. One of my students, Stephen Lloyd, designed such a system in our laboratory at Rush-Presbyterian-St. Luke's as his psychology doctoral research project. With additions from psychiatry resident Bret Schneider, then a medical student at Rush, it provides goggles that detect the rapid eye movements of dreaming. When the eye movements reach a preset number, the system buzzes to wake the dreamer and turns on a tape recorder for the dream report. The system records the time of night of the report and resets itself for the next dream.

Volunteers who used this device in our laboratory and in their own homes recorded an average of four dreams per night in both places. The device is being readied for commercial distribution and may be available in electronics' stores by the time this book is published. While it may never become as familiar a fixture on the nightstand as an alarm clock, it may prove useful to people trying to solve creative problems or psychotherapy patients stuck in treatment.

⇨ SELF-HELP: Interview yourself about your dreams

Once you have captured a dream, how do you decode it? When we awaken sleepers in our laboratory for dream reports, we first let them tell all they can remember on their own. Then the technician prompts them with questions designed to flesh out details. The questions help clarify the who, what, when, and where, of what has been in the sleeper's mind. You can ask yourself similar questions at home.

Who was in the dream? Did you recognize any of the characters?

Figuring out who is present in a dream is not as straightforward as it sounds, as we have seen in my previously mentioned dream about Michael Young. Specific characters may be amalgams of several people or may stand for certain traits that concern us in ourselves or others. Although recognizable in a dream, a person may be present only to serve as some attribute of ourselves or others.

We may use animals the same way, much as we do in waking life, when we describe someone as "sly as a fox" or "grouchy as a bear." Objects may represent human characteristics, too. One woman dreamed of a pencil being sharpened. She was the pencil, getting "sharp" to write a new chapter in her life.

Even the clothing of someone in a dream may provide the key to unlock the dream's meaning. One woman dreamed she was in prison, watched over by a sadistic guard. The guard's uniform was the same as that of the security guard at the apartment building where she lived with her parents.

What was going on?

Were you involved in the action or watching it transpire? If involved, what were you doing? Did someone else do something to you?

Here is the dream of a depressed woman:

A co-worker was taking all my things out of my desk and I couldn't do anything about it.

Contrast that dream of helplessness with this one from a person coming to terms with having a life-threatening illness:

I almost missed my bus. The driver was starting to pull out, but I ran up and banged on the door until he stopped.

Where did the action in the dream take place?

Have you seen the setting or any part of it in real life, or was it all fantasy? Sometimes the setting of the dream, a vacant lot in which you used to play as a child, for example, provides a big clue to the feelings that prompted the dream.

What was the time frame?

Were the events in the dream taking place in the past, present, or future? Were you the same age as you are now? Or older or younger?

One man reports a dream that begins:

I was eight years old and living at home with my parents. My parents were fighting, and my mother was threatening to leave.

He woke up sobbing. A little dreaming of the past, to review, is healthy, but to continue in the past, dream after dream, night after night, is a bad sign. It suggests a person is stuck there.

Who's responsible for what happens in the dream?

Do you take the blame for everything that goes wrong? A depressed man dreamed:

Some men were threatening to rape my girlfriend. We were out in the desert and it was my fault for exposing her that way.

Who are you in your dreams?

Do you play a role you like, one consistent with the "possible you," or is your dream self someone you'd rather not be? One woman dreamed she was the inept captain of a sinking ship. She called on a nearby ship for assistance, and its captain, also a woman, came to her rescue. She recognized that she played both roles, one helpless and ineffectual, the other a competent person who knew what to do.

Depressed women going through a divorce often see themselves in their dreams as a "maid" or "slave." By contrast, those who are not depressed or who are happily married, are more likely to see themselves as a "hostess" or "lover."

Did you know you were dreaming while you were dreaming?

Were you aware that this was going on in your own mind or did you feel it was really taking place? Dreams usually fool us by their here and now immediacy. By becoming a participant-observer in the dream process, using the RISC method described in Chapter 6, you can, if you wish, recognize when you are dreaming and even rewrite the endings of your dreams.

What are the dimensions of your dreams?

Figuring out the polarities in your dreams will give you a concise summary of the issues with which you currently are wrestling. As you get better at recalling dreams, you may be able to capture two or even three from a single night. Here, you'll have the opportunity to see various themes and their opposites appearing across the night and to judge their progress. However, even if you record dreams only occasionally, you can expect to see the same themes appearing over and over, more or less prominently, reflecting your current concerns.

What were your feelings, both while you were dreaming and now?

As Snyder found in his study of healthy volunteers, dreams tend to be more unpleasant than pleasant. They ask us to pay attention to our emotional problems in much the same way that a headache or an upset stomach makes us pay attention to aspects of bodily functioning we normally take for granted.

In recounting our dreams, many of us focus more on the story than on the feelings. However, it is the feelings that usually provide the key to understanding the dream's meaning. Were you scared, angry, excited, or frustrated? Feelings usually provide the fuel for the dream's story line and serve as the stimulus for its images. We can't understand why we think or act as we do without examining the feelings attached to our thoughts and behavior, says psychoanalyst Walter Bonime. "An emotion experienced in a dream never symbolizes anything," he notes. "It is always an authentic response to something in the dreamer's life."

Common Dreams and Normal Nightmares

$\mathcal{A}$LL DREAMS, even seemingly simple ones, are open to many different interpretations. All may be valid—or none. Only the dreamer can say for sure which explanation feels right, which version of a dream's meaning provides the inner sense of satisfaction that comes from seeing new connections.

It would be convenient if we could turn to a standard dream dictionary to learn the significance of various images. However, the only valuable volume is the one we write ourselves. Just as we give meaning to our experiences in waking, we also define for ourselves the meanings of the symbols we frequently use in our dreams. We can understand these best only by paying attention to our dreams over time, particularly to the images and dimensions we use again and again.

We often draw on familiar images for our dreams when new events, particularly those that threaten basic aspects of our identity, stir up old feelings. Such crises may represent challenges to our physical health and safety, our sense of competence and self-esteem, or our ability to trust, love, be close to others and earn their respect. These are the three big issues that arouse our strongest feelings and that we deal with not just once but repeatedly in our lives. That's why a serious accident or illness, a failure to receive a promotion, or an encounter with a hostile person may cause us to realize when we wake up, "I had that same old dream again last night."

The specific drama, the people, the setting, and the themes, will vary from time to time and certainly from person to person. Each issue may have its own dream expression. Although we all wrestle with similar problems as we grow up and indeed throughout our lives, we write our dream scripts with our own unique vocabulary.

We draw on images from many sources. Some we have only imagined, others we have seen on television, in movies, or with our own eyes. Sometimes we reach back into childhood to fairy tales or folklore, especially if those images evoked in us strong sympathetic feelings for the characters. The image of Mary Poppins calmly in command while sailing though the air perseveres in dreams of many young women; and Mike Ditka, coach of the Chicago Bears, often appears as an image of masculine strength in the dreams of young Chicago men.

Much as we learn to express more abstract and subtle thoughts as we grow, we also learn to use idioms and less perfect forms of speech for everyday communication. If you've ever listened to a tape recording of your own spontaneous speech, you've probably winced over the false starts, the "you knows," and the mistakes of grammar. In dreams, too, we often speak colloquially, using pictorial shortcuts to convey meaning faster and usually far more vividly than we can with words.

One man dreamed he missed the bus. For many people, "to miss the bus" represents a lost opportunity. For this man, a professor of Elizabethan literature, "bus" was a visual pun. In talking with his analyst, Walter Bonime, he saw that the dream highlighted problems in his marriage. He missed the "buss," his wife's kisses. A woman dreamed she stepped in a puddle on her way home, tracking mud onto the carpet. In the dream, she said to herself, "My sole is dirty," but it was her "soul" that occupied her mind. She was feeling guilt over marital infidelity, a problem she dragged into her home. Some dreams—and some dreamers—are more eloquent than others.

People who share a language and a culture understandably may use certain symbols in the same way. "We all borrow the images in our dreams from society at large," Montague Ullman and Nan Zimmerman write in *Working with Dreams.* "Since we all swim in the same social sea, it should come as no surprise that we may use the same imagery to express the same meanings."

Freud viewed certain symbols as universal. The primacy of sexual concerns in his thinking led him to assign sexual connotations to many objects and activities that appear in dreams. Guns, snakes, umbrellas, and other long or pointed objects, as well as fountains, faucets, and other objects from which water flows, he suggested, represent the penis. Containers, doorways, and circular objects stand for female sexual organs. Activities such as climbing or flying represent masturbation or intercourse.

Symbols in a dream must mesh with their applicability to each dreamer's life. Hair in a dream, for example, may hold vastly different import for a teenaged girl fretting over her appearance, for a woman who has lost her hair after chemotherapy for breast cancer, and for a person who works as a hairdresser. The same symbol, of course, may hold different meanings for the same person at different times.

Every dream is unique. Nevertheless, you may hear someone else's dream and think, "I've had a dream like that myself." Because most of us share some basic concerns, it should come as no surprise that we also share certain expressions of those concerns in dreams. For example, I dream of losing my purse with all my important identification papers and car keys, symbols of who I am and my access to mobility. I call this my "incompetence dream." When I dream it, I am warning myself that I am "losing it." Another woman might use the same image to represent being locked out of a marriage or other relationship. For another, it might represent a loss of financial security.

Take the common dream:

I was supposed to take an examination, but I didn't know the subject and couldn't answer any questions.

For many of us, this old school memory surfaces in dreams when we encounter situations that stir up feelings about being tested. In the case of some people, the psychologist Alfred Adler says, such a dream may mean, "You are not prepared to face the problem before you." For others it may mean, "You have passed exams before and you will pass the present one, too." For the first group, the dream sounds a warning to work hard or face the consequences or shame. For the second, the dream offers the reassurance that, ready or not, you can make it.

Examination dreams may involve situations out of the classroom. Psychoanalyst Wayne Myers describes one man, an expert skier, who dreams repeatedly of "wiping out" on a familiar, challenging ski slope before important business meetings, sexual encounters, or matters of family dispute. Concern about failing when tested remains the salient feature.

Recovering alcoholics often dream about having their sobriety tested. Such dreams suggest they still are struggling with surrender and their powerlessness over alcohol. Sociologist Norman Denzin describes a typical dream report heard at Alcoholics Anonymous meetings:

"I was sitting in front of a pitcher of beer. Three glasses, all mine, in front of me. I drank them real fast, then I woke up, shaking and crying. I haven't been able to get this dream out of my head."

Some alcoholics worry that such dreams signal an impending relapse. However, other former drinkers, Denzin says, offer a more positive interpretation. "I'm an alcoholic," one says. "I'll be an alcoholic until the day I die. I'm powerless over alcohol, even in my dreams. Hell, I still have those dreams. Last year on vacation I dreamed I was back with a bottle of gin and the boys at work.

"They remind me of how bad it was," he continues. "They also tell me that my primary purpose is to stay sober. If I have to drink in my dreams in order to stay sober when I'm awake, that's O.K. Better there than in real life."

Such "exam" or "test" dreams are only two types of common dreams with many possible interpretations. We are more apt to recognize the same theme and feelings of being scared and unprepared than to reexperience the identical dream. A dream's significance may not be apparent immediately. We may discover that an event or another dream years later adds new meaning to an earlier dream. Sometimes we need the help of a spouse, a friend, or a therapist to get past our blind spots.

Here are opposing versions of several of the most frequently reported dreams, dreams that often surface in times of emotional upheaval in our lives.

COMMON DREAMS

Falling and flying

Falling is the earliest dream many people can remember. It's easy to understand why. In the first months and years of life, we have to master many physical skills. We bump into things and stumble and fall. Even as adults, we may dream we are falling a long way down a hole like Alice in Wonderland. Or we may be falling off a cliff or out of an airplane. We may not even know how we came to be up in the air but there we are, sinking fast.

Folklore holds that if you hit bottom in a dream, you die. But plenty of people have had that dream and lived to tell. One woman told me she dreamed she was thrown off a very high building. "As I was falling, I wasn't terrified," she recalls. "I told myself, 'You can't die because this is a dream.'" Being aware that you are dreaming while you are dreaming can be quite reassuring.

Falling dreams appear throughout our lives, often at times of threats to our basic sense of security, such as the loss of a job or a failed love affair. In falling dreams, feelings run high. We feel helpless, out of control. We often recognize that we are doing something unusual, taking a flyer or going over the edge, defying rules. Sometimes we get away with it. More often we awaken with a thumping heart, sweaty palms, and a profound sense of relief that we are safe in bed. We calm ourselves by saying, "It was only a dream."

Flying dreams, by contrast, usually are exhilarating. In these we escape the physical laws of gravity and the demands of the waking world. While we dream, we are above it all. Some people remember swooping around like hang gliders or flying down staircases without touching the steps.

As the poet W.H. Auden writes:

"Since he weighs nothing
Even the stoutest dreamer
Can fly without wings."

Flying dreams often accompany a "good" crisis, when we feel the pride in accomplishment, such as graduation or a job promotion. We feel pleased with ourselves, "high" in self-esteem, superior to others. Flying dreams also may have their anxious moments. We may discover we are going too far or too high, too fast. Or perhaps we try and can't really get off the ground. At a time of uncertainty, one woman dreamed she was a baby bird, tossed about by raging winds. Anxious flying dreams are close to falling dreams; they arise from our early concern for our physical safety. We need to be aware of whether the image is positive or negative in feeling to understand the meaning.

Being chased or embraced

Being chased by thieves or killers, or stalked or attacked by animals, suggests a different kind of concern. Here, the danger comes from other people, from their aggressive intent. Such dreams may warn us, "People are not always trustworthy." Some current crisis may be stirring up feelings we had in childhood, such as the expectation of being punished by an angry parent or when confronted with a lie.

In these dreams we may hide, but we hear the approaching footsteps. We try to call for help but cannot make a sound. We try to run but cannot move. We may feel trapped and see no way out. We are helpless to alter circumstances or to protect ourselves from those who intend us harm. Like one of my patients, who dreamed his wife tried to smother him with a pillow, we often escape only by bolting into wakefulness.

Being embraced in a dream is the opposite of such experiences and usually it is a positive event, a way of reaffirming to ourselves, "There are people whom I can trust." We may meet friends, relatives, or lovers, even wished-for lovers, such as movie stars.

While we sometimes read a sexual dream as a simple wish fulfillment, sexual images may relate to many kinds of feelings, both positive and negative. Imagine the differences in the dreams of a young, single woman the night before embarking on a vacation cruise, compared to the night after learning a friend was raped. The latter may involve feelings closer to being chased than embraced. Attaining satisfaction from others or being at their mercy are only two of the possible themes of sexual dreams.

Failing or winning

In *failing* dreams, the negative feelings are our own fault. We let ourselves down. We forget an assignment, lose a wallet, miss the bus, get lost. These often are dreams of self-doubt or self-reproach. We didn't do all we could have done to prevent some bad event. We fail, and it's our own fault.

One man in our divorce study, Craig, dreamed he was cleaning out his garage.

I piled all the summer furniture and other equipment at the end of the driveway while I swept the place out. Another man came along in a pick-up truck and helped himself to my furniture. I yelled at him, "Hey that's my stuff." The man replied, "Then you shouldn't put it out there for anyone to take."

The cheeky action of another man made Craig focus on his losses. He might be clearing out, leaving his wife and kids, but his dream reminded him that some other quick-thinking man might come along and get the good stuff he was not yet ready to throw away.

The flip side of this type of dream is one of success. We discard our self-doubt. We accomplish an important task. We may even dream of being more able than we really are, doing something well that we don't truly know how to do. We may fly a plane or play great blues on the piano. A law student, anxious about a paper she had to write, had this dream:

I had been appointed to the Supreme Court. I was sitting there talking to Thurgood Marshall. Suddenly I remembered I had a paper to write and jumped up. Then I realized I didn't have to worry about it any more; I already was on the Supreme Court. I sat down and happily continued the conversation.

She awakened thinking her upcoming assignment would not be as tough as she initially had thought.

Ashamed or proud

In *social embarrassment* dreams, we are caught naked where everyone can see or we find ourselves in a public bathroom designated for the opposite sex. These may be dreams of shame and exposure to the ridicule of others. In such dreams, we may be both literally and metaphorically caught with our pants down. Such dreams are more common at times when we are worried about being seen as we really are, before a job interview or a date with someone special, for example.

Dreams of glory sparkle with pride. We win a gold medal in the Olympics or a thunder of applause for our performance at the Metropolitan Opera. Sleep researcher Allan Rechtschaffen told me a dream in which he brought about world peace.

I invented a device to stop all wars in their tracks. At a touch of a button, I could put everyone in the whole world to sleep until they got over their urge to fight.

He awakened with a great feeling of accomplishment.

Birth and death

In certain situations, such as pregnancy and terminal illness, dreams of birth and death may help us rehearse the future. (See Chapter 9.) However, dreams of birth and death usually go far beyond their literal implications. Births may represent beginnings, growing awareness and understanding, religious salvation, a remodeling project. Deaths in dreams, even the dreamer's own, may serve as a metaphor for the end of a relationship or activity. Deaths also may reflect anger. "I'm so mad I could kill you," we might say in waking life. In dreams, we can do it.

DREAMS OF MEN AND WOMEN

Being male or female is the major organizer of who we are. Men and women dream differently, too. Women's dreams typically have more characters than those of men. This disparity reflects the roots of how our self-image develops. Women more often define themselves through their interactions with people: I am Sally's mother, Rosa's daughter, Jenny's friend. Men more often define themselves through how they perform in the world: I am an engineer, a golfer, a commuter.

Women traditionally have gotten what they need to sustain their sense of self by relating to others, and men by manipulating objects, money, and machinery. Women are brought up to be more nurturing toward family and others. Men are trained that to be successful they must be competitive and winners, not givers.

In a study of 1000 dreams, half from each sex, psychologists Calvin Hall and Robert Van de Castle found that women have more friendly characters in their dreams than men do. In men's dreams, people more often are hostile, aggressive, and competitive. Among participants in our divorce study, one man dreamed that ski-masked figures robbed him, and another that his friends blocked his path. By contrast, a woman sat down in her dream to talk things over with her ex-husband's new partner.

Women typically dream about their homes and families. Men seldom do, unless this subject becomes a "hot" issue for them. Women dream of shopping, doing things with the kids, seeing old friends. Men dream of traveling, fixing something, working. Explicitly sexual dreams, in both sexes, are relatively infrequent.

Women's dreams are more likely to take place indoors, and men's outdoors. In our divorce study, the settings for some of the women's dreams include their parents' homes, their offices, restaurants. By comparison, the action in the men's dreams occurs at a gas station, overlooking the ocean, paddling on an open sea, out in the desert.

Women express a wider range of feelings in their dreams than men: more surprise, anger, fear, anxiety. Our society generally expects women to be more emotional than men and to express their feelings more freely. Men's dreams are more action-oriented than women's.

These basic differences in dreams of men and women persist in the face of societal changes. Hall and his colleagues compared dream contents and sex differences in dreams of American college men and women in 1950 and 1980. This thirty-year period was the time of the active feminist movement in this country when there was a widespread liberalizing of attitudes about sexual behavior. Yet the researchers found little change over the years in what students dreamed about. They also found that the differences between men and women did not change at all. "Despite social changes," the researchers observed, "human nature has not changed."

Whether you are male or female is a far more potent determinant of the nature of your dreams than whether you are young or old, or black, white, or another race, according to psychiatrist Milton Kramer, who studied a representative sample of the dreams of 300 Cincinnati adults. "Internally, privately, subjectively," says Kramer, "the concerns of your sex role are more pervasive than that of your racial category or age group."

Age and race do produce some differences, Kramer's study shows. Anxiety appeared in dreams of those aged 21–35 as guilt over issues of right and wrong. In people aged 65 and over, anxiety focused on death and dying. The dreams of whites showed more covert hostility than those of blacks.

NORMAL NIGHTMARES

Although bad dreams are more common than good ones, most bad dreams do not wake us. Nightmares are the frightening heart-pounding ones that propel us from sleep.

Flight attendant Susan White dreamed of plane crashes for months following the 1989 crash of her plane at Sioux City,

Iowa, in which 112 people died. "I'd dream about the woman who was crying and the children who were alone," White told *The Wall Street Journal.* Sometimes, her nightmares, while not literal reenactments, were close to the actual situation. "I'd dream that we were doing a safety demonstration, and a man was lying in front of the emergency door and I couldn't get him to move," she recalled.

White's dreams reflect both the anguish she felt in waking life over the tragedy and her helplessness to prevent it. Flight attendants are trained to feel personal responsibility for the safety of their passengers. After accidents, Richard Gist, a consultant to the Association of Flight Attendants union, found they "rehash the things they did, the things they should have done, the what-ifs, the maybes and the hows—every instruction they gave to every passenger."

Like Susan White, any of us may suffer nightmares after some devastating event. These nightmares sometimes force us to relive the terrible event over and over again. Common examples include sudden injuries or serious accidents, physical assaults, seeing someone seriously hurt or killed, news of the sudden death or injury of someone close, house fires, and natural disasters such as tornados or earthquakes.

A man whose daughter was murdered saw every gruesome detail in his nightmares, even though he had not witnessed the actual event. Night after night in his dreams, he saw his daughter walking from the bus-stop to school. Powerless to cry out and protect her, he watched in agony as a man grabbed her and dragged her into a car. He saw the assailant tie her up, gag her, and drive her to an isolated house, where he raped her, beat her, and branded her with cigarettes. He told Seattle psychiatrist Edward Rynearson that as the attacker slit the girl's throat, he would awaken gasping and screaming.

Sometimes, nightmares don't present the actual event but rather a distillation of its emotional impact. A rape victim, for example, might dream of being pursued by a knife-wielding attacker down a deserted street, or of being smothered or of drowning, rather than of the rape itself. Some people dream not of the recent shock but of horrible events from earlier in their lives, never-healed wounds that the recent event has torn open. Some come to dread dreaming so much that they barely sleep.

Nightmares are a predictable—and normal—response to traumatic events that are beyond our control, especially those that fill us with intense fear, distress, helplessness, or horror. The accident or earthquake victim who is pinned down by rubble, the mother who sees her child struck down by a speeding car, the innocent bystander shot in the arm during a grocery store holdup, the child who sees his father strangle his mother—these people almost certainly will suffer disturbing nightmares. The more severe the trauma and the bigger the threat to life or our sense of security, the bigger the load on the dream system will be. The more helpless we are to cope during the day, the greater will be the fear left over for dreaming to handle at night. Yet somehow we must restore our confidence that we can cope.

Almost everyone experiencing a traumatic event dreams about it in the days and weeks that directly follow. Ernest Hartmann, a Boston sleep researcher and psychiatrist, has found that a person who flees along with the rest of the family from a burning house, for example, might dream about the fire and the smoke and the fright nearly every night for weeks. Following that first stage of dream response, the person's dreams might involve being with other members of the family and looking at the burning house. Weeks or months later, the dreams might expand to include other houses the person lived in. However, with time the person's dreams most likely will return to the way they were before the calamity.

The severity of our involvement in an event influences its impact on our sleep and dreams, although severity is, of course, highly subjective. We each have our individual Richter scale. Some events, including serving in combat, torture, long-term childhood sexual abuse, and imprisonment in death camps—horrors so extreme that those who have not experienced them can never fully comprehend their magnitude—often leave particularly virulent aftereffects. These include not only disrupted sleep and nightmares but daytime flashbacks, emotional numbness, and other symptoms collectively called Post-Traumatic Stress Disorder (PTSD). We will explore PTSD in Chapter 11.

The younger we are when trouble strikes, the fewer our resources. The fewer successful strategies for coping with life-threatening crises that we have in our memory networks, the more likely it is that anxiety will overwhelm our dream mechanism and awaken us.

Between the ages of three and eight, 5–10% of children experience disturbing dreams at least once a week. The frequency declines gradually. College students, according to a recent study at the University of Arizona conducted by James Wood and Richard Bootzin, may suffer nightmares as often as twice a month. In adulthood, most of us experience the kind of disaster-filled dreams that wake us in fear only about once a year. As we become older and more competent to cope with the world during the day, our nightmares subside.

Adults who suffer frequent nightmares are not inevitably people who have not developed good psychological and practical coping skills. In his book *The Nightmare*, Hartmann suggests there are two types of adult nightmarers: those who have suffered from nightmares all their lives, and those who develop them only after experiencing some crisis of unexpected, unavoidable, and major proportions. Defenselessness in the face of real trouble is the common thread that binds the nightmare sufferers together. For some the assault on personal integrity started early and prevented the development of a self-image with confidence and self-esteem. Others had their confidence knocked out of them by some later blow.

We'll look at nightmares during and after particular crises and see how we can understand them and go forward with our lives. These are crises of loss—a threat to our own life; a threat to or actual loss of life of a child, spouse, or another to whom we are close; and loss of job, home, belongings, crucial aspects of our basic security and identity. Such losses when we are adults stimulate memories of unresolved anxieties from earlier in life.

The death of someone close

The death of someone close produces feelings of intense grief in just about everyone. Overwhelming sadness is a normal response, indeed, a healthy one. However, such strong feelings can trigger sleep disturbances, melancholic dreams, and trouble concentrating during the day. All are common and predictable consequences. Feelings of loss can persist for months or even years, mixed with anxiety over whether we did all we could, guilt if the survivor feels he or she left some tasks undone, relief if the person was suffering, or anger at the one who died for abandoning the survivor. The intensity of such feelings diminishes with time. The stress a death brings will be intensified if the death occurs at an early age or is the result of an accident, suicide, homicide, or sudden illness.

Some people suffer acutely from the death of a pet or even of an idol whom they have never met: Rudolph Valentino, John Kennedy, Elvis Presley, or James Dean. If these emotional connections made life meaningful, their loss may have as much impact as the loss of someone close.

Our reactions to death, like any other event, are uniquely our own and do not follow invariably predictable stages. Our dreams may highlight for us aspects of our relationship with the person who has died that we overlooked while he or she was alive. They may help us to reconcile feelings that troubled us then and remain troubling now. They can help us accept the finality of the event and prepare us for life without that person.

Using a collection of 10,000 dreams recorded by one woman over a 50-year span, Margarete Gerne of the University of Zurich found that dreams following the death of someone close fell into three phases of variable duration. In the first phase, dreams focused on death, the person who died, and sadness. In the second phase, themes such as "work" and "new orientation" emerged, and living characters began to make appearances. In the third phase, dreaming subsided, a sign, she suggests, of relief in the mourning crisis.

The loss of a parent is the most common type of bereavement we experience in adult life. Although this loss may be painful, unless it occurs at an early age, it does not usually prompt prolonged or intense grief. Rather, it is accepted as an expected life-cycle event, for which we usually have had some preparation through the shared experiences of other family members and friends. Around the time of the death, dreams about the dead parent are common. Although they seldom turn into nightmares, they may cause intense distress. "Right after my father died," one woman reports, "I dreamed my father was standing outside my bedroom window, talking to me clear as day."

"I woke up screaming and crying in grief," she recalls. "The dream made me believe he was there and then when I woke up, he wasn't there, so I lost him again." Even though her bedroom is on the second floor, she didn't find her father's presence at the window unusual during the dream. Now, several years later, her father appears in her dreams around the time of his birthday or other meaningful anniversaries, and sometimes for no apparent reason at all. He doesn't talk much to her anymore. "He's usually just looking at me," she says. "Or maybe he's throwing me a kiss from his car as he drives off, just as he used to do."

The death of a spouse usually is much harder for most people to accept. Research shows that for several years after the death of a spouse, young and middle-aged people are at increased risk of dying themselves. A National Academy of Sciences report says that men who do not remarry have a higher rate of death for perhaps six years than men who do. For women, the risk of death may be higher in the second year after a husband's death.

Some 800,000 people in the United States become new widows and widowers every year. According to the Academy report, some 10–20% of the widowed are still seriously depressed a year or more after the spouse's death. While this is a lower figure than we see in people going through a divorce, it is still a large number—perhaps 80,000–160,000 people.

The loss of a child is even more devastating and may be an event from which one never fully recovers. Therapists working with groups of parents who have lost a child often report that new members will ask the others, "How much longer will we suffer this way?" Someone else in the group almost invariably will reply, "It takes time. My child died 20 years ago and I'm not over it yet."

I know that answer to be true. It is now seven years since my daughter Christine was killed by a speeding driver while she walked across a poorly lit rural road. She was 28, a brand new Ph.D. She died instantly. I was awakened at 1:30 A.M. with this news by a phone call from the police. I still feel fear each time I get a late-night phone call.

At first I could not dream of Christine at all. After a few weeks, I started dreaming of her as a toddler, in trouble. I would hear her cry and rush to rescue her. In one dream, she was falling down a toilet and I pulled her out. In another, a car hit her, but her padded snowsuit protected her. I lifted her and comforted her. In each dream, she became a little older.

After some months, I had this dream:

I was at a big convention, waiting for an elevator with a crowd of people. Now an adult, Chris joined me there.

"Christine!" I said. "I'm so glad to see you. I thought you were dead."

"I am," she said. "I only came to be with you until you are used to the idea."

That was so very like her, I found the dream comforting. I recognized finally that I couldn't save her, but she could stay with me in a way that gave me some peace. That was the last dream of the grieving period. The threat and rescue dreams turned to acceptance and appreciation.

Unnatural dying

The manner of death may alter the nature of the mourning. If a person dies peacefully with members of the family present, survivors most likely will have feelings that are categorically distinct from those they would have if the same person were stabbed to death by an assaultive thief or run over in a crosswalk by a drunk driver.

Rynearson, a psychiatrist, interviewed 15 members of a local support group for those who had lost a relative by homicide at least three years earlier. Seven had lost children, five had lost siblings, and three had lost spouses. Six of those murdered had been shot, four stabbed, three strangled, and two beaten to death. In 12 of the cases, the murderer was caught and sent to prison. Three murders occurred at the hands of immediate family members.

All of the people he interviewed had experienced bereavement previously following the death of a relative from a cause other than homicide. All reported that grief after a murder was distinctly different. Like the man we described earlier who continually replayed his daughter's death, they were haunted by images of the homicide, awake and asleep. None had witnessed the crime, so the pictures they put together came from the reports of witnesses or the findings of the police, mixed with their own imaginings of what must have happened. They focused on the terror and helplessness their relative must have experienced.

All reported vivid, recurring nightmares about the event. Often, as I did, they dreamed they tried to save the victim. Ten of the group reported that they had both waking fantasies and nightmares about murdering the murderer. Some became fearful of being attacked themselves, and a few came to view the future as less secure and fulfilling than before.

For the man who continually reconstructed his daughter's murder, the horror of her dying seemed to eclipse memories of her warmth. Her dying isolated him from the rest of his life, including other members of his immediate family, on whom he kept strict tabs. He was furious with the police for not finding the killer. In therapy, Rynearson helped his patient to recall positive experiences in his daughter's life. The man gradually replaced the horrific images with those that brought comfort. His terrible dreams diminished in frequency and intensity. Indeed, he began to dream of a reunion with his daughter, a type of dream that Rynearson says is common in survivors as they come to terms with their loss.

Suicide brings other problems for the survivor. The victim and the perpetrator are one. Edward Shneidman, an early researcher in the field, said that "the person who commits suicide puts his psychological skeleton in the survivor's emotional closet—he sentences the survivor to a complex of negative feelings and, most importantly, to obsession about the reasons for the suicide death."

Such obsessing often shows up in dreams, adding to the survivor's pain. Unfortunately, the need to cope with a suicide is not rare. Some 30,000 suicides occur in the United States annually and more than one quarter are of persons aged 24 or under who leave several surviving family members.

Close relatives of persons who committed suicide may have certain experiences not usually seen in those whose family members died from other causes. These include a sense of shock, a need to search for an explanation, and difficulty in sharing feelings about the suicide. Psychiatrists David Ness and Cynthia Pfeffer of the New York Hospital-Cornell Medical Center report, "the suicide remains an incomprehensible fact about a loved one." Relatives of those who commit suicide appear to be at higher risk of committing suicide themselves, a good reason for caring friends to step in, avoid blaming survivors, and help them to air their feelings. Asking about their dreams is a direct route to those feelings.

Threats to personal safety

When we find ourselves in danger, even if the event lasts for only seconds, even if we emerge physically unscathed, the repercussions may last for years. Columnist James Kilpatrick describes the persisting impact of his mugging five years after the event. He had left his office at noon and walked to his car a couple of hundred yards away. Two teenagers then held him up. "They threatened me with what I thought was a pistol; they robbed me of money, watch and self-respect. Then they fled," he relates.

"Not a week has passed in these five years that I have not relived those terrifying moments," Kilpatrick writes. "Other victims have told me of the same experience. Nightmares cannot be banished," he says. "They come wildly racing through one's sleep."

Becoming a victim is related to feeling bereaved, but it differs in some important ways. "The bereaved feels loss. The victim feels like a loser. The bereaved feels sad. The victim feels humiliated." This is the way psychiatrist Frank Ochberg puts it in *Post-traumatic Therapy and Victims of Violence*, "The bereaved may feel as though a part of himself or herself has been ripped away. The victim often feels diminished, pushed down in a hierarchy of dominance, exploited, and invaded." Such feelings are particularly prominent when the crime is a sexual one and takes away a person's sense of autonomy and control.

We'll explore the impact of sexual assaults on dreams and the sense of self in Chapter 10.

Natural disasters, despite the magnitude of their destruction, leave surprisingly few long-lasting emotional scars. A key reason is that whole families and communities usually experience the disaster simultaneously. When many are victims, people can help each other to rebuild their lives. In virtually every study ever conducted of the psychological impact of natural disasters—the eruption of Mount St. Helens, the Johnstown, Pennsylvania, flood, Hurricane Hugo, and others—survivors universally report a period of disrupted sleep and nightmares.

After the earthquake that struck northern California in 1989, next-day conversations almost invariably included questions about sleep. Because of frequent aftershocks, many people acknowledged feeling jittery and anxious, particularly when driving on double-decker bridges. Younger children wanted to sleep with their parents. Older ones were afraid to leave for school. However, many people used the quake as an impetus to reinforce or brace their homes; to stock up on water, canned food, and flashlights; or to rehearse for future quakes, by planning escape routes from home or workplace if that should become necessary. Six weeks later, psychiatrists reported that nightmares were still common. But six months later, most people queried reported that their nightmares had subsided or stopped.

Witnessing natural disasters or the aftermath of events such as plane crashes or building collapses in person, on television, or through stories related by others, may prompt nightmares even in those not directly involved. A woman living on the East Coast, unable to reach her sister in San Francisco by phone the night after the 1989 earthquake, reported this dream:

"I was in the middle of the earthquake. I was standing outside my house, and all these buildings were on fire all around my house, and this shower of sparks was falling on my house. I remember putting my *parents and my cats in the car, and we just started driving. We just kept driving to get away from it. Then I woke up and started crying."*

Her dismay at not being able to help her sister, not even to talk with her sister, prompted her dream of escape.

Disaster workers are not immune. In fact, because of the frequency of their contact with life's tragedies, those in the helping professions know that nightmares may go with the job. One study of police officers involved in the aftermath of an airliner crash found that one in five received treatment for symptoms of stress.

One disaster worker recalled the scene of a plane crash. "It was an Inferno, intense fire and smoke, the most profound emotional experience I ever had. There were body parts all over the place, heads, legs, torsos with no limbs attached, people torn in half, covered in blood, some burned beyond recognition. These dismembered parts were scattered in the flotsam and jetsam of crash debris—books, suitcases, clothes strewn everywhere. There was no one I could help, nothing I could do for anyone.

"Night after night when I dreamed, I saw this terrible scene," he reported. Then, finally, the dream changed.

I was back at the accident but it was daytime. There was no fire, no smoke. The bodies were there. I knew the people were dead, but they were whole.

This man could not deny that the accident occurred. However, by making death more acceptable in his dream, he could continue to perform his needed community work.

⇨ **SELF-HELP: Making use of nightmares**

Horrible as they may be, nightmares that follow a death or disaster have an important purpose. They proclaim, rudely but emphatically, that the calamity is still with us, still inflicting its damage upon us. One earthquake survivor put it this way, "It's not as if I can choose to be through with the earthquake. The earthquake isn't through with me."

Nightmares are a cry for resolution, for finding a way to incorporate the terrible experience into our lives. They goad us to create and accept a new picture of ourselves, one that takes the disaster into account, and to move on. This is a tall order, and we cannot always do it quickly or alone. We may need help from someone we trust, a spouse or close friend perhaps, or a therapist, someone who will help us to express our feelings and grieve for the loss of our way of life as it was before.

Exploration of bad dreams can be particularly useful when grief is prolonged or intense. When the survivor finds it hard to concede the reality of the event, use of dreams to access feelings for further examination may have important benefits for that person's health. You may provide enormous help to someone who is grieving simply by conveying your recognition that what they are thinking and feeling most likely is showing up in their dreams and by listening to any dreams they wish to share.

If nightmares awaken you more than once or twice a year, you can learn to defuse them by thinking about such dreams while awake and designing better endings for them. In the next chapter, we'll explore a method for coping with troubling dreams, a way to improve their endings by incorporating positive dream dimensions. This approach can make nightmares less threatening and help them subside.

6

From Everyday Dreams
to Crisis Dreams

WHEN LIFE IS CALM, most of our dreams contain a little of this and a little of that. Our dreams don't have much work to do other than hold the picture of our present self in a steady state. They may lack a single unifying theme across the night. Often they are no more memorable than what we thought about at breakfast this morning. At such times, we simply may not have much of importance to say to ourselves.

If we are open, uninhibited, and creative, our dreams may be fanciful. One man relates that in the middle of what for him was a familiar dream—that of watching a procession of people in elaborate Renaissance costumes—he suddenly had a commercial break. A big, smiling mouth appeared on his mind screen. A toothpaste ad!

When our daily lives fit well with our established sense of self, our nightly dream work runs on automatic pilot. Our dreams do their work silently whether we pay attention or not. They sort out our current emotional experiences, compare these to older memory files, and on this basis think ahead to imagine new scenarios. This dream system is self-regulatory, like many other systems in the body. Dreams always represent some integration of new information, but there may be no need for them to change our basic picture of ourselves.

In times of crisis, however, when we are under stress or are thrust into some new role for which we are not prepared, dreams go into action. In our dreams, we search through our memory files, looking for material we can extrapolate from the past to the present. When the new information finds no match in memory or when bad dreams break through, we need to listen to what our dreams have to tell us.

CRISIS DREAMING

When he was in high school, one of my patients lost his eyesight while experimenting with firecrackers. Months later, he still dreamed of driving a car and playing football, just as he had before the accident. It took a couple of years, he told me, before he became aware in his dreams that he should not be driving because he was blind.

Not until 25 years later did he start to see himself in his dreams carrying a cane or reading Braille. Even today, 45 years later, he doesn't always see himself in his dreams "as is." Nor are his dreams invariably set in the past. Rather, on his mind screen, he may appear at his present age yet able to see normally.

His story is not unusual. Indeed, it is more typical than not. His experience is analogous to that of people who have undergone amputation of an arm or leg. Even in waking life, many of them occasionally experience some sensation, usually pain, that they perceive as coming from the missing limb. In their dreams, many see themselves as still having intact limbs. Similarly, men who have suffered injuries that left them paralyzed from the waist down continue to have sexually explicit dreams. Some who are unable to experience orgasm while awake may do so in their dreams.

In waking life, my blind patient knows he cannot see. He

would never get behind the wheel of a car, although he might wish it were possible. However, in his dreams, he sees himself not as he is but as his emotions dictate.

Seeing or not seeing in a dream may be, of course, a metaphor for recognition of some important fact. Walking with a cane may symbolize an impediment to progress, and reading in Braille may reflect "getting in touch" with some feeling. The same metaphors may appear even in the dreams of the normally sighted. But when such metaphors appear in the dreams of someone who is blind, the blindness offers one more dimension to explore.

Psychologists Nancy Kerr and David Foulkes of the Georgia Mental Health Institute studied adults in the sleep laboratory who had lost their vision in their teens. Many years after the event, these people still reported their dreams in visual terms. Some created visual images of people and places known only since they lost their sight. One, for example, described a picnic at a friend's house. She remembered noticing that the friend had gotten fat and that her hair was "very, very, blonde," although neither was actually the case. "Dreams," the researchers point out, "never are simply simulations of seeing; they are simulations of living." Our dreams don't reflect life only as we currently perceive it, but rather as we feel, imagine, or want it to be.

Even those of us who are normally sighted have emotional blind spots. We may take a long time to revise our internal self-identity, especially if the changes are ones we are forced to make and don't like. In dreams, we draw from both memory and current experience to create a blend that expresses our current feelings. The combination may accept or ignore reality, wholly or in part.

Kerr's and Foulkes's study suggests that the process of changing our inner vision of ourselves to reflect what is happening in the outside world is a slow one. We can hasten this process and use it to our advantage in waking life by actively intervening in our dreams. That is the reason I developed the dream therapy described in this chapter. I wanted to help those whose lives and dreams were stalled.

DREAMS THAT GO NOWHERE

One of my patients, Tony, came to see me in the throes of depression. Before his marriage crisis hit him, Tony thought he had it made. An engineer, he had a good job, a nice home, an attractive wife, and three sons. Physically, he was a fine figure of a man—tall, trim, resplendently bald, and well-groomed. His face, however, was frozen and somber. Essie, the woman who had left him four months before he joined our study, was not merely his wife; she was his "dream girl."

Tony's childhood had been emotionally bleak. His parents showed no affection to each other or to him. When Tony was 15, his mother left home to live with a younger man. She continued to live in the same neighborhood, however, and her presence made Tony the constant butt of jokes. From adolescence on, Tony fantasized about a beautiful girl with long, soft, blonde hair who would walk hand-in-hand with him and make up for all his early loneliness. When he met Essie just before he was sent to Vietnam, he thought she was that girl.

They married on his return. Accustomed to being a free spirit, Essie wanted none of the homey fireside life that Tony yearned for. When they disagreed, she would jump up, leave the house, and stay with girlfriends. She made many threats of divorce, but Tony, a deeply religious man, refused to consider it. They finally agreed to try to make the best of their marriage. After having three children, Essie insisted that Tony get a vasectomy. Although they stayed together for 19 years, their problems continued. Essie started going out again and staying out all night.

Tony was so committed to the idea of keeping the family together that it took him a long time to recognize that his wife was involved in a long-term love affair with another woman. When Essie finally confronted him with her need for this outlet, he could not face it. He screamed at her and called her ugly names. She kicked him hard, and left, taking their youngest son. Tony still lives in the same house with the two older boys, although Essie is suing him for half of it. He does not know where she lives.

Despite his many strengths, Tony fell into a major depression. His long, unhappy dreams, recorded one night in the sleep laboratory, show how the loss of his wife severely damaged his self-image. They also suggest what needs to change to help him feel good about himself and to love again. They illustrate how dreams illuminate current concerns and integrate them with memories of earlier events.

As is typical of many depressed people, Tony's first dream did not begin in the present. It took him back to an earlier time, to Vietnam, and the start of his troubled marriage.

Dream 1

I was in a small boat, a 15-man rubber raft. I was trying to paddle ashore, and a storm came up and caught us in a sort of open sea. It was some kind of military operation that had something to do with a submarine that dropped us there. It was a big raft, but only two other people were there with me. The raft was being tossed around. It was an amphibious infiltration. Something artificial about it, like a mock-up of a battle being filmed in a tub. It was dark and stormy and the raft was spinning and the water was boiling.

The dream showed Tony "at sea" with two others, trying to land safely. It was a smaller crew than was needed to man the raft. Clearly, he and his sons were trying to survive on their own.

In describing the dream, Tony said he was in a sham situation. That was how he felt about his marriage; he had been deceived. His picture of a happy family was a pretense. Even though the plot sounds dramatic, he said it was artificial. It was not real to him. Following his separation, he was remote from any feeling. In talking about his dream, Tony identified several dream dimensions: real/sham, safe/dangerous, and in control/out of control.

This dream gave us Tony's problem statement: "How can I and my boys make it safely through a sea of trouble, after I have been unmanned and abandoned by a bisexual wife?" He partly answered his own question in the dream by drawing on memories of his service experience for images of the competence and strength he needed to get through this crisis.

Dream 2

It was a very domestic type of dream. Something to do with a large thermos jug sitting on a table. I think I was moving this stuff. There was a big truck involved. I was watching it on a TV monitor. This stuff had to be moved from one house to another.

Here, too, Tony was in transition, a theme that often appears in dreams of people going through a life change. This time it was a domestic move from one house to another. Again, there was something disengaged and remote about his viewing it on a monitor, perhaps a reflection about how he felt about being on view in the laboratory.

Dream 3

It was a sexual dream. I was in a foreign country. I was in the army. I'd met a much younger woman, a girl almost. I was staying in a strange hotel and she was staying there, too. She let me know she liked me. I was trying to decide what to do about it. I was trying to tell myself, "This girl is much too young for you, so don't be fooling around." That would be typical of me.

Finally I got tired of that and went to her room. It was fashioned out of a cave. All of the rooms in the hotel were fashioned out of caves, with plastic strips hanging down instead of doors, like curtains so you could walk through them instead of opening a door. I knew I had done the wrong thing by going there, but the farther I was into it, the harder it was going to be to turn back. I was thinking there was still time to get out of it.

Her mother was staying in another room. She'd already indicated that she didn't approve of this, and I had to agree, but I was thinking of breaking a rule because the girl seemed pretty interested in me sexually. We were sitting on a bed and she said she had to go to the bathroom. They didn't have bathrooms in these cave rooms. She was gone a long time.

I went to find her and passed her mother's room and overheard her mother saying, "Did you know what she's doing now? She's in her room with that old guy." It's very pleasant that a girl that age would find me attractive.

Tony was caught in a moral dilemma. He felt exposed and embarrassed by his surrender to an inappropriate sexual desire, but he also felt pleased and flattered. He was being tempted, led astray, and was rescued only by the girl's action when she vanished to use the bathroom.

The subterranean hotel reminds us that his first dream found him on a raft launched from a submarine. In the second, he had to take a thermos, a container for fluid shaped like a submarine, to a different house. According to Freud's theories, the submarine and the thermos are both symbols for Tony's sexuality. In the third dream, the appearance of the cave rooms with hanging strips may be a graphic representation of female genitals. This interpretation was consistent with what we knew of Tony's concerns, but it is important to note that Tony was the only one who could tell us what the symbols represented to him.

This dream found Tony in trouble in a heterosexual situation when he passively went along with a young girl's advances. He was asking, "What is it appropriate for me to do about my sexuality, now that I'm getting older?" We remember that he condemned his mother for running off with a younger man. In Dream 3, he added the dream dimensions domestic/foreign, young/old, and moral/immoral.

Dream 4

I was trying to meet some people in a restaurant. I was with my wife's family. My wife's aunt picked me up from work and was taking me there for a family get-together. We were meeting two dwarfs, twin sisters. We went to a little toadstool apartment they lived in. They came out disguised as a couple of guys, but their disguises weren't very good, as all they did was put mustaches on their faces and they were both wearing dresses. They were very old and looked unusual with artificial mustaches on their upper lips.

My mother-in-law was trying to coordinate everything, get everyone to the meeting place. She was upset that everything was going wrong. The dwarf twins were going to the wrong place. They came charging out of that little toadstool, basement apartment, where they lived. Their faces were weird, like squashed together, compressed looking. They thought their disguises would work, and we wouldn't recognize them. When my wife's aunt found they were going to the wrong place, she started screaming and said, "The heck with it, I'm going home."

The original restaurant we were supposed to meet in belonged to Mike Ditka, the coach of the Bears. There were swimming pools all over. I was dressed in a suit. A guy led me down to a pool beneath Mike Ditka's office where he swam. It was dark, and I walked right into the pool between these steps, and I found myself waist deep in water with my suit on.

Before that, I was at the zoo, looking for bears, and I ran into this guy I suspected of being queer, because he was following me. He sort of picked me out of the crowd and took me to Ditka's. It made me mad to wind up in the water.

When we talked about this dream the next morning, Tony quickly explained the meaning of some of its images. The dwarf sisters with squashed faces reminded him of the feud between his mother-in-law and his aunt. They had had a falling-out over their mother's care when she became elderly. Their mother was a tiny person whose face had become distorted and squashed-looking as she aged.

We also see in this dream his concern about his wife's "coming out" as a bisexual person, with the image of the two women escaping as false men and rushing off to the wrong place. Tony also dreamed about a very masculine man, Mike Ditka, and a frankly homosexual male, who pursued him, led him into an inappropriate act, and got him all wet.

In this dream Tony said: "Family things go wrong, people fight and misunderstand each other, and I am left with a dilemma about my masculine identity. Having a bisexual wife, what does that make me? Where do I belong?" Again we see his use of the dream dimensions real/sham, and in control/ out of control. This dream added the dimensions straight sex/gay sex, active/passive, pride/shame, and exposed/private.

In the last dream of the night, Tony finally dreamed directly about his wife.

Dream 5

My wife had injured herself somehow and she was showing me a surgical scar. It was on her leg. We were talking to each other. She showed me the scar and told me she needed more surgery.

Tony dreamed that his wife was damaged and not right yet, perhaps expressing his wish that surgery would repair Essie sexually and restore her to him.

In reviewing his dreams the next day, Tony made many fruitful connections as he searched for their origins in various aspects of his waking life. The surgical scar brought to mind the vasectomy Essie required of him after the birth of their third child. He also recalled that one evening recently while he was at a social event at the army base where he serves on reserve duty, two teenaged girls approached him and a younger man. He danced with one of the girls and thought she enjoyed his company. He was encouraged that a young girl found him sexually attractive. He thought this recent exposure to sexual temptation showed up in his dream of the doorless cave hotel.

The more immediate day residue stimulus most likely came from being put to bed that night by an attractive young female sleep technician in a hotel-like laboratory, an experience that may have triggered the earlier army base memory. This dream also reflected the still older memory of the basement apartment his mother occupied with her lover after she left home. Tony remembered that the door to that apartment had had a window in it. In the laboratory, he knew a video camera would be trained on him. His dream reveals his feeling of a loss of privacy.

The restaurant dream reminded him of his wife's family, a large, close, and emotionally volatile clan. It was their custom to meet for big family dinners at a restaurant. This pleasant routine broke up when the two sisters, his mother-in-law and aunt, stopped speaking to each other. He missed the closeness very much.

Tony related his dream of moving household goods in a truck to a trip he had made recently to deliver some donated clothes and furniture to a mission for AIDS victims run by nuns. He admired the dedication of these good "sisters" to gay people so much he thought he might try to find Essie and make a go of his marriage to a gay woman one more time.

Throughout his night's dreams, we saw Tony's self-image as passive and disengaged. He observed and only pretended to act or let others lead him. He wondered if he were masculine or feminine, as he dealt with the dangers of straight sex and sexual ambiguity, morality and immorality, youth and age. He juggled his dilemmas this way and that from dream to dream.

Tony lacked the ability to cope well in all of his dreams. He was stalled in his inner world, just as he was in waking reality. He got into trouble by letting things happen according to other people's wishes. He saw himself as an onlooker, an outsider, a victim who tried to do the right thing. He doubted his manliness and felt helpless. He was "guilty as charged" for having sexual desires and for being abandoned by his damaged dream girl. Tony didn't work these problems through in his dreams. I worried that he would continue to have emotional trouble unless he got some help. It was nearly two years before Tony entered therapy and started to work on his dreams.

REWRITING DREAM SCRIPTS: THE RISC METHOD

The premise of dream therapy is straightforward: If bad dream scripts make you awaken discouraged and downhearted, rewriting the scripts to improve the endings should lead to better moods.

Dream therapy has just four steps that you can learn on your own:

- *Recognize* when you are having a bad dream, the kind that leaves you feeling helpless, guilty, or upset the next morning. You need to become aware while you are dreaming that the dream is not going well.
- *Identify* what it is about the dream that makes you feel badly. Locate the dimensions within your dreams that portray you in a negative light, as, for example, weak rather than strong, inept rather than capable, or out-of-control rather than incontrol.
- *Stop* any bad dream. You do not have to let it continue. You are in charge. Most people are surprised to find that telling themselves to recognize when a bad dream is in progress often is all it takes to empower them to stop such dreams when they occur.

◆ *Change* negative dream dimensions into their opposite, positive sides. At first, you may need to wake up and devise a new conclusion before returning to sleep. With practice, you will be able to instruct yourself to change the action while remaining asleep.

The first letter of each step forms the acronym RISC to help you remember that the idea is to "risk" stepping in to change the endings of your dreams and to work toward a more positive self-image.

Troubled dreamers seeking help usually can master these four steps in just eight weeks, and often sooner. Working with a therapist may speed up the process or help you focus on aspects of your dreams you might not otherwise see, but it's reasonable to try to initiate dream repair on your own and see how far you can go.

The RISC treatment, like other techniques of psychotherapy, works both by what it does and how it does it. In most psychotherapy treatments, therapist and patient focus on changing waking attitudes and behavior. The therapist helps the patient generate the "right stuff" to talk about and work on. In the RISC program, we also seek to change waking attitudes and behavior, but we do it by spotlighting the negative aspects of the underlying identity displayed in each patient's dreams. I meet with my patients for hour-long sessions at weekly intervals, usually for eight weeks or longer.

In RISC therapy, patients do not have to search for topics to discuss. Right from the first session, the dream transcripts from their previous night in the sleep laboratory are on the table to give a compelling account of what is on their minds at night. We work as a team on the problems these dreams reveal. As therapy proceeds, I ask patients to bring in their home dream diaries so that we can work on dreams they currently are having. I urge those who initially are poor dream recallers to take the test of personal constructs included in

Chapter 3 and to talk about any dreams they may remember; these acts usually foster better memory for new dreams.

Patients are not passive recipients of treatment. They serve as co-investigators to discover how their dreams relate to both their present crises and their earlier life experiences. During our sessions, they then practice creating healthier and happier conclusions for troubling dreams. "Make up a better ending," I urge them.

The way they define "better" sometimes proves surprising. One meek young man often had a nightmare in which a bus ran him down. When he changed this dream, he gave himself a machine gun so that he could attack the bus and shoot its driver. He felt much better afterward and never had the dream again. Why not? In his dream, he could retaliate aggressively against the bullies who had picked on him when he was a youngster and destroy them. His dream success rebuilt some pride he sorely needed.

The differences between RISC treatment and other types of psychotherapy become even clearer in the second through the eighth sessions, when patients bring their home dreams to the therapy hour for us to study together. Only they know what they have dreamed at home. They decide what to share with me. While they can practice the most important part of this work in my office, changing the ending of a dream, they must accomplish the task on their own at home.

Often people discover through their dreams that their present crises have reawakened distressing feelings from events earlier in life. At such times, they need therapists who are skilled enough to recognize the emotion-packed inner pictures of a damaged self and will stand by to monitor how safe it is for their patients to look at them. Therapists also must be able to help patients find images of strength to build on. In general, however, patients take a more active role in dream therapy than in most traditional forms of psychotherapy.

Altering the outcome of a dream is a tall order, but our

studies show it's an achievable goal. There's an active give-and-take between the conscious and the sleeping mind. Even if you don't change a particular dream while asleep, your waking exploration of the depressive elements of your dreams, and your awareness of what you can and should change, may have a payoff. People who do their homework, who devise several possible solutions to familiar dream dilemmas, report that they often manage to incorporate some of these new waking attitudes into their dreams.

Such success reverberates with waking life. Becoming more active in dreams helps people to become more positive about the future. A successful night of dreaming produces immediate benefits for mood in the morning. Stopping a bad dream and changing it lifts the spirits. People gain a sense of empowerment from knowing they are not at the mercy of their bad dreams. Then, as they begin to change the image of a rejected, helpless self to one that is more in control, waking behavior begins to improve. They start to try out the new roles, the underdeveloped, better aspects of themselves, that they first practice in dreams.

Some people have both scant memory for their dreams and scant insight into their waking feelings as well. They have a breakdown in communication between their outer lives and their inner lives. They may go through the motions of living but feel slight satisfaction with their lives. Often they have lost track of themselves in trying to please other people.

Sometimes these people seek psychotherapy, but their dissatisfactions are so vague they have trouble articulating their discontent. They can't put their finger on what they want nor can they say how they feel. They lack a vocabulary for talking about themselves. For such people, dreamwork can offer rapid and remarkable rewards.

More than a decade ago, I undertook a project to help a university counseling service that had a problem: Nearly half of the students seeking help there and deemed in need of long-term individual psychotherapy failed to return or dropped out of therapy after the first few sessions. Those most likely to drop out proved to be those with difficulty expressing why they had come. All had trouble sharing their thoughts and feelings.

I wondered if potential dropouts who had the opportunity to become familiar with their inner life through their dreams and who had practice discussing their dreams would remain in treatment longer and make better use of it. With the assistance of the counseling service's social worker, I selected 48 students considered poor risks for staying in treatment.

I offered them the opportunity to participate in a program designed to help people utilize the opportunity for psychotherapy more fully. Thirty-two of the students spent eight nights in our sleep laboratory. The other 16 went directly into treatment. My technician awakened half of those who slept in the laboratory only during REM sleep episodes. She awakened the others only in NREM sleep. She asked both groups to tell what was going through their minds at that moment. Every morning, I asked those who had spent the night in the laboratory to recall whatever they could of the dreams they had told during the night. I offered no interpretations but prompted those who forgot any dreams to remember them. I asked them two questions: "Do you see any way these dreams relate to each other?" and "Do you see any way they relate to your life?"

The aim was to get these students to recognize that what was going on within was understandable and related to their problems in daily living. They did remarkably well. Those awakened during REM sleep who reported dreams more than half of the time proved most likely to remain in treatment through the first 10 sessions and to dig in and work hard at making needed changes in their lives. Even those awakened in NREM sleep who reported only a few dreams seemed to bene-fit from the morning-after conversations about their night thoughts. The majority of those who did not come to the laboratory first but entered treatment directly dropped out of therapy much sooner, without making progress.

The dream recallers had one complaint: Because we did not want their therapists to know which group they were in to avoid any bias in rating their treatment progress, we kept the records of their nighttime reports. However, the students wanted to discuss their dreams. When they tried to bring the subject up, the therapists discouraged them, saying, "Dreams are not my bag," and turned the hour toward dealing with reality problems. Even without a therapist's help, access to their dreams helped them to identify their emotional issues and increased their comfort in discussing their disturbing feelings.

Because sending patients regularly to a sleep laboratory is not practical, we followed this study with a small pilot study using a simpler approach. We invited eight poor-risk students to join an hour-long daily dream-modeling workshop. Instead of sleeping in the laboratory, these students first viewed a different 10-minute videotape each day for eight days. Each tape showed a morning dream discussion session with a student who had been in the REM interruption group. We encouraged the students to first look for meanings the dreamer had missed and then, for the remainder of the hour, to work in a similar fashion on one of their own dreams. This method of learning from watching others proved promising. Once their own treatment began, five of the eight stuck with it for 10 or more sessions, almost as high a proportion as those we had awakened in the laboratory during REM sleep.

Researchers in Finland adapted our study to treat a different problem in psychotherapy—getting through a dry period. They found that sending a group of patients, whose progress in treatment had been stalled, to the sleep laboratory to have their dreams collected revitalized the therapeutic process. Gaining access to their dreams made the patients more open to exploring their emotional lives.

⇨ **SELF-HELP: Using RISC to change your dreams**

Mastering the RISC method takes motivation and practice, but it is not difficult to do. These are the steps:

◆ With your dream diary and your day journal in hand, start by reviewing the dreams that trouble you the most and try to figure out why. As you learn to identify negative self-talk, you will become more proficient at doing so.

◆ Look at the message each dream displays and focus on its dimensions. Each dimension will have numerous images that illustrate its opposite pole. Initially, you may see more negative dimensions in your dreams, but as you explore in your waking life the positive side of the dimensions you habitually use, you will program yourself to incorporate more self-confident images into your dreams at night.

◆ When you locate a problem dream, imagine different endings. You're the scriptwriter. How else could the dream have turned out? Consider several endings. Which do you prefer?

◆ Think of times when you've been in a similar situation that turned out well. If you can't find many positive images in your memory bank to draw on, you will need to create new images for yourself. If you're stuck in the past, for example, mentally rewrite your dream scenarios so you are an adult, not a helpless child. If you find yourself a victim in your dreams, practice standing up for yourself in fantasy, where you can do it safely. Ponder the new possibilities at bedtime.

◆ Tell yourself, "Next time I dream, I want to recognize that I'm dreaming." Even more importantly, tell yourself, "Next time I have a bad dream, I want to recognize it, stop it, and change it." You always can stop a dream just by opening your eyes.

Here is an example of the RISC method in action.
Judith was a single woman in her forties who had lost her

job as a traveling sales representative when her company made sweeping recessionary cutbacks. After searching unsuccessfully for months for a new job, mainly by responding to newspaper ads and sending out dozens of resumes, she was feeling depressed about the lack of opportunities and was running out of money. The longer Judith was out of work, the more she began to feel that something must be terribly wrong with her, that she was unemployable. She felt disgraced, and she was embarrassed to see her former workplace friends; she stopped calling them, and they stopped calling her.

Judith frequently dreamed that her car had broken down and that she was in a remote spot, far from help. She would awaken feeling beaten down before her day even started. After learning the RISC method, she reported this dream:

My car was stalled at a ferry debarkation point. It was rapidly getting dark. The car was completely dead and I was standing at a distance from it, full of despair, looking at the rough waves and menacing skies, desperately wanting to go home, needing my car to do so, feeling utterly powerless and deflated.

"I woke up feeling a sense of emptiness and failure, let down, very disappointed in myself," she said. "I was thinking, 'Here comes another bad day.' But then I thought about the dimensions I kept repeating in my broken-down car dreams: dead versus alive, helplessness versus taking charge, stuck versus moving forward. I kept thinking, 'What can I do to help myself?'

"The next thing I knew," she reported, "I was back in the same dream":

It was the next morning. My car now was in a garage. A mechanic approached me and said, "Take your car. It's fixed and we threw in a full tank of gas, free." This meant to me that the garage service was apologetic about having taken a full overnight to fix my car. I needed my car badly; it was my vehicle to getting on with my life. I was sur-prised and grateful.

This dream is a good example of the benefits of dream therapy. It showed Judith's gratitude for the "overnight help" she received. In the dream she turned night into day and her broken-down car into a functional one. Her dream dimensions came up on their positive side. She also saw that she didn't need to struggle entirely on her own. She recognized it was no disgrace to ask others for help, especially when they, like the man in her dream, had knowledge she lacked.

After this dream, Judith realized it was necessary to swallow her pride. Although she cherished her independence and didn't want to be in anyone's debt, she took out her address book and contacted her former co-workers and clients. She returned to a businesswomen's lunch group she always had enjoyed and told everyone she could buttonhole that she was looking for work. Within two weeks a job offer came from what Judith thought was a surprising source: one of her former clients had long thought she was one of the better sales representatives calling on him and now wanted her to represent his company.

In one of Judith's most recent dreams, she was driving across a big bridge. In another, she was traveling down a busy highway, keeping up with traffic and enjoying the trip. She now has new images of strength to store in her memory bank. The more such images you can create for yourself, the more likely you will be to draw on them, and the more likely it is that the dream process will function well on its own when you next find yourself in a situation in which the same emotional buttons get pushed.

Facing the Crisis of Divorce

E HUMANS are ill-equipped to live alone, as so many now do. We are born needing the care of others. This need continues in different forms throughout our lives. Both psychological and physical health reflect the quality and quantity of our loving ties to other people. Health statistics confirm that people with few or poor-quality personal relationships run a greater risk of accidents, diseases, psychiatric disorders, and death. The death rates from every leading cause are highest for divorced people and lowest for married people, in both sexes at all ages.

Why is health so strongly tied to having a partner? The answer lies not so much in what a mate does *for* us, as in what the loss of a mate does *to* us. The loss of someone who gives meaning to our life typically provokes a stress reaction, a state of psychological alarm and body-wide arousal, just as if our own lives were under threat. In Chapter 1, Laura questioned, "If I am not Jim's wife, who am I?" This reaction is even more intense if the tie to the lost mate involves a strong commitment and emotional dependency, as is true in most marriages, at least at their start.

If this kind of emergency reaction lasts for some time without resolution, as often happens when a marriage goes bad, then bodily changes, such as increases in blood pressure and frayed sleep, may persist. Such changes make us vulnerable to a host of diseases. A state of persistent threat also may produce psychological changes. After the initial shock and anxiety pass, a state of helplessness may set in, a feeling of resignation that nothing can be done to change the situation. A collapse into depression may follow.

More than one million Americans divorce each year, about 50% of all first marriages. While about four out of five divorced people remarry, three out of five of them divorce a second time. "Divorce is deceptive. Legally it is a single event, but psychologically it is a chain—sometimes a never-ending chain—of events, relocations, and radically shifting relationships strung through time, a process that forever changes the lives of the people involved," say Judith Wallerstein and Sandra Blakeslee in their book *Second Chances*. "There are winners and losers in the years after divorce," they go on. "In some families, particularly where there has been long-standing conflict or physical violence, everyone may be better off. But in most families, divorce tends to benefit one of the adults much more than the other. For that one person—most often the one who sought the divorce—the quality of life can be greatly enhanced, even beyond his or her expectations. But for the other person, divorce can have tragic consequences—five, ten, and even fifteen years after the event."

Even under the best of circumstances, when both parties are ready to part, untangling the many threads that unite two people who swore to cherish each other for a lifetime is a painful process. Virtually everyone who divorces experiences feelings of sadness, disappointment, and regret, even those for whom divorce initially brings welcome relief.

According to psychologist Mavis Hetherington of the University of Virginia, the adverse psychological impact of divorce hits women and men at different times. "For women, the hardest time is right around the divorce, in the agony of the months leading up to it and just after it," she says. "Men have more lingering feelings of regret," she notes.

By the end of the first year following the divorce, 65% of divorcing persons who also are parents say they regret having done it. Even those who thought their marriages were terrible wish they had worked harder to resolve problems. However, Hetherington notes, they do not communicate these feelings to their former spouses in an attempt to patch things up. "In my experience," she says, "things get worse before they get better."

Soon after divorce, she says, both men and women report strong feelings of failure, social incompetence, and loss of self-esteem. Women feel helpless and unattractive; men, rootless. Both feel depersonalized, having lost the identity that marital status confers, and both feel extreme loneliness. Women often lose a network of social contacts based on their former husbands' occupational associations, although increasingly women have their own occupational networks to draw on.

Fortunately, not all spiral downward from anxiety to depression. Some prove much more adept than others at putting the divorce behind them and establishing a new life pattern. Why do some bounce back fast? Why do others take so long? What boosts recovery? What retards it? Can we speed the recovery process?

With funding from the National Institute of Mental Health, we launched a large study to try to answer those questions. We enlisted the participants—100 men and 100 women—by advertising in local newspapers. We asked them to share with us within a year of their separation what they felt led to the dissolution of their marriages and how they were coping. We hoped to learn what they were thinking and feeling about themselves, both awake and in their dreams, and how these two views helped or hindered their moving on with their lives.

Our only qualifications were that the marriage must be their first one and that it must have lasted at least three years.

The women who joined our study ranged from 25–45 years of age; the men from 25–50. The majority were in their mid-thirties, with two children. One in four, however, had no children. They were white, black, Hispanic, and Asian-American, with a wide range of occupations, incomes, and education. Two thirds had attended college, and nearly one in five had some postgraduate education. They included equal numbers of spouses who walked out and spouses who were left behind. All promised to come back one year later so we could see how they had made it through this time of transition. Julie, Harold, and Tony were among those who took part in this study.

Some of the participants came for the money, even though they received only a small fee to cover their time and travel. Divorce is an expensive business, and many were so short of funds that they welcomed anything extra. Some came for the opportunity to learn more about their dreams. Most came for the chance to talk about what had happened to their marriage, with the hope of gaining some better understanding and a sense of support.

People often cried during the first interview, but most said they were glad they had come. They were faithful about returning one year later for the follow-up, even those who moved out of state. Most responded to a survey we conducted as long as four years after their first visit, and many write with periodic updates.

All of the volunteers started the project by talking with me about the marriage for an hour. They reviewed how the marriage began, developed, and died. They completed many questionnaires to describe themselves, their moods, and their social networks, both during the marriage and once they were on their own.

All participants met with a psychiatrist who interviewed them to determine whether they currently were depressed or had been previously, and whether they had a history of depression in their family. Their answers gave us a picture of their personality patterns, coping styles, degrees of depression, and strengths and weaknesses. The answers also told us how they interacted with others and how they hoped to change.

To assess their sleep and dreams, we chose 70 people, representative of the entire group, to spend three nights in the sleep laboratory. They included 30 participants who were doing well and 40 who were having trouble coping, with equal numbers of men and women in each group.

On the first two nights, the volunteers slept without our awakening them. We wanted them to become comfortable with the laboratory and our procedures. We, too, had to familiarize ourselves with their particular sleep patterns. Were they sound sleepers or did they toss and turn? Did they have normal amounts of NREM and REM sleep? Did these sleep states occur at the normal times?

On the third night, before they went to sleep, we told them that we would awaken them several times to collect a report of what had been going through their minds at the time. We explained that they might be dreaming or thinking or not aware of anything at all, and that any report was fine. We also told them that we would ask a series of questions about their dreams before they went back to sleep.

By awakening sleepers during each successive REM period, we averaged four dream reports in a single night. The next morning, participants reviewed their dreams and talked with me about how the dreams related to each other, to help reconstruct the story line of the night. We gave participants transcripts of their dream reports. Many told us the transcripts further sparked their interest in dreams and helped them to recall more dreams at home.

Meanwhile, our research team carefully reviewed the dream scripts for clues as to how our study participants were weathering this stormy time. We wanted to find those who managed well, to learn what kinds of dreams they had, to see what their dreams told us about the coping process. We also sought to identify those in the process of divorce whose dream system hindered their adaptation to their new role. We hoped to find strategies used by the successful copers that we could teach to those whose progress was stalled.

DIVORCED BUT COPING

Maggie was successfully surmounting her marriage crisis. She and her husband, Matthew, had married young, when she was 21 and he was 19. When Maggie was 32, Matthew announced that he was in love with another woman.

Maggie described their marriage as troubled from the start. During the first two years Matthew attended school and she worked as a secretary to support him. They had agreed that once he finished his degree program, he would go to work and give her a turn at school. After he graduated, however, he became a free-lance writer and did not bring in enough income to permit Maggie to stop working.

"I was totally focused on him," Maggie reported. "I was devastated when he said he intended to leave me, but it jolted me into realizing a lot of things about my own assumptions. I grew up feeling the man always comes first. I patterned myself after my mother, who always catered to my father. Matthew liked to go out late and stay out late, while I was basically a homebody. A few months ago, when he first left, I was afraid to go out by myself, and I was scared of being alone. There was no one to talk to when I got home.

"I got two cats for company," Maggie said. "Gradually I'm learning to use my free time for myself. I'm finally taking some classes at the university, where I've met some nice people. I have a new sense of freedom. I don't have to fix dinner if I'm not hungry. I've also got some pride that I can take care of myself."

Maggie already paid attention to her dreams. "When Matthew first left, I used to have a repetitive nightmare that I had lost my purse with everything important to me in it," she said. "I ran through the hallways begging people to help me. Now that dream has finally stopped." In the laboratory, Maggie's first dream looked toward the future rather than the past.

Dream 1

I was with a man. It was really beautiful. We were sitting out on a cliff at sunset over an ocean, then the scene changed to a stark hospital room, where we were lying on the bed, fully clothed. We were talking, not doing anything sexual, but I had those strong feelings that something was about to happen. I was sure that the sexual feelings I was having toward him were going to lead to something and I wasn't sure if I wanted to have those feelings or not, those feelings of attachment to somebody.

In this dream, Maggie expressed the wish for an idyllic, romantic relationship. She also displayed some conflict over following these feelings through to form a new attachment. She needed love, but she was wary and worried that these feelings would be exposed in the laboratory setting and perhaps judged harshly. This was a rehearsal dream in which she tested how it would feel to let it be known that she was ready for a new relationship.

In her last dream of the night, a long, detailed narrative, Maggie put her relationship with Matthew to rest. She accepted not having a place in his life any longer.

Dream 4

I had keys to the apartment of the woman my ex-husband is with now. I went into the apartment, to her kitchen table, because there were three or four small pages, like scraps of paper with notes on them, that were from my job, from my office, and I was going to get them from her kitchen table. I didn't know how they ended up there, but I was there picking them up, and she came out of the bathroom.

She didn't hear me in there and I didn't know she was in the apartment. She got really freaked out. She ran out of the bathroom into the living room and I ran after her. She was very upset and couldn't understand why I had gone in there without telling her or letting her know I was going to be there, and I said I was sorry, I didn't know she was there or I wouldn't have done it, but I was there to get some things she had on the table.

I remember feeling guilty, like I'd picked up stuff that maybe wasn't mine, and maybe stuff of hers that I was going to take and I told her I was sorry, but I really needed the stuff. So then she said she was really scared that I was able to come in there without her knowing, and she was afraid.

She and my ex-husband were both afraid that I would come in and take valuable things or take a lot of stuff sometime when they weren't there. I told her I didn't intend to do that, that I was just as afraid that they would get some of my stuff, and I guess they maybe had access to my apartment, too.

So we were both acknowledging our fears and kind of came to an understanding that we both weren't going to do something like that to each other. I remember we were sitting in her living room and there was a big picture window, and it was really nice outside, it was really beautiful, real sunny.

Maggie's dream settled something: the past was the past. She realized that she had to stay out of her ex-husband's life, and he out of hers. The main dimensions of Maggie's dreams had to do with hanging on to the past or giving it up, and approaching or withdrawing from new contacts with others. In her dreams, the balance was away from the past and toward the future. Maggie was managing well; she needed no special help.

Robert was another good coper. He had been quite ready for his divorce; in fact, the wonder is that his marriage lasted as long as it did, some 20 years. Robert was only 19 years old and his wife, Karen, 18 when they married. She had made a full-time career out of being sick. Over their years together, she had been treated for a host of ailments, most of them imaginary. She constantly took medications and frequently overdosed on them.

She played the sick role so well that Robert became locked into a pattern of dropping everything to stand by her through many hospitalizations and surgeries. One day he reached his limit, threw out all her pills, and left. His first dream in the sleep laboratory showed clearly that he was willing to give up taking care of Karen and was at peace with his decision:

I was in a driveway, where cars were parked. It looked like California, with the ocean below. Two guys wearing ski masks suddenly appeared and wanted all my money and my wife's money. One of the guys grabbed Karen. I hit the horn and he said, "There's no sense in doing that, nobody hears anything out here." I laughed and said, "You're probably right, go ahead, take whatever you want."

The most important dimension in this dream is protecting versus giving up. Robert felt that this dream said, "I give up on her. I can't help her and no one else will come to our aid." As Robert noted, "She cost me a lot of money, which I now willingly give up."

Robert and Maggie had both cleared the decks from their old marriages and were ready for a new phase in their lives. Their dreams showed it. Neither had any history of depression in their families. Both had good stable work histories and good friendships. One year later when they returned for follow-up interviews and testing, both reported new romances. With the help of their good friends, good genes, strong self-images, and the reorganizing work of their good dreams, they successfully negotiated their transition from married to single life.

Most of those who were emotionally stalled in depression when they first enlisted in the divorce study improved both their lives and their dreams by the time they returned one year later. We were curious about this group. How did some who were stunned by the initial blow manage to stop reeling and move forward with their lives?

DIVORCED AND DEPRESSED

Helen, a woman who was so depressed when we first saw her that she was thinking of ending her life, was one who improved on her own. A hard-working paralegal aide, she longed to go to law school. Hers was a big, close, religiously-oriented family in modest economic circumstances. Her parents had expected their children to go far, but they could not provide the fare. Helen had put herself through college. Helen's husband did not have her strong moral fiber. He was an immature, self-indulgent pleasure seeker who lived for the moment. When Helen discovered he was having an affair, she was indignant. He was casual about it and told her it was "no big deal." It was she who said, "Choose." He did. He left her.

On her first dream-collection night in the laboratory, Helen had these dreams:

Dream 1

I got on the El and tried to get someplace, but I kept on coming back to the same place. I kept on making this big loop. I wasn't going anywhere. I kept winding up back where I started from. And then I was suddenly at work and this guy asked me how come I wasn't working. I remember feeling very, very guilty, wondering why I wasn't working.

Dream 2

Someone asked me when did Dick ask me for a divorce and I was explaining it to them. Then it all came to life. This isn't how it really happened, but in my dream we went to a restaurant, me and Dick and my younger sister and some others. We sat in the booth and were hav-

ing beer and a co-worker said, "Oh, they have lager. I wonder if they will warm it up?" So I asked the waitress if she would warm up the beer. She said, "Yes, we have a microwave." So I got a beer glass and warmed it up and when I came back, Dick said, "I'm divorcing you. I'm leaving you." He got up and walked out.

Dream 3

I was walking past a school, and I saw a child playing with a puppy. It was so little, real tiny. I went over to play with it and it shit on me. My sister was there commenting on how cute he was but puppies do that.

The theme here, "Something I thought would be fun has backfired and it's all my fault," is one we often see in dreams of people with depression. Their dreams are full of self-blame. Indeed, the more severe the depression, the more prominent the motif of self-reproach.

In all three dreams, Helen's picture of herself was not a happy one. She was going around in circles and not doing her work. Her husband publicly discarded her while her back was turned, and an immature animal defecated on her. In these dreams she was, in turn, unable to get ahead, blameworthy, abandoned, and besmirched. She portrayed only the negative sides of her dream dimensions. She saw herself as stalled, not progressing, guilty, not innocent, humiliated, not praised, serving others, not caring for herself, and sullied, not cleansed. How did she manage to revise this view of herself on her own?

While initially devastated, Helen had all the strengths she needed to recover: a good set of genes from her parents, a strong support system in her sisters, friends, co-workers, and supervisors, and a highly creative dream system. When Helen returned a year later, she told me several pieces of good news. She had been accepted into law school and given a partial scholarship. She had a new boyfriend who was older and more mature than Dick. Dick's girlfriend had dropped him, and now he wanted to come back. Helen had the satisfaction of finding she was better off without him.

Helen's later dreams show how much better she had begun to feel about herself and demonstrate her ability to manage on her own. They also illustrate how dreams help us to revise our self-image and to rehearse a possible future. Here's one of them:

I was on a trip with about 30 people, an adventure trip in Japan. We were going to climb a mountain. We were in a valley with very steep walls and it was very, very foggy and no one could see. Everyone was wandering around with their arms out in front of them, like they were sleepwalking and trying to figure out where to go. Finally I said, "This is ridiculous, I'm going to find my way out of here." So I put my arms down and opened my eyes. I found a rock that went up like a stairway. And everyone started to argue about who should go first. I thought I should go first because I found it. So I started to walk up the stairs going up the side of the mountain, and everyone started to follow me walking up the stairs single file, slowly. I remember feeling very anxious and afraid at first, but when I found the staircase, I felt very, very good, real strong. I felt I was the only one that could do it. I had to do it myself. So I did.

This dream showed how much Helen's sense of her own competence had improved. "If I find myself trapped and going around in circles, I can find my way out. I just need to trust myself to open my eyes and face reality," she told herself. Look at the changes in her dream dimensions: she now was progressing, not stalled, praised rather than disparaged, serving herself, rather than going along with others, and uplifted, not humiliated. She had flipped all of her important dimensions to the positive side.

Not all those who at first were depressed over the breakdown of their marriage were able to make this kind of change by themselves. Harold, the truck driver, was among them. His self-image as an in-charge guy had suffered a devastating blow when his wife walked out. He did not have good resources to help him through his crisis: he had few friends. An adopted child, he knew nothing of his genes. His dreams were stalled; they portrayed only his troubles. In his initial dreams in the sleep laboratory, he had no money, he couldn't keep a girl from leaving him, and he couldn't get his hose in the tank.

"I'm worse than I was when you saw me a year ago," Harold told me when he came back for his one-year visit. Because trucking offered more income than other job options, he had returned to the work he disliked. Unfortunately, he suffered an injury on the job and was laid off.

"My ex-wife got remarried with no warning," he related. "My kids told me they had been to a wedding. I asked, 'Whose wedding?' and they said 'Mommy's.'" Harold said that he now recognized that he and his wife had not worked hard enough to resolve their difficulties.

The struggle to accept his wife's departure was even tougher for Tony than for Harold. Tony suffered a self-image crisis when his wife, Essie, left him after 19 years of marriage to live with another woman. In Tony's first dreams in the laboratory, he constantly had found himself in deep water, quite literally in a sea of trouble. His dreams had showed no progress across the night. I anticipated then that he would continue to suffer emotional trouble unless he received help. However, it took Tony some time to discover that for himself.

Tony had built his first dreams in the laboratory around the issues of masculine/feminine, old/young, active/passive, surface/underneath, moral/immoral. He had portrayed himself on the positive side on only two of these dimensions, action and morality. He played an active role only in his interaction with other men. He demonstrated his morality with both sexes, despite temptations. His dreams of positive action came largely from his experiences of competence as a military officer in Vietnam. His morality reflected his strong religious background, which also gave him a commitment to winning favor by being a humble, giving person.

One of the key characteristics that interfered with Tony's personal happiness was his inflexible, all-or-none, right-or-wrong view of the world, particularly of women. He did not see women as human beings with the usual blend of strengths and frailties, but rather as goddesses or whores.

When Tony returned for his one-year follow-up visit, he reported that he had found another perfect love and that he had lost her, too. Again, he had idolized the woman, smothering her with gifts and affection. When she turned down his proposal, he plunged into a deep despair and even thought of suicide. Tony still sought perfection. He based his entire self-worth on being the head of a loving family. He kept trying, but he couldn't make things work out.

His rejection by the second woman he adored prompted Tony to seek conventional psychotherapy and to take antidepressant medication. However, after six months of this treatment, he was no better. He called me. By then I had developed the RISC program and invited him to participate in dream therapy. I felt he could benefit from recognizing how his old emotional history still actively shaped his self-image and behavior.

In the more than 18 months since Tony had first come to the laboratory, he had had many new experiences. His two older sons left for college, where they were doing well. Tony had to sell his home for the divorce settlement and now lived alone. While he saw some of his old friends and worked at the same job, he agonized over how to improve his life. He kept going over the past to find how he could have given more to win the love he needed so much.

He began his first RISC session by relating that he repeatedly had violent dreams.

I was on a cattle drive. We were fighting the toughest-looking Indians I ever saw. We wanted to bargain with them and they said they wanted to bargain, but the first thing they did was to kill the bugle boy who was standing at attention blowing his bugle. He just fell apart.

We pulled back and slept on the side of a mountain and went to talk to the Indians the next day and offered them some gifts. They said they were going to take the gifts and kill us anyway. They said, "We are going to have everything that you have, so why should we bargain?"

In this dream, Tony failed to win peace through passivity and giving of gifts. His enemies were going to take everything—including his life. This dream revealed Tony's view of his circumstances at that time. He had to give both money and his home to the wife who had deceived him. He even had to give up one son, the one who had gone to live with Essie, the bugle boy in his dream. His new girlfriend took his lavish gifts but ultimately turned him down. His saintly passivity had driven him to despair and to the brink of suicide. Tony thought the main dimension of this dream was deceit versus trustworthiness. It also showed his struggle between power and helplessness.

With these issues on his mind all week, Tony came to his second RISC session with a report of success. He had managed to recognize that he was having a bad dream and to interrupt it by waking himself. He described the dream:

It was the army again. A basic training company. The gang of recruits were from the inner city, blacks, whites, and Hispanics. They were off to a very bad start, disobedient and hostile. I knew I could fix it by the power of my leadership ability. There were people hanging around the outside egging them on and screwing up the formations. The recruits were starting to laugh at me and I was getting very angry.

"I was starting to feel so uncomfortable that I stopped the dream," Tony reported. "I couldn't get back to sleep so I made up a new ending while I was lying awake. I made the crowd go away and the troops behave properly."

The important dimension of this dream was the feeling of being in-control versus out-of-control, with the out-of-control feeling as one of potential physical violence. The risk of killing others or being killed himself was close to the surface in Tony's dreams. The recruits in this dream, Tony thought, might be the sons that he felt responsible for shaping up. He fretted that they might turn bad despite his discipline. He worried that his ex-relatives laughed at his inability to control the boys.

Tony's dream showed his fears of defeat and humiliation as well as the anger toward his former wife and her relatives that he could not acknowledge even to himself. In this dream, even his generosity and leadership skills let him down.

In another dream Tony reported:

My son spilled food all over a brand new carpet. All over everywhere, milk and peanut butter, mixed together. I grabbed him and started yelling at him to clean it up. In the dream he was only about six or seven. He was crying. It was awful. I already started feeling guilty in the dream. So I picked him up and comforted him and told him I'd help clean it.

Tony's perfectionistic personality was hard on everyone. It masked a lot of inner anger. He felt he had to be good to earn love, but he paid a high price for not expressing his anger in waking: it erupted in his dreams. Visualizing new endings to his dreams gave him courage. In the next few weeks, he began to have more positive dreams.

One happy dream he remembered during this period found him back in his old neighborhood where blacks and whites lived together.

I was a member of a group that was trying to rid it of gangs and fix things that had been destroyed. I was so happy that I could fly. I had to take a big jump to get going, but several times in the dream I was flying about the neighborhood on my own power.

In his dream Tony made things work out so people could live together despite their differences. When he awakened, he found his mood better than it had been for some time. He knew that nurturing young people and helping to solve other people's problems gave him great pleasure. The flying made him feel exuberant.

"A couple of times I'd say, 'Wait a minute, I can't do this,' then I'd say, 'Yes I can. Go ahead and try,' and then I'd be flying," he explained. "I took off and flew around the old neighborhood. It was almost like I could see it was getting better for me."

What of his rigid, all-good or all-bad feelings about women? Wouldn't they continue to give him trouble until he acknowledged and accepted that everyone has flaws, even himself?

Tony brought in two landmark dreams at about this time. They showed some of the roots of these feelings and how these feelings, too, were changing through our work together on recognizing and confronting the dream dimensions that troubled him. Here are Tony's dreams:

Dream 1

I was in church where several older women were smoking. People kept asking them to stop, but they refused. The trouble was, these ladies were also the ones who made the best desserts for the church meal, and I wanted another dessert. I snuck up to the room where the desserts were, hoping no one would see me, but a younger girl caught me. She was smoking, too. She knew I liked desserts and thought I should be on the smokers' side because I was eating their desserts. I was afraid that would happen. That's why I tried to sneak up there.

"These women seemed to represent a mixture of good and evil," I observed. "And in your dream, you were not all innocent either. You wanted some of the good stuff they could provide."

Tony paused before replying. "You are right," he said. "My mother was a very heavy smoker. She always was smoking in the bathroom. It would leave a terrible tobacco smell. She did provide me with many wonderful things. What good there was in our childhood came from her."

"You want more of the sweet things women can provide, but you don't know how to get them openly, legitimately. You also want to stand apart from their dirty part," I suggested.

"I remember being very torn in the dream wanting that dessert and not wanting to be associated with them," Tony said.

"How can you relate to someone who has both good and bad sides, things you want and don't want?" I asked.

"My mother caused me a tremendous amount of unhappiness," Tony insisted. "I still haven't forgiven her for running off with that young man. It humiliated me. They stayed in our neighborhood, and my friends all knew about it."

"Women are a mixed bag for you," I told him, "but in your dream, you recognize that so are you. You are stuck between accepting and rejecting your own feelings and desires."

Tony then reported another dream:

Dream 2

I had moved into a commune where my three best friends and their wives were also living. Somehow all the wives in this community had become blind. I had a powerful sense of being alone. Everything we did had to be geared to the blind women. It was becoming annoying to go so far to accommodate them.

"Do you think you did that in your own life, accommodated too far?" I asked him.

"Yes, with my wife and with the other woman, too. I accepted things I didn't want to see. I was deaf and blind, intentionally. It was inconceivable to me that someone I perceived as close to perfect could do those things."

"You didn't really accept them. You put them out of your mind, ignored them, and built up a false picture of these women. How would you change this dream to make it work out better?" I asked.

"The blind people would stop expecting that accommodations would be made for them. They would demand to be treated like everyone else. We would be able to communicate without these bizarre rituals."

Tony himself was visually impaired, the result of an injury received in Vietnam. The severity of his dysfunction proved a source of contention in his marriage. His wife often insisted that at times he simply was choosing not to pay attention to her.

"In your dream," I said, "your three best friends were married and stayed married despite the fact their wives were blind. But you were alone. Others managed to accommodate to deficits better. When I asked you how you would change the dream, you said, 'The wives would demand not to receive special treatment. They want to be treated like everyone else.' Is that the way you want to be treated?"

"Me? Yes. I think so. No." Tony searched to clarify his feelings. "I want more sympathy from my boys, some understanding that the divorce was their mother's fault. I did the same thing to my father when he was going through this with my mother. I would not give him any sympathy at all."

This dream unlocked a flood of related, emotionally painful memories. His annoyance at the blind wives, who got too much consideration, stirred recall of his wife's early anger and rejection of him, his failure to comprehend the significance of her anger, his wish for more understanding from his sons, his failure to give it to his father, and his humiliation over his mother's sexuality.

The dream showed clearly both Tony's need for self-deception in matters of love and his tendency to withhold love as a punishment. These were the keys to his troubles. His model of perfect love was the all-giving love between mother and child. He, too, wanted the total acceptance one gives a baby on the basis of his moral purity.

Tony suddenly recognized that what he could give and get as an adult was something different. The dream solution that he put into the mouths of the blind wives, "to be accepted and loved like everyone else," faults and all, may work better for him. If Tony could hang on to this insight and begin to act on it, he would make a big change toward health. Reading our dreams gives us rapid access to the sources in our emotional history that lead to repetitive errors in present-day relationships.

Tony's mother, his only source of love in his early years, ran off and left him. He had struggled to be good ever since to try to keep other people he loved from escaping. However, to do so, he had to blind himself to their faults and to build phony, idolized relationships. He had not been able to accept himself or others as real, imperfect people. Now that he understood his dreams, he could begin.

Tony was an extreme case of someone with little insight into how his past still controlled his present emotions in ways that undermined his mood and relationships. By heeding his dreams, he rapidly recognized that his rigid moralistic stance was no match for unscrupulous people. He began to relax and accept himself as an imperfect person who had the right to be loved whether or not he was perfect.

The dreams of our divorce study participants, both those who were depressed and those who were doing well, illustrate the impact of a crisis on a person's inner identity. Dreams show big differences between those who remain trapped by their old problems and those who are ready to leave them behind.

For Tony, the divorce was an attack on his basic sense of manhood. His response was one of helplessness. Harold saw his divorce as a crisis in which he was powerless to get his needs satisfied and to control the actions of others. His response, as reflected in his dreams, was to continue to try to do things in the old way. To Helen, the divorce brought a surprising besmirching. Her response was to open her eyes to solve her own problems. Maggie and Robert, who were not depressed, both said in their dreams: "I invested enough and lost. Now it is time to cut the losses."

Tony and Harold were not mature, healthy adults making a reasoned decision to change a pattern of life that was not working well for them. As with Julie, their early emotional ties had set them up for marriages that were hard to sustain. The failure of their marriages then brought into question their whole styles of loving interaction. On their own, they floundered like abandoned children.

Both needed to revise their internal self-images extensively to avoid future difficulties. For both, the roots of their emotional traps were much clearer in their dreams than they were in their waking minds. The unfinished business reflected in their dreams slowed their transition toward becoming strong, self-respecting, single persons. Their marital failures rekindled their old problems. In effect, they had double trouble.

⇨ SELF-HELP: Weathering the crisis of divorce

If you are in the process of divorce, you quite likely will find feelings in your dreams that you are experiencing in waking life, such as anger, humiliation, despair, helplessness, self-blame, and abandonment. If you find that your dreams are repetitive and that they leave you feeling worn out and unhappy the next morning, try the RISC method.

◆ *Recognize* when you are having a disturbing dream while it is in progress. Some examples from participants in our divorce study include:

Dreamer 1: Someone was yelling at me in court, accusing me of lying.

Dreamer 2: My former husband was tramping mud all over my white rugs. I was down on my knees scrubbing them.

Dreamer 3: I was in bed with two women, one of them my ex-wife.

◆ *Identify* what's gone wrong in your dream.

Dreamer 1: I felt falsely and publicly accused of dishonesty.

Dreamer 2: I had to cope with the mud my former husband was throwing at me.

Dreamer 3: I felt guilty of infidelity, even though I'm really free.

◆ *Stop* the action, then change it by taking charge of what happens in the dream.

Dreamer 1: I kept my cool and asked the judge to cite the person for contempt.

Dreamer 2: I told my former husband to get out and sent him the cleaning bill for the rug.

Dreamer 3: I introduced my ex-wife to my new girlfriend.

◆ *Study* the messages you are sending yourself in your dreams and identify their dimensions. Then strive to create new images on the positive side of these dimensions.

Dreamer 1: The message: I'm passive when attacked, even wrongly. The dimensions: Passivity/activity. Homework: I'll identify dreams as well as waking situations in which I was passive and devise ways in which I could have taken a more assertive stance.

Dreamer 2: The message: I take on the responsibility of

correcting the messes others make. The dimensions: Assumes responsibility/assigns responsibility. Homework: I'll find ways to assign responsibility to others for the troubles they create.

Dreamer 3: The message: I feel guilty about my sexuality. The dimensions: Guilty/innocent. Homework: I'll imagine enjoying sexuality without guilt, discuss my fears with any new partner, and introduce sex into a new relationship slowly.

8

When a Crisis Leads to Depression

WHEN WE STUDY the sleep of people with depression in the laboratory, we find that their nights have a distinctive look. They are not like the bad nights that many of us experience, say, after a shock or before an exciting event, or simply when we are away from our usual routine, traveling or changing workshifts. At such times, insomnia is common. We may take much longer than usual to get to sleep. Once sleep begins, though, it is normal. We go through the usual cycles with the usual proportions of REM and NREM sleep. Laboratory studies show, however, that the sleep of depressed people differs from that of people who are not depressed and even from ordinary insomniacs.

Most of us start the night with an hour or more of sound, deeply relaxing sleep. Only then do we enter the excited brain state of REM sleep. The first REM period normally lasts only about 10 minutes before we plunge again into deep sleep. We repeat this pattern of resting first, then dreaming, several times throughout the night. Not until morning nears, after we have had enough deep sleep to refresh the body, do we begin to have lighter sleep with longer dream periods and more active eye movements. These are the times that refresh the mind.

By contrast, in people who are depressed, the first REM episode of the night may be the longest. Research by psychiatrist David Kupfer and his colleagues at the University of Pittsburgh shows that some depressed persons have only light sleep, no deep sleep at all, before entering this first REM period—sometimes after as little as 20 minutes of sleep.

Relatives of people with depression, particularly those who have experienced depression themselves, often have early REM periods, too. Kupfer and many other researchers in the field view early REM periods as a warning of vulnerability to depression, a biological marker. They hope that identifying and studying people with such markers may lead eventually to ways to keep depression from emerging or to alert patients as well as their families and physicians to the need for treatment when symptoms first appear.

Melancholy prompts dreaming to begin too soon. What is worse, the night also ends too soon, often at 2, 3, or 4 A.M. It looks as though people with depression skip the restful first half of the night, start in the middle, and then awaken after only three or four hours' sleep. About one third of those with depression participating in our divorce study showed this characteristic pattern.

If the REM sleep is out of phase, what is happening to dreams? "To sleep, perchance to dream. Aye, there's the rub," Hamlet said, describing his depression over his father's murder and his mother's remarriage. Dreams during depression often reflect the "rub" of frustration. They restate the dreamer's problems but they don't solve them. Tony, you'll recall, found himself adrift on a raft on the open sea. He reported, "It was dark and stormy and the raft was spinning and the water was boiling."

Awake and asleep, the depressed view the world as a hostile place where their needs go unmet. The dreamer wants something—money, a better job, direction in life, connection with other people—but can't satisfy any of these needs, even in dreams. The dreams of the depressed tell of disappointment, rejection, and pain. (*See* Appendix for "Depression Symptom Checklist" p. 281.)

Having early REM periods does not, however, condemn people to a lifetime of depression. Quite the contrary. Participants in our divorce study who had this sign recovered faster than those who also were depressed but did not have it. Dreams that start unusually soon seem to go right to work. We don't call them "good" dreams, for they rarely are happy. However, they often display the emotional issues that preoccupy the dreamers, typically loss of their relationships, possessions, and homes. "Too early" first dreams in people with depression are higher in emotion, with more imagery, more bizarreness, and a more elaborate story than dreams that start at a normal time. They incorporate the cause of the blue feelings—the spouse; and they highlight the need for the dreamers to take care of themselves.

By contrast, the dreams of depressed people whose REM periods occurred at more normal times often are flat in feeling and dull in content, rather bland and mundane. They contain themes of being helpless, abandoned, guilty, and of being alone and unable to cope. They show little action, and they rarely deal with the spouse. They are much like the first dreams of people who are not depressed.

Here are some early first REM dreams in depressed people:

I was at work and a guy was asking me why I wasn't working. I felt ashamed and worried that I hadn't been concentrating.

I was watching someone cross-examine a man who was very angry. I was being yelled at in court.

I was being conned by someone. I felt scared and my husband was making me feel guilty.

I was watching my husband having trouble at airport customs about taking something through that belonged to me.

Here are first REM dreams occurring at the normal time in depressed people:

I think I was selling a book.

I was with friends talking about traveling to Minnesota.

I was on an aircraft carrier. There was damage to the ship.

These are first REM dreams in people who were not depressed:

I was watching a baseball game on TV with my mother.

I was off to the side watching my son grocery shop.

I was sitting at a table with people.

The second and third groups of dreams are quite similar. To appreciate their import, we have to see the rest of the night's dreams. People who are depressed, whose REM periods occur at normal times, show little progress in facing problems in dreams across the night. Every dream is like their first one. Indeed, like Helen, the woman who let the puppy defecate on her in her dream when she was depressed, they repeatedly concoct events that go awry. Their dream dimensions are negative, negative, negative.

When researchers at the University of Pennsylvania asked 287 psychiatric patients to tell their most recent dream, they found that people with depression consistently reported more dreams of self-blame than those with other emotional disorders. Dream themes in the depressed, as in the rest of us, reflect waking thoughts and actions, according to psychiatrists Aaron Beck and Clyde Ward. Moreover, the patients in this study told Beck and Ward that they remembered having had dreams like these all their lives, long before they became depressed. They were set up for depression by their negative dreams and, most likely, will experience future episodes of depression unless their dream program changes.

People who reproach and criticize themselves and believe they deserve punishment often dream of being reproached, rejected, or punished. Those who set up barriers against any goal-directed activity and have a general attitude of indecisiveness or ambivalence in their waking lives often dream of trying to attain some goal and consistently being thwarted by circumstances. Conscious self-destructive urges may prompt dreams of being injured or dead.

Such dreams are not necessarily a sign of illness, Beck and Ward say. In times of crisis, any of us may have a few such dreams. However, they occur more consistently in those who are depressed.

Psychologist Peter Hauri of the Mayo Clinic confirmed this picture. He found that the same themes continued to haunt formerly depressed patients even after their waking symptoms subsided. When he compared dreams of 11 people who had recovered from depression with those of 11 nondepressed people of the same sex, age, education, and occupation, he found that the formerly depressed patients reported four times more unhappy dreams than the healthy subjects. They dreamed more about crying, feeling sad, deserted, rejected, or being thwarted.

Additionally, Hauri found, inanimate objects played a larger role in the dreams of the depressed. In their dreams, storms blew, motors ran, and gunshots were fired, suggesting a view of the world around them as much more violent and threatening than that of people without depression.

In short, the dream scripts of people subject to depression constantly undermine the confidence that they can cope with new waking problems. Over and over in their dreams, they match new experiences with memories of old failures. They maintain a self-image that is inadequate, hopeless, and self-punishing. It's no wonder that those who have one depressive episode often have others.

The past had a strong hold on Jerry, a soft-spoken, poetic man who was 32 at the time of his marriage break-up. A gentle soul, this high school social studies teacher was ill-equipped for a nasty divorce. Jerry's wife, Lois, an emotionally unstable woman subject to tantrums, still needed Jerry to take care of her. Their fighting focused on the custody of Mark, their four-year-old son.

After Jerry left Lois, he found Elaine, a warmer, less demanding love. Their future was not without complications: Elaine lived far away and also was separating from a bad marriage. Elaine still was unable to choose between her love for Jerry and her attachment to her husband. Jerry faced a long period of transition before he could hope to get out of his old marriage and into a new life pattern. Although he was too sensitive to be a match for the enraged woman he had left, he had to continue to relate to her as the mother of his son.

When Jerry joined the divorce study, his depression was intense. His dreams were full of the conflict between his romantic hope for a new life with Elaine and his fears of his wife's anger. Yet Jerry rapidly learned to use the RISC method to recognize his bad dreams while they were occurring and to stop them. He was given these instructions: "These are your dreams. You create them and only you can change them. If you don't like the way things are going, pop your eyes open and stop the dream. Then go back to sleep and make it come out better."

After four weeks of discussions concerning his troubles with Lois, his sadness over being separated from his son, his frustration over his unresolved relationship with Elaine, and his hopes for the future, Jerry had his first success with the RISC method. He reported the following dream:

I took Elaine to a forest preserve for a picnic. It was a gray fall day. As I unpacked the picnic basket on an old wooden table, a wind picked everything up. It whirled paper plates, food, napkins, and all, like leaves above our heads. I jumped up trying to catch them, but they were beyond my reach.

This dream reflected his frustration that Elaine was not free to be with him. Her stormy marriage kept their happiness together out of reach. But Jerry managed to stop his dream and change it.

"I realized in the dream that I didn't like what was happening," he reported, "so I woke up. I lay there for a while and thought about the dream. Then I drifted off to sleep again."

This time I dreamed it wasn't fall, it was spring. The colors were bright instead of dark. The sun was shining, and the flowers were out. It was like a postcard. We were driving in my red car to a brand new picnic place that had just been opened. No one had been there yet. Everything was shiny and sparkling. I felt really good that I found this great place.

Jerry told this dream with a good deal of pride. He had had real success in mastering his feeling of not being able to control things. He changed the dimensions of fall to spring, dull to bright, and old to new. Most important, he changed his self-image in the dream from being passively at the mercy of forces beyond his control to arranging a new and better experience for Elaine and him to share. Now they were the first to enjoy something together.

Jerry's success in changing this dream did not mean he really would be able to transform his relationship with Elaine. However, his dream success lifted his mood and encouraged him to try to change aspects of himself that hindered coping with his present crisis.

In the next session, Jerry reported another success in changing a dream. It was an important breakthrough that dealt with his guilt about leaving his son, Mark. He recalled:

Elaine and I were living in a new house. I could smell the odor of varnish, it was that fresh. It was early in the morning, a frosty morning, cold and clean. I came to the front door and opened it and found a baby. There was an apple crate, a box. I opened it and there was a baby inside almost frozen to death. I pulled it inside and called Elaine. "What are we going to do?" I asked her. We took it to the emergency room of the hospital and they put it on a shelf. The woman there asked me, "Who is going to sign to be responsible?"

"I woke up at this point," Jerry related. "My heart was thumping and I said, 'Well, that was a scary dream. This is a dream I should finish,' so I went back to sleep and let it go on."

The woman said, "Who is responsible for the charges?" and we looked at each other and I said, "I'll sign," and I did. They took the baby to resuscitate it, and Elaine and I sat in the waiting room doing crossword puzzles, alternating helping each other with the clues. I went back to see the baby and it was doing okay. The baby was in a crib with its leg up so I couldn't tell what sex it was.

"Maybe it's about Mark," Jerry suggested. "The morning after I had that dream I called Elaine about her visiting me while I have Mark for the weekend. We talked over whether she should put off her visit. I said, 'Let's do it the hard way, with Mark here.' Maybe now I'll be able to dream of him inside the house!

"Grand as it is to be in a new house together, I have an abandoned baby that I can't just put on a shelf for someone else to take care of," he said. "I have to declare that I want him to be part of my new life with Elaine. Mark is not nobody's baby. He is mine." Jerry's dreams then began to deal with the future. He had learned how to turn his bad dreams to good ones and then translated them into good waking actions.

A year later, after completing his dream-reshaping work with me, he came back to the laboratory for a dream checkup. His divorce was final, but he still was in limbo with no firm commitment from Elaine. These are three dreams from the same night in the sleep laboratory:

Dream 1

It was a nightmare! I thought I was in some big city like New York. I was sleeping in some kind of a research place, but someone there was very jealous of the work we were doing and was trying to destroy the results and kill me. It was a woman. She was trying to suffocate me. She put a pillow case over my head. I was just starting to fight back. It was dark and hard to see. I had to do it on my own. My throat was tight and my whole body was hot. I was about to call my research associate to come back and help me when you woke me up.

In this first dream Jerry saw himself as vulnerable to his ex-wife and unsure about his new partner. He couldn't count on her to be around when he needed her. There he was, flat on his back, having to fight for his life on his own. This dream stated the night's problem: "Lois would rather kill me than let me go. I have to protect myself."

When Jerry walked out of the marriage, he relinquished an important part of his identity as a protective caretaker. This choice left him with a good deal of guilt. He also felt guilty about his extramarital "experimental sleeping." What was new for him came in the last two dreams of the night.

Dream 4

Mark and I are returning from a trip to Alaska where we enjoyed the wild flowers. As we drive into the driveway of my old house to drop Mark off for his birthday party, a neighbor accosts me, saying I don't have a permit for the party to be held outdoors. I tell him confidently that Lois took care of that.

Dream 5

I was driving my car. I had just dropped off some money, a child support check for Lois. She asked me to take her shopping at a big clothing store. Before we got started, she swung her legs over across my lap. I had to put her legs back on the floor before I could put the ignition key in the lock and start the car. I was angry that she always took advantage of every opportunity.

As the night ended, Jerry dreamed that he could trust Lois to care for Mark and that he could cope effectively with Lois. He was no longer a helpless victim. He was in the driver's seat and handled her provocativeness calmly. He saw that what he wanted was to get going, to "put his key in the lock," to start a new sexual relationship, and not go back to Lois. Through the night he had worked at defining what he was willing, and was not willing, to do for her: He would take her to the store, but he would not be manipulated physically. He would supply child support, but he would not be threatened or seduced. In his last dream, Jerry took a self-respecting, ex-husband, supportive father role. This was a good dream program at work.

This dream didn't quite square with reality, however. It was more of a rehearsal, a wistful wish for a future competent self-image, one that still remained to be achieved. Lois had found someone else and was about to remarry. Jerry was angry with her for upsetting their son by this change, just when the boy seemed to be getting comfortable alternating between their two households. Jerry himself was a child of divorce, who suffered greatly from feelings of abandonment. Jerry's father and mother had threatened divorce all through his childhood. The possibility hung over him as a persistent peril until his teenage years, when his parents finally parted. When his father left, Jerry stepped into his father's supportive role with his mother, and he hated it.

Jerry felt that Lois's new man was a threat to his own ability to perform his familiar caretaking role, to be a good father. He worried that the introduction of a stepfather would interfere with his plans to be a better father to his son than his father was to him. His relationship with Elaine still was uncertain. They saw each other, but she had not left her husband.

Jerry still had real deficits in the resources he needed for coping with his life crisis. His male friends had little patience with his need to talk about his feelings. His female friends, he said, "all have marriage on their minds." Like many of those in our study suffering from depression, he had leftover emotional issues concerning his parents that influenced his marriage choice and contributed to its failure. Wanting to get free of his smothering mother, he married young. He had chosen Lois, he told me, because she was strong enough to defy his mother and help him escape from his mother's powerful hold on him. Nonetheless, Lois was the same kind of woman as his mother. He then had to fight his way free of her.

Jerry went from a seductive mother, who bullied him into taking care of her after his father left, to Lois, only to realize he was playing the same role all over again. Moreover, he left his wife just as his father had. At 32, he was still an adolescent, leaving home for a second time. Jerry's dreams showed vividly the depth of his feeling that he deserved his former wife's anger for having abandoned her and having experimented with another relationship. He still expected to be seduced by her or punished as if she were his mother.

The divorce may have been final legally, but the emotional separation was incomplete. Jerry knew that his former wife was competent to take care of herself and their son, but in his dreams he was still a caretaker. Jerry was a man in transition. He had more internal work to do before he could forgive his father and himself for their desertion, so that he could live fully in the present.

RISC THERAPY FOR DEPRESSION

Some of our divorcing dreamers did not need the RISC program: they were not depressed. Some who were depressed worked through their depression on their own or with the aid of family or friends. Some benefitted from other types of psychotherapy, while some, unfortunately, did not get better. Because people entered the study at different times, we have information on some from only their one-year checkup. Others, whom we first saw soon after the study began in 1988, continue to write or call from time to time to let us know how they are doing and how they are sleeping and dreaming. None of those you've met in this book have remarried to date. Those who were not depressed initially and those who participated in RISC therapy both show the most success in moving on with their lives. Their dreams reflect their progress.

Laura, the woman who dreamed her husband discarded the sock with a hole in it, was deeply depressed when she entered the divorce study. We felt then that she was bound to have trouble adjusting without help. Sadly, she did not get it. She moved to another state, where she worked as a book-keeper and tried to provide a decent home for her children. When she came back for her one-year checkup, I asked if she were dating. She said firmly: "No way. I've no ambition to. I'll be happy when I have grandkids; that'll be enough for me."

"How are you sleeping?" I asked.

"I sleep only 20 minutes here and an hour there," she replied.

"Are you dreaming?"

"Yes, sometimes, sad dreams."

This was a dream she remembered:

I was walking on a sidewalk on a street that bordered my old school. I was thinking I wouldn't get in a car with anyone, even to save my life. It was dark out, evening. I was hurrying, rushing because I was kind of afraid of that area. I was trying to see if there was someone coming. I was going the opposite way on the block because a car was approaching. I was my usual cautious self.

Laura saw herself in her dreams as alone and vulnerable to danger. Her dream dimensions, being alone instead of with others, in danger instead of safe, and fearful instead of self-confident, showed that her anxious, timid self-image still was undermining her recovery.

Julie, also fearful and withdrawn when she entered the study, made substantial progress toward revising her negative self-image after only six sessions of RISC therapy. At her one-year checkup, she was a much more self-confident young woman. She dreamed she recovered from a fall and from the embarrassment of being seen undressed in public.

When Harold, the trucker, returned for his one-year visit, he still suffered from blue moods. "If I can keep my depression at bay," Harold said, "I can think more clearly, but I think to myself, 'You come up short here, and you come up short there.' I come on strong, but I can't follow through."

"How are you sleeping?" I asked him. "I generally don't have any trouble, but my dreams are real vague now," he said. He couldn't remember one to tell me. Even in the sleep laboratory, his dreams were scanty. In one he reported:

I was fighting with somebody, wrestling. They were trying to take something away from me.

This was another:

I kept hearing a song called "My baby just wrote me a letter."

The dimensions in these dreams were winning/losing, closeness/distance. The fragments showed Harold was still experiencing a sense of loss and disconnectedness from his family. Harold had lost touch with his inner self. He might have benefitted from RISC therapy, but he chose not to pursue it. He had, however, entered psychotherapy and was learning, he said, "to do one dish at a time, instead of trying to handle the whole load of dirty dishes at once." Harold saw his children frequently, and he felt they were adjusting well to having two households.

Tony, deeply depressed when he entered the divorce study, made good progress after working on his dreams in RISC therapy. Three years after joining the study, he reported his life was much better. He was proud of his work performance and of his boys. Here is a dream that showed his progress. He called it "the happiest dream I have ever had."

I was married with a big family. We were living in a primitive environment, but we were very happy. We had a baby girl, and I remember adoring this baby, holding her in my arms and feeding her soft, creamed corn with a tiny spoon. She was smiling, and she loved me because I was feeding her. It was almost like I was nursing her.

We lived next door to some priests who told us of another baby born to a woman who didn't want her, so I started out to see if she would give us the baby. She did and we raised the two babies as sisters. There was just total love in this dream. When I woke up, I felt loved and loving.

The change from his earlier dreams of bad boys who were out of his control to the loving little baby girls was dramatic. In this dream, Tony let himself start over. Even if he could no longer father children because of his vasectomy, he saw a way he could raise them. His dream dimensions, caring versus rejection, closeness versus distance, reflect his newer, more positive outlook. This was a future-oriented dream rehearsal of successful fatherhood and love.

Jerry also benefitted from the RISC program. "I've come out of my depression and faced the reality that Elaine is just not moving to join me," he reported two years after joining the study. He said he had started dating four other women and was enjoying his life as a bachelor.

"Are you sleeping better?" I asked.

"Oh, yes," he said. "And here is a dream you might like."

Elaine was supposed to come but didn't show up. I was in this house and wanted to go to the bathroom. I went to a basement bathroom where there were wooden slats. You could be seen through them. I was sort of exposed. I needed to have a bowel movement. I took my pants down, but the commode was filled with sand. I thought, "Well, what should I do with all this shit?" There were some teenaged girls starting to come down the stairs. They looked at me and offered to help clean me up. I said, "I can do it myself."

"I laughed when I woke up," Jerry reported. "I have plenty of women offering to help me get over all this mess." The dimensions here, exposed versus private, messy versus tidy, independent versus dependent, showed Jerry was moving toward relying less on women and feeling better about himself. He acknowledged that the physical side of his life made him susceptible to dependency on women and was messy; at the same time, he said in this dream, he could clean up his act and make his own decisions about his life. Both Jerry's dreams and his good self-image speeded his recovery.

Helen was one who initially had been depressed but worked her own way out of it. In a key dream in the laboratory when she returned for her one-year visit, Helen had opened her eyes in a dense fog and found a way to climb a mountain. Two years later, Helen reported further growth.

"I am much happier and more optimistic about the future," she said. "When I first came here, I was desperate. I wanted to die. Now I know I will never kill myself. I really wanted to die, but God wouldn't let me do it. Now I don't want to."

"I had a dream that was a turning point for me," Helen related.

I was in an old house with a ghost, a woman ghost. You could see right through her. I lived there all alone and the ghost was calling me. I lived in a closet. I think that it was the ghost of a "single-woman-living-alone" and I had to confront it and say, "That's okay."

"Now I have faced it and I am okay," Helen asserted. Her dreams showed that she had overcome her fearful earlier pattern. Her dream dimensions, substance versus shadow and confrontation versus avoidance, proclaimed that she had the self-confidence to be on her own, if she had to. She had successfully resolved the self-image crisis that her divorce precipitated.

Maggie, who dreamed during her first visit to the laboratory that she worked things out with her husband's new girlfriend, never was depressed. Two years later, she wrote to tell me she was quite satisfied with her new life. She was close to graduating from college. She had several male "friends," but was not ready to settle down with any of them. She had no trouble sleeping or dreaming. "I am more confident about who I am, and I have accepted myself," she said. "I am taking charge of my own life." She reported a recent dream:

I was much younger and still living at home. I told my parents I was joining the Peace Corps. They were shocked and told me they always wanted me to go to Bible school, but I refused. I decided for myself to go to the Peace Corps.

"That was a good dream," Maggie said. Her dream dimensions, independence versus dependence and defiance versus compliance, mirrored her practical, helpful self and her readiness for new experiences, including new relationships with other people.

Robert, another good coper, had had a near fatal car accident in the year after leaving his hypochondriac wife. He spent several weeks in the hospital, and when he recovered, he decided it was time to live. He found a new woman, a healthy one, and eventually moved in with her. "We talk and have real communication," he told me at his one-year visit. "I take a hand with her children. I have a real sense of family now. I cut down on my drinking. I'm in better contact with my friends. I feel really good about myself. I still have pain from the accident," he said, "but when I'm free of pain, I sleep fine. I never was aware of my dreams before the lab," he recalled, "but there I got five. I'm just not a good recaller on my own." Robert didn't need to remember his dreams; everything was going well for him.

Stimulating depressed people to take charge of their lives by teaching them to play an active role in their dreams improved their outlook toward the future. As coming chapters describe, the RISC approach has many applications beyond divorce. It can even be used to ward off trouble before it gets out of hand. One example:

Barbara, a woman in her sixties, sought relief from a recurring nightmare:

I'm a passenger on a train, going through a mountain pass. The train speeds up. I can tell it is out of control and going to crash. Just before it crashes, I wake up.

Barbara had never married and spent her entire life working in relative isolation as a librarian. She wasn't amenable to making life-style changes and thought she didn't have enough money to permit her to retire. The key dimension in this dream is the one of being out of control versus being in control. In waking life, this woman might not have identified herself as being "in crisis," but her repeated nightmares and her decision to seek therapy gave strong hints of trouble coming to the surface. Her depression was deepening. Her therapist, David Calof, suggested that the next time she had the same nightmare, she could try to change the ending. The woman accomplished this task. As she reported:

When I realized the train was about to crash, I said to myself, "I have to do something to keep this from happening." I walked to the front of the train and discovered that the engineer's compartment was empty. Although I debated whether or not to touch the switches, I decided to try to take control of the train. Within a couple of moments, I came to a "Y" in the track. One branch continued the path I was on. The other led up and out of the valley. With a great sense of excitement, I took the path leading up and out.

Within six weeks, Calof reports, she consulted with an accountant, found a way to retire, and now travels to see places she'd long known only in books.

⇨ SELF-HELP: Calling for the dream doctor

Breaking the depression cycle—making people well and keeping them well—is the challenge of treatment. Depression is a complex illness that displays its symptoms in many ways. Over the years, doctors have tried dozens of different treatments with varying degrees of success. These include both biological treatments, such as medication and electroconvulsive (shock) therapy, and psychological treatments, such as psychotherapy. At present, therapists often use a combination of approaches. A person might, for example, take antidepressant drugs every day and see a therapist once a week.

Many antidepressant medications help the user to sleep through the night, but most do so at the cost of some REM sleep. Many also suppress the first early REM period. Indeed, some specialists think that these drugs improve their patients' waking mood precisely because they prevent abnormal dreaming. They assume that an early REM period is *unhealthy*, a symptom of trouble, rather than a healthy response to it.

However, perhaps we can take advantage of the changes that occur in sleep in depression rather than suppressing them. When dreaming begins sooner than is normal, it may be responding to the extra heavy emotional work load. In the laboratory, we find that these early dreams start an active search process for a helpful answer. Indeed, we find that people who experience early REM periods are more likely to be over the worst of the blues a year later than equally depressed people who do not. Those who do not show the biologic response in sleep to upsetting life events need extra help to find the inner strengths they require to move on with their lives.

We need to work to change dream scripts that persistently show images of helplessness and hopelessness to those that provide more optimistic views. If dream dimensions remain stuck on their negative poles, depression quite likely will recur. The ability to change the characteristic ways we see ourselves in our dreams can affect profoundly our waking moods. Our best source of help in troubled times may simply be ... to dream well.

9

Crises of Health

$\mathcal{T}$HE WAY WE VIEW OUR BODIES is central to our sense of self-identity. "I am pretty," "I am fat," "I am crippled," "I am dying," all tell a different self-story. Since dreams carry forward our waking thoughts and feelings, it's no surprise that when we undergo major changes in our physical selves, both good and bad, in pregnancy and in illness, for example, our dreams serve as a report card on how we're adapting. Dreams do more than reflect these changes: they actually may help us integrate them into our life story. Dreams during times of bodily changes add to our understanding of how dreams help us surmount major life crises.

DREAMS DURING PREGNANCY

Some women report dreaming that they have conceived even before they confirm their pregnancy. This is true of both women who wished to become pregnant and those who did not. Since sexually active women of child-bearing age know the possibility of pregnancy exists, it's incorrect to think that these dreams foretell the future. However, the dreams may reflect recognition of subtle bodily cues well before they enter conscious awareness.

Dreams in both mothers- and fathers-to-be reflect concerns

about the well-being of the baby and about being a good parent. They also express anticipation about how the birth of the child will change the marriage, the couple's relationships with their own parents, and both partner's daily lives.

In a study of dream diaries of more than 150 pregnant women, psychologist Robert Van de Castle of the University of Virginia found distinct differences in dreams in each trimester. Dreams during pregnancy, he says, help clarify the intimate relationship between body and mind.

Early in pregnancy, references to the condition often are veiled. A woman might dream of planting seeds in a vegetable garden, for example. Some women dream of small fish, a clear symbolic representation of the fetus bathed in amniotic fluid. These are usually the first of a plethora of dreams about fish, rivers, oceans, floods, swimming, sea monsters, drowning, and even washing machines, so extensive are the water metaphors that appear throughout pregnancy in dreams of both women and men.

Small animals often appear in early dreams, both cuddly ones like puppies and rabbits, and threatening ones like rats tunneling through walls. Women often dream of farfetched changes in body size, both literally, as in dreams of massive obesity, and symbolically, as in dreams of tugboats or walruses. Even those who are thrilled with their pregnancy may have anxious dreams. Fears of the unknown set the agenda.

Dreams of expectant fathers also follow a predictable course, as men explore and adapt to the changes their new role will bring. Luis Zayas of Columbia University compared dreams of expectant fathers throughout pregnancy with those of nonexpectant men. The dreams of the expectant fathers contained more references to the fetal environment, enclosures and other containers. They also reflected more feelings of being lonely and left out. By contrast, the dreams of the nonexpectant men had more references to sexual anatomy and money.

Dreams of fathers-to-be early in pregnancy display their awe and curiosity about the pregnancy. One man dreamed he was going to a house under construction, and another, about visiting a basement apartment, Zayas reports.

In their second trimester, women dream more directly of the coming event. Once the baby starts to move, it becomes more "real." A woman realizes that what she imagined would happen someday actually will happen soon. A writer dreams her husband takes her typewriter to the playground in the park and leaves it there. The dream addresses her fear that the baby will keep her from her work.

Psychologist Alan Siegel reports that expectant fathers dream of babies and birthday parties far more often than married men whose wives are not pregnant. The prospective fathers' dreams included wonderful images such as floating scuba divers with umbilical cord-like hoses attached and animals emerging from the sea.

Women experiencing their first pregnancy commonly see the new baby in their dreams, not as an infant but as a small child, someone easier for them to handle. Van de Castle believes this transformation reflects fears of competency to handle a newborn. During this time, especially around the fifth month, women may dream of dropping, accidentally killing, or losing a baby.

In *The Dream Worlds of Pregnancy*, Eileen Stukane describes many such dreams. In one, a woman and her mother were doing the laundry. They put one load in the washing machine and were dividing the rest into piles on the floor. The woman reported:

"All of a sudden, to my horror, I can't find my child. I start to become hysterical because I'm afraid that we mistakenly put him in the washing machine. He is only five inches long. We stop the machine but can't find him. Finally, we go through all the clothes, and there he is, in a pillow case. I was frantic until we found him."

Refrigerators, a frequent metaphor in mid-pregnancy dreams, may reflect ambivalence about the pregnancy. On one hand, a refrigerator keeps foods fresh until they are "delivered" to the table. On the other, the chilly environment may symbolize a woman's worries about her ability to give her unborn child the warmth it needs to grow and develop as well as a possible coldness toward her husband.

In dreams of fathers-to-be, once a woman's figure starts to change, recognition of the pregnancy shows up more often, Siegel reports. One man, for example, showed his delight in the pregnancy and his desire to share the experience with his wife in this dream:

"I am standing on a street corner, carrying my baby fetus under my shirt against my chest. I have my hand cupped over the fetus to protect it. It is moving and people ask what it is. I say, 'It's my baby.'"

Fears of being excluded appear in men's dreams throughout pregnancy. One man graphically depicted his worry that there would be "no room for daddy" in this dream:

"In the middle of a baseball game, I get up to get some beer. When I return, I can't find my seat. I look around for a new one, but many of the women in the stands are pregnant and they are taking up two seats. I have to go to the back of the stadium and stand. I am very annoyed."

In the third trimester, a woman must contend with still further changes in her appearance. She may wonder whether her husband still finds her sexually attractive and whether she'll regain her former shape after the baby's birth. These concerns often trigger dreams about husbands and former boyfriends. One woman dreamed she had no date for New Year's Eve. Husbands, too, have more sexual dreams, covering such topics as pride in their potency, fear of loss of their wife as a sexual partner, and concerns about maintaining their masculinity while expressing nurturing, so-called "feminine" feelings, toward the new baby.

Some women celebrate the fact of pregnancy with dreams that they are the center of attention, a queen or a princess. One woman, Stukane reports, dreamed her pregnancy was a newsworthy event.

"I am pregnant for 12 months. Doctors from all over the world come to examine the situation, but they are baffled. At the end of the dream I give birth to 10 babies."

As delivery approaches, dreams often focus on anxiety about the birth process itself, particularly for those expecting their first child. Dreams of being trapped in caves or closets and of negotiating dark passageways or tunnels are common. Some women anticipate the contractions of labor with dreams of earthquakes or volcanic eruptions. They may have frightening dreams of drowning or of buildings collapsing.

A commonly reported dream is that of having the baby but losing it or forgetting it, setting it down somewhere and going off without it, for example, or finding that the crib is empty. Such dreams address fears about not being a competent parent. Many women report they dream of babies who are deformed or are monsters. They may witness their own death or that of their child.

In a study of 70 pregnant women at the University of Cincinnati, Carolyn Winget and Frederic Kapp found that women who had anxious dreams beforehand had faster and easier deliveries. Perhaps such dreams serve as useful rehearsals. Once labor begins and it becomes obvious that a woman's horror-filled dreams are not coming true, that all is proceeding normally, she may be better able to concentrate on her delivery. Conversely, a woman who has denied her anxieties and not worked on them in dreams or in therapy may be less able to relax during labor.

In men's dreams late in pregnancy, themes of camaraderie, support, and closeness increase, Zayas says. Depictions of the imagined baby become quite realistic and men display their growing sense of what it will be like to be a father. One man, for example, dreamed the baby was keeping him and his wife up all night, but "we didn't mind at all." Another saw a baby who was "big and healthy" and "looked like my wife and myself." Such dreams do more than reflect the external reality. They help prepare a man to expand his self-image to encompass the role of fatherhood.

What if either of the parents-to-be are anxious, ambivalent, or even opposed to the idea of a new member of the family? Could dreamwork identify those who may have trouble coping early enough so that they could receive counseling before problems emerge? In Chapter 14 we will introduce you to the work of dream groups and the support they can provide. Dream workshops might prove a useful addition to childbirth preparation training sessions, offering reassurance and a new perspective when most useful—in advance.

DREAMS OF ILLNESS

Do dreams serve as a seismograph for illness, registering subterranean tremors long before the earthquakes of noticeable symptoms jolt our outer surface? Much as some women dream they are pregnant before their condition is confirmed, can dreams tell us that an illness is developing in our bodies even before we experience symptoms or before our doctors can detect signs of the illness? If so, we could use our dreams to obtain treatment earlier and perhaps to improve our health.

Aristotle suggested the role of dreams in recognizing illness some 2300 years ago. Hippocrates also discussed the impact of illness on dreams. And in this century, the psychoanalyst Carl Jung observed, "What we consciously fail to see is frequently perceived by our unconscious, which can pass the information on through dreams." While many contemporary scientists greet this notion with skepticism, some do not find it so farfetched.

Psychologist Robert Haskell of the University of New England notes that the body undergoes numerous changes in REM sleep. Heart rate and breathing fluctuate more, for example. Certain hormones are released, while others are suppressed. Blood pressure rises. People with duodenal ulcers secrete more gastric acid. Dreams from which we awaken, heart pounding, palms sweaty, offer a good illustration of the impact of mind on body. The reverse also may be true. "It is quite possible, and reasonable to assume," Haskell asserts, "that just as simple external and internal physical and somatic stimuli are worked into dreams, that more complex 'cognitions' are also worked into the dream process, cognitions about the state of physical health and illness."

Stanford University researcher Ernest Hilgard personifies the dream system as a "hidden observer," an internal self-monitor, that supplies us with a steady stream of information and scrutinizes bodily cues that we otherwise might miss or dismiss as inconsequential.

Evidence that dreams serve this function, while sparse and often anecdotal, is nonetheless intriguing. Surgeon Bernie Siegel writes that patients sometimes report dreams that tell them they are ill, that reveal even the cause of their illness, long before symptoms appear. In *Peace, Love & Healing*, he describes a patient who awakened from a terrifying dream in which torturers placed hot coals beneath his chin. The man reported:

"I distinctly felt the heat start to sear my throat and I screamed, the sound becoming hoarser, a raw, animal desperation, as the coals gnawed my larynx."

The dream convinced the man that he had cancer of the throat. He went to his doctor, who was skeptical, particularly after a physical exam and blood tests were negative. The man had another dream in which medicine men surrounded him and stuck hypodermic needles into something called "the neck brain." Several weeks later he developed a lump in his throat, eventually diagnosed as thyroid cancer.

In *Love, Medicine & Miracles*, Siegel describes a nurse who had had a mysterious illness for weeks. One night she dreamed:

"A shellfish opened, a worm stood up inside it, and an old woman pointed at the worm and said, 'That's what's wrong with you.'"

The nurse awakened, certain that she had hepatitis. Her self-diagnosis proved correct. One might say, "Oh well, she's a nurse. She knows that contaminated shellfish may cause hepatitis. She just put two and two together." Perhaps. But she solved the problem while asleep, not while awake. Her dreaming mind saw connections that her waking mind did not.

Scientific journals contain numerous examples of this same phenomenon: A woman with rheumatoid arthritis dreamed her arms were bound in a straitjacket. Her illness flared. Later, she dreamed that she fell down on ice but got up easily. Her symptoms subsided.

A patient with long-standing kidney disease dreamed of "a core meltdown of a nuclear power plant—it goes completely out of control." Within the week, the patient suffered a severe collapse.

A woman overwhelmed by work dreamed of looking at her watch, only to find its faced covered over by strips of paper. Soon afterward, she became so exhausted she could not continue working. After taking time off, she recovered. She then dreamed she looked for her missing watch and remembered she had put it on a shelf. When she took it down, she found the face "quite clear."

Like the patient with thyroid cancer who dreamed of being tortured with hot coals on his neck, dreams often metaphorically, even poetically, illuminate the specific illness affecting the dreamer. A woman with multiple sclerosis dreamed of stepping on a big tarantula that did not die. Instead, its legs were spread out and paralyzed, as were her own. Another woman dreamed of a disease demon who forced her to sit on a hot pipe. She had a bladder inflammation. A man with AIDS dreamed of fish. Every fish he touched died. A woman with anorexia nervosa dreamed she used full cans of carrots and peas as curlers to set her long hair. She didn't put food in her mouth, even in her dream, but she got pretty close.

Such images often reveal the psychological meaning of the illness to the dreamer. Thus, they may alert the dreamer as well as his or her physician to aspects of the dreamer's life in which changes in medication or environment, for example, might prove beneficial. The woman with rheumatoid arthritis who dreamed her arms were bound in a straitjacket, for instance, might describe her illness as keeping her from pursuing normal, everyday activities. A different type or dose of medication or physical therapy might improve the quality of her life. Patients with disturbing dreams also might benefit from using the RISC method to find images of strength to help them cope better with the vicissitudes their illnesses impose.

Research suggesting that dreams may have diagnostic validity and even may predict the course an illness will take is just beginning. Robert Smith and his colleagues at Michigan State University interviewed 49 hospitalized cardiology patients about their dreams. One member of the research team asked the patients to tell them a dream occurring in the past year, any dream at all. The researcher then rated the dream for references to death or separation.

Another member of the team supervised a physical test in which a catheter was inserted in a vein and passed into the heart to measure the blood flow out of the heart during a beat. This measurement, known as the ejection fraction, indicates the severity of heart disease. The researchers then compared the results of the two assessments.

Patients who reported no dreams at all had the most severe illness. In the dreamers, there was a good correlation between the severity of their cardiac disease and the content of their dreams, with an interesting sex difference. Men who had the highest number of references to death in their dreams also proved to have the most severe disease. The women who were the sickest dreamed the most about separation or disruption of a personal relationship. The men's greatest fear was loss of life; the women's, a loss of connectedness. Because many of the patients underwent corrective coronary artery bypass surgery, the researchers were not able to correlate the types of dreams with the likelihood of survival.

Several studies of dreams in patients with asthma illustrate the interaction between mind and body as well as the successful use of dreams in treatment. Harold Levitan of McGill University notes that 40% of asthmatic attacks occur during sleep. He suggests that disturbing dreams may trigger such attacks by provoking changes in both the body's autonomic nervous system, which controls breathing and heart rate, and the hormonal system.

Levitan studied 45 dreams preceding asthmatic attacks. The dreams fell into four categories: dreams in which the dreamer is the victim of a violent act, perpetrates a violent act, is involved in a sexual act, and dreams that contain disturbing memories. These preattack dreams often involve extreme situations, he says. Dreams in which the dreamer is the victim, for example, involve injury and pain rather than mere threats. Dreams of perpetrating violent acts involve murder. Sexual dreams tend to be incestuous or at least perverse. And dreams embodying disturbing memories focus on the patient's worst recollections. He found no instances in which a bland dream culminated in an asthma attack.

In waking life, Levitan points out, sudden intense emotion

such as anger or sadness frequently triggers asthmatic attacks. "It is possible," he says, "that dreams simply reveal more clearly forces that are also present during the day but which are obscured by the various complexities associated with wakefulness."

Psychologist John Meany of Atascadero, California, and his colleagues reported intensive treatment of a 61-year-old man with asthma so severe that he had to be admitted to a hospital's intensive-care unit. The evening after entering the hospital, the man reported a frightening dream in which the patient in the next bed died during heart surgery conducted by a team of several doctors.

During 14 therapy sessions, the man wore biofeedback devices to monitor his hand and cheek temperature. Once he learned the association of warm temperatures with relaxation and lower ones with tension and stress, he used the biofeedback devices to get in touch with the effect his feelings had on his body. He learned to recognize that anxiety provoked feelings of tightness in his chest, which in turn made him more anxious. Talking with his therapist about his fear-inducing dream gradually diminished its power over him. He became more adept at mobilizing "the doctors within," who were there all along, to help him get better.

DREAMS BEFORE SURGERY

Even when we regard surgery as a healing procedure, one that will rid us of pain and illness and restore us to health, we may experience it emotionally as a physical attack. It's normal to approach surgery with trepidation. No matter how reassuring and experienced the surgeon, how certain we are that surgery is the right step or perhaps the only step to take, "going under the knife" almost always elicits some apprehension. We think about it during the day, and we dream about it at night.

Our worries resonate with long-buried childhood fears and

fantasies. We worry about suffering unbearable pain, something going wrong during surgery, not getting good results, and the grim possibility of dying. We become anxious about what the doctors and nurses will do to us and think about us. The indignities of being hospitalized, such as having our clothing taken away, being sent to our rooms, and losing our privacy, make us retreat to childlike helplessness. Studies of dreams in patients about to undergo surgery offer another glimpse at how we integrate a crisis experience into our existing sense of self. These studies also suggest steps we can take to promote a faster recovery.

In the mid 1960s, psychologist Louis Breger postulated that dreaming plays an important role in helping people to master the stress aroused by impending surgery. In a landmark study, the first to use a sleep laboratory to explore this theory, he and his University of Oregon colleagues, Ian Hunter and Ron Lane, collected dream reports across the night from five people scheduled to undergo major surgery.

The patients spent four nights in the laboratory before their surgery and three nights afterward. The researchers used the standard methods of recording sleep and making REM sleep awakenings, the same methods we continue to use in our divorce study today. Additionally, they interviewed the patients to determine their characteristic coping styles and gave them a battery of psychological tests.

One of their patients, Melvin, a 34-year-old shipping clerk and part-time beautician, had a long history of peptic ulcers. He had been hospitalized because of his ulcers in each of the previous 14 years and had had two previous operations. He was in the hospital at the time of the study for a vagotomy, a procedure in which the vagus nerve to the stomach is cut to decrease the flow of stomach acid.

Although one might think the prior operations had prepared Melvin for the surgery, that was not the case. Melvin expressed open fear of the coming operation and needed constant reassurance that his surgeon was competent. He worried that he would lose the support of those on whom he depended and that his doctors would not care adequately for him.

Melvin's description of his childhood gave the researchers some clues about the source of these concerns. Most notably, he suffered an early loss of those who normally would have taken care of him. His mother died in a fire when he was only eight months old. He lived with his grandmother, a warm and giving woman, until her death when he was 15. The older woman may have found it hard to keep up with an active, young boy and encouraged his passivity. During those early years, Melvin saw little of his father. Melvin said his father "didn't care much about me." Smaller in stature than his father, Melvin described himself as less outgoing and "shy and meek."

Melvin habitually coped with a threatened loss of care by exaggerating his weakness and helplessness. In this way, he induced others to take care of him. Indeed, he depended on his wife for this kind of nurturing. "She's always taken good care of me," he said.

On his first night in the laboratory, Melvin had three dreams. In the first, he was on his way to catch a bus to work. His neighbor passed him in a car and waved, but wouldn't give him a ride. "He didn't pick me up," Melvin reported.

In the next dream he was unloading heavy boxes and a heavy trunk from a truck. The driver, "a big guy," like Dr. A., his surgeon, was going to just drop the trunk. The dream continued:

"The owner told him no, he didn't want it dropped, he wanted it handled carefully. So he [the driver] said he was going to open it and take it down piece by piece. The owner was stuttering and stammering, 'Who told you you could open it? That stuff is mine and I don't want it opened.'"

The dream went on:

"I lost my truck. I called the wife to come and get me. The big guy that was driving the truck was husky, quite strong, and I seemed to envy or wish I were like him."

In the last dream that night, Melvin told the researcher:

"I was dreaming that this study was over and you came in and asked if I slept comfortably. I was complaining about the bed being too soft. But I felt almost like I shouldn't have said anything because it wasn't really that bad. I had some apples and was eating them and reading a comic book like I used to."

In all three dreams, Breger and his colleagues note, Melvin was poorly treated, first by his neighbor, then by the driver who reminded him of his surgeon, and finally by the sleep researcher. In all three instances, he was put in a helpless position, dependent on others who disappoint him. His fears of bodily damage also were obvious. The trunk in the second dream was a metaphor for his own body. The doctor-like person said he was going to open it up and take things out piece by piece. No wonder the owner objected!

Melvin portrayed himself as helpless, and he looked to others to assist him. Not everyone did, not the neighbor, or Dr. A. He could count on only his wife. His dreams showed his envy of strong men and the fear of his own weakness. The impending surgery heightened his childlike vulnerability. His solution at the end of the last dream was to become even more childlike, to regress to a time when he read comic books. He attempted to nourish himself by having something to eat.

In dreams on other nights preceding the operation, Melvin elaborated the same themes. He symbolized his fear of losing support as a loss of actual physical support. In one dream, he was on a shaky ladder, blown about by the wind. In another, he was on a bicycle that skidded about in the snow, causing him to have "trouble in keeping my balance." He described a tree trunk being eaten by moths, a ball stuck in telephone wires, and a woodworking shop, all, Breger suggests, references to his ulcerated stomach and the impending surgery to cut a nerve.

As Melvin's dreams showed, the psychological stress of the expected surgery brought out his characteristic dependent style. Melvin had many strengths, however. He had managed to marry, be a father, hold a job, and provide for his family. The night before the surgery he displayed some optimism about a potentially possible outcome. He dreamed he bought a new car. The situation was not unambiguously positive—he needed his wife with him and when he looked in his wallet, he couldn't find a card he needed to close the deal—but it was a good sign.

Once the surgery was completed successfully, Melvin's mood improved. He felt more optimistic that this would be his last trip to the hospital. His dreams changed for the better, too. In one he saw "a crippled man who was completely healed." He pictured this man "building his own house." He dreamed again several times about buying a new car. He made a real shift from fear of loss and damage to his body to hope for rebuilding a shiny, new, and more independent future.

Melvin built his preoperative dreams around the dimensions of dependence/independence, weakness/strength, high/low, active/passive. His first dreams all emphasized the negative sides of these dimensions. His neighbor left him behind, he depended on his wife for a ride, he was weak in relation to his doctor, in a low bed. After his successful surgery, he drew his images from the positive side of the same dimensions. He was more active, independent, and strong.

Surgery does not always evoke as much fear as it did for

Melvin. Another participant in Breger's study, 18-year-old Penny, looked forward to her gallbladder surgery. A high school senior, Penny was obese, shy, and harbored strong feelings of inferiority. She had never had a date. While she did have a few close girlfriends, she impressed the researchers as being overinhibited and lacking the enthusiasm and buoyancy usually found in girls her age. Her parents' overprotectiveness, combined with her own insecurity, slowed her transition from adolescence to adulthood.

Penny entered into the hospital with high hopes that the surgery would change more than her health. She believed it would enable her to lose weight, increase her attractiveness, overcome her shyness, and gain enough self-confidence to become independent of her parents. That's a lot to expect from losing one gallbladder! The important point is that her preoperative mood was very different from Melvin's. Before the surgery, she spent time sewing new clothes for her future, thinner, self. The meaning of the surgery to Penny was less of potential damage than of a positive reshaping of her body image.

Her first dream in the sleep laboratory had only a single image, a cross section of a house, like a doll house, where she could see people upstairs and downstairs. This "opened-up" view continued into the next dream. Here a party was going on, and everyone was happy.

"You could see into all the rooms and someone was cooking dinner in the kitchen. Everyone had nice-looking clothes on. I was going around talking to everybody, and everybody was laughing and having a good time."

In her third dream, the mood changed to a darker tone. Penny was at a fair where a fat man kept trying to feed her Mexican food that she didn't want. He "has hold of me, so I couldn't go," Penny related.

In the last dream that night, she reported:

"One of my aunts was supposed to get married and everyone was coming and deciding what to wear. Then at the last minute nobody turned up. There was a phone call from South Dakota, where my grandmother lives, and some material was sent from there, to make my aunt's dress, but it was real old. The styles had changed. She started to cut out the material, but it was way out of style. All the people were trying to decide how they were going to get the dress out of that material. I was kind of let down in the end because nobody came."

Penny's dream sequence took her from being a happy, social success to anticipating that things might not work out so well. Her issues as revealed by her dream dimensions were approaching/resisting, open/trapped, up-to-date/out-of-style, happy/let down, attractive/fat. Her first two dreams carried her optimistic hopes that her surgery would literally open her up and change her into being a happy person, unafraid to be seen, well-dressed, and someone who could approach people easily. Her last two dreams showed her fears of being trapped into being fat, out-of-style, and let down. Her wish to be thin was mixed with fear about sexual advances that might come her way. Food, weight loss, and clothing, all of which represented her image of herself, were on her mind awake and asleep.

In other dreams before her operation, the same symbols recurred. Penny dreamed of taking money from a father, children being fed by their mother, and a mother fixing lunch for her children. She dreamed of opening a restaurant, a house with "a great big kitchen," and a "rickety hot dog stand." She dreamed of freshly washed clothes, a remodeled banquet room, and a museum in which old torn drapes were replaced. These dreams underscored her troubled relationship with food and her hopes for a make-over. They explored the dimensions of dependence/independence and old/new.

Penny's fears were realistic. After her surgery, she realized she was essentially unchanged in both her shyness and physical appearance. She also had to cope with having lost a body part and, a further complication, with having a drainage tube and disposal bag that, even though temporary, added to her woes about looking different from other people. Feelings of grief and anger are common in people who experience actual bodily damage in surgery. Penny's dreams after the operation showed concern over getting rid of something. They focused more on body imagery than they did before. Now she faced the reality of herself as she was: Obese, unattractive, and, she felt, unlikely to marry and live happily ever after.

Melvin's and Penny's dreams illustrate my belief that dreams during crises are easy to understand. When we identify the dimensions that underlie the dreams, we see the emotional issues clearly. The trend across the night shows the direction of the dreamer's adaptation to the current crisis.

The aim of Breger's early study was simply to describe what happened in dreams before and after surgery. The dreams were not utilized in any therapeutic way. Both Melvin and Penny might have approached surgery more realistically if their doctors had helped them to address the issues their dreams so clearly reveal. Surgery involves pain, feelings of helplessness, and a change of body image. Melvin's dreams showed his need for emotional support; Penny's, her unrealistic expectations of a miraculous transformation. Melvin saw his body as a trunk being opened and its contents removed, despite the owner's objections. Penny viewed herself as old material that couldn't be cut up and reshaped into a modern wedding dress.

Today we might employ the RISC method to identify and confront these concerns in hopes of easing Melvin's and Penny's pain and boosting a speedier recovery. Melvin needed to be reminded to use his coping strengths, and Penny that the surgeon could not correct her weight or dispel her shyness; she needed to take on those tasks herself. There is a real place for presurgical dream work; it's a new frontier.

Patients are not the only ones who feel anxious as surgery approaches. People close to them may feel stress, too. If they can confront it, they may be better able to give their loved one support to get through this difficult time.

Recently, my husband was in the hospital for coronary bypass surgery. I tried to reassure our daughter Carolyn by telling her that the surgeon, who had a foreign name, was a very "big man" in the field, and senior to all others in the hospital. The night before the operation, Carolyn had this dream:

I was riding in a taxi through a bad ethnic neighborhood of Chicago. While the cab was stopped at a red light, a gang of foreign-looking men approached. One, a dwarf, appeared to be the leader. He had a long knife. I yelled to the driver, "Lock the doors."

The driver said, "The doors on this cab do not lock." The foreign man pulled open the driver's door, plunged the knife into his chest, and killed him. He then opened the passenger door to get to me. I jumped out the other side and ran into a dress shop, where I ducked into the dressing room to hide. He pursued me. The people in the dress shop turned out to be the dwarf's allies. Trapped in a small space, I fought back. I picked up the dwarf and found he was soft, only a Cabbage Patch doll. I tied his arms behind his back and left him there.

The dimensions Carolyn used in her dream are obvious: big/small, dangerous/safe, foreign/familiar, passive/aggressive. The dangerous, foreign, aggressive, knife-wielder kills the safe, familiar, passive cab driver. In her dream, Carolyn coped with her fear of a deadly attack by first changing the big man into a small one. When that proved insufficient, she ran away. However, she then found herself in an "undressing" place where the villain had allies, a symbolic representation of the hospital. At last, she stood up to him and actively defended herself. This worked. She "disarmed" him. She converted the aggressor into a safe familiar object, a toy.

This is an example of a successful dream. In spite of her concern for her stepfather's safety, my daughter found her dream reassuring. It told her she could master her fears. She woke up feeling amused, ready to face the day in a calmer mood.

"But," you might ask, "didn't her stepfather get killed in this dream?" The answer provides an interesting insight into the dreaming mind. My husband does not drive. Having the taxi driver killed is another way to say, "It is not my stepfather who is in danger. It's someone I don't even know."

DREAMS OF DEATH

While people may dream about their own death throughout the life cycle, such dreams occur more often when the threat of death is real and pressing. Even those who have not been told that they have a terminal illness or who consciously deny this knowledge may show their awareness of it in their dreams. One woman, from whom the truth had been withheld, reported these dreams:

"My watch was broken. I took it to the watchmaker, but he told me it could not be fixed."

"My favorite tree lay on the ground."

As the end of life nears, dreams of death may help prepare us for the end, enable us to say goodbye, and help us strengthen ties with those who will survive us. Death dreams sometimes are quite explicit, as in this example cited by psychoanalyst Marie-Louise Von Franz from a 29-year-old woman whose cancer had spread throughout her body:

"I am standing beside my bed in the hospital room. I feel strong and healthy. Sunshine flows in through the window. The doctor is there

and says, 'Well, Miss X., you are unexpectedly cured. You may get dressed and leave the hospital.' At that moment I turn around and see, lying in my bed, my own dead body!"

"Dreams of death are often beautiful," writes psychoanalyst Martin Grotjahn in an essay he calls "Being Sick and Facing Eighty: Observations of an Aging Therapist." "It always has struck me as sad that when people finally have beautiful dreams, they are dreams of death," he says. "In these dreams, people dream about beautiful castles, which represent the houses of the parents, frequently of the dead parents. I dream frequently of the university in the City of God, the city of learning for me.

"In these dreams I have the vague feeling I don't belong there, or I do not find my room, or my room has been given away to other people," Grotjahn adds. "When I dream about beautiful landscapes, fountains, and streams, I associate immediately with fantasies about the marvelous life hereafter, in which I seem to believe only in my dreams."

Psychiatrists Harvey Greenberg and Robert Blank report a remarkable series of dreams chronicling a 50-year-old man's gradual acceptance of his terminal illness. The man, whom the therapists call Mr. E., had entered psychotherapy for depression following his mother's death. Several months after beginning therapy, he developed lower back pain. The source of the pain proved to be cancer of the colon which had spread to his liver and bones.

Mr. E. began chemotherapy but referred to his illness as a mild liver problem. As he had no close family, his doctors decided not tell him his prognosis unless he asked for it, but at the same time to help him prepare for death. Despite his seeming denial of the seriousness of his illness, the dreams he told his therapist showed that he knew he was dying. In one, he reported:

"I'm trying to get to your office and can't make it. I'm already late for my appointment and am becoming more and more desperate."

The psychiatrist reassured Mr. E. that if he had to be hospitalized, the psychiatrist would hold sessions with him in the hospital and would try to help him with various problems the illness might present. Shortly afterward, the man lost sensation and movement in his legs, presumably because the cancer had spread to his spinal cord. He entered the hospital. While there, he reported this dream:

"A shadowy stranger, dressed darkly, stands by my bedside. I find I can walk. He leads me out of the hospital to a place I've never been to before. He is somehow very comforting. I'm extremely interested in what he shows me."

Mr. E. envisioned for himself a peaceful death. Over the next several weeks, his condition didn't change much and he remained in the hospital. His brother came from out of town to visit, then returned home. Mr. E. dreamed:

"I was being tortured, battered about by several people who were supposed to be my friends—they pushed me back and forth amongst themselves playfully, but it was all very painful."

Then he began to deteriorate rapidly. He had high temperatures and lost a great deal of weight. His speech became slurred. He dreamed:

"I am negotiating to buy a small plot of land—it is not clear how small. This is part of a bigger plot."

The therapist saw the dream image as a graphic depiction of a grave, but supported the patient in his bucolic fantasies.

Mr. E. came ever closer to death. In one dream he showed his impatience with being sick and his wish for an end to his suffering:

"I'm in a room with Michael and Dolores. They are talking animatedly and seem to be enjoying themselves immensely. They put on a record, a Spanish opera. It is as if I am a ghost; they cannot see me. The record ends but the turntable keeps spinning and they make no move to stop it. I am very angry. I shout: 'It's all over, turn it off.' But they cannot hear me and keep talking and laughing."

He died a few days later.

Sam, a man dying of inoperable cancer, bolted from bed one night in a confused state of mind. He thought his son was a giant who wanted to kill him. In a state of partial arousal, Sam chased the boy around the house with a sword until his wife's screams finally awakened him. This event was so dramatic and so frightening that Sam could no longer deny his fears of his imminent death. He finally began to talk about them and to deal with them in his dreams. One that occurred soon before he died included another image of a giant, this one benign, a bringer of peace. Sam reported:

Here was a big, big hand, reaching out to me. I touched the hand. It was warm and strong. I felt very calm, peaceful. I fell asleep after that in the dream.

⇨ SELF-HELP: Coping with bodily changes

Whether dreams herald conditions such as pregnancy or illness at their earliest stages or simply reflect them as they progress, they show how we feel about what is happening to us, a message that we ignore at our peril. During pregnancy, they help prepare parents-to-be for the roles they will soon assume. In illness, they highlight the issues most salient to us, the emotional meaning of what is happening in our bodies. They provide the opportunity for us to assess how waking behavior and attitudes contribute to physical problems and to call on our own internal doctors to help speed the healing process. By keeping tabs on what our dreams tell us when facing major threats to our body-integrity, such as surgery, we may be able to quell some of the energy-draining anxieties surrounding our treatment. We then will be freer to mobilize our strengths. As we approach the end of life, dreams may help us accept the inevitable. The important point is not to wall off the messages in our night scripts from our waking recognition; our best healing is done with help from within.

10

Rape and Incest: From Victim to Survivor

*A*NNA-MARIE was cutting across a park when a stranger blocked her path and dragged her into the bushes. She struggled, but he overpowered her, held a knife to her throat, and raped her. She was a teenager, and this was her first sexual experience. A month later, a boyfriend who previously had been pressing her to sleep with him claimed he had the right to have sex with her now that she was "deflowered." Although she protested and struggled to fight him off, he raped her, too.

Anna-Marie felt betrayed, ashamed, and humiliated. The first rape was bad enough. The second left her devastated. She hated to sleep. Terrible dreams engulfed her at night. She often awoke sobbing and terrified. She sank further and further into a black mood and began to obsess about killing herself. Finally, she talked with her high school counselor who helped her to obtain psychiatric help. She was so depressed that her doctor felt she had to be admitted to a hospital. While she soon improved enough with support and medication to be discharged, she did not return home.

During her hospital stay, Anna-Marie had realized that if

she returned home, she might never recover. Anna-Marie and her brothers and sisters had lived with their mother after their parents separated, when Anna-Marie was 10. Her mother and the others in her family not only failed to provide sympathy but also blamed her for somehow inviting the rapes. "You should have known better than to be in that park alone. You must have led your boyfriend on …," they insisted. They constantly told her she was at fault. Anna-Marie wondered if they could be right.

With the help of a social worker at the hospital, which was in California, Anna-Marie came to Chicago to live with her father. She didn't discuss her decision with her mother, whom she believed would be so furious with her for "joining the enemy" that she would never be permitted to see her brothers and sisters again.

A pretty young woman with soft blonde curls, Anna-Marie came to see me a year after the rapes. She wore no makeup. She dressed in sloppy jeans and oversized shirts to conceal her femininity. She told me that her bad dreams were not about the rapes but rather about being abused as a child by her mother. Until these dreams occurred, she said she had "forgotten" these early episodes. They resurfaced only after her second sexual assault. She dreamed that her mother tried to drown her in the bathtub and that her mother smashed her head against the pew while the family was in church, experiences that she now said actually had happened.

The earlier threats to her physical safety laid down basic images in her memory network, images linked with feelings of pain and vulnerability. The most important figure in her life, her mother, hurt her and told her that she deserved the abuse. Anna-Marie concluded that she must have done something very bad. When she grew up, she retained her childhood sense of herself as a bad girl. The rapes reactivated this misperception. Her self-esteem was near zero when she began dream therapy.

Along with her nightmares, Anna-Marie had another serious problem. Every night, she cut her wrists with a razor blade. She made cuts that were deep enough to cause pain, although not deep enough to endanger her life. She felt compelled to perform this act, without understanding why. By hurting herself, she could mollify her fears of being hurt by others. She imagined that by punishing herself she could stave off future attacks. Her arms were laced with white scars from old wounds and red ones from more recent injuries.

In our therapy sessions, Anna-Marie and I soon came to see that most likely she was the target of her mother's rage only because she was her father's child. Her mother railed against the husband who left her by attacking the child who most resembled him. Once Anna-Marie realized that, she also began to see herself more objectively. She had flaws, like everyone else, but she was not "bad." While she could not alter her mother's feelings, she could stop punishing herself. I told her that she could change her mother's behavior in her dreams. Although she was skeptical, Anna-Marie reported success after only our second session.

I dreamed I was a little kid. My brother was teasing me viciously. My mother stepped in and told him, "You are grounded for attacking her."

Anna-Marie was amazed by this dream. She said her mother never used the word "grounded" and never used this measure to control her children. Blows and curses were more her style. "I turned my family into a normal family!" Anna-Marie said with enormous delight. While the dream was in progress, she shifted its dimension from helplessness to one of protection, a good sign.

This and similar dreams that followed helped her to gain a sense of control. She stopped seeing herself as a victim in her dreams, and her mood began to lift. The cutting, however, continued. Inflicting pain on herself calmed her fears of being victimized again. I worked with her to help her express her rage in her dreams rather than by directing it toward herself this way. I told her that the next time her mother or anyone else attacked her in a dream, she could take action. "They are your dreams," I said. "Make them come out better." I suggested she remember that she was no longer a little kid but full-grown and could tell her mother off. Happily, Anna-Marie succeeded in doing just that. Here is her dream:

I was about eight years old, dressed up for church, when my mother lost her temper with me for wearing my best shoes on a rainy day. She started to hit me. That's when I remembered what you told me. I turned and faced her and said, "What the hell do you think you are doing?" My mother was so surprised that she stopped.

Anna-Marie shouted excitedly when she reported this dream. She said over and over, "What the hell do you think you're doing?" and laughed with glee at how her protestation took the steam out of her mother.

This was the first of a series of dreams in which she saw herself in a new way, as a person with power to confront those who intended harm. She began to change her view of herself as a target for others. In the following weeks, Anna-Marie broke off a relationship with a girlfriend who had been wearing her clothes and even taking food from her refrigerator without her permission. She called her mother and arranged for a sister to visit. Her cutting slacked off and then stopped altogether. She didn't need to hurt herself anymore.

Today, Anna-Marie works in an art store, a job she enjoys. She writes poetry of haunting beauty, expressing in waking images the feelings that once haunted her dreams. If she ever encounters another situation where events are beyond her control, her early dreams may resurface for a time. However, I hope she will remember that she can stand up for herself, both in her dreams and in reality.

Rape often is termed "the ultimate violation of the self," short of murder. With a knife or gun pressed against her, or overwhelmed by brute strength, a woman fears for her very life. She is forced to yield the most private parts of her body. The rapist renders her helpless and powerless. That troubled sleep and nightmares follow a rape is not surprising. The persistence of these symptoms months and years later testifies to the enormous impact a rape may have on a woman's sense of self.

Psychiatrist Carol Nadelson—the first woman president of the American Psychiatric Association—and her colleagues at Tufts University interviewed 41 women some 15–30 months after they first sought help at a rape crisis-intervention center. The majority of these women still reported a pervasive suspiciousness of others. They had continuing feelings of fear. More than half said they would go out only with friends. Some said they feared walking alone even in the daylight. Although most reported that their sleep problems had lessened, they still had nightmares and awakened during the night without being able to fall back to sleep.

However, many of these women also described some positive changes in their lives. They felt they had become more serious, more careful, more self-reliant, more independent, and, to some degree, stronger. "This reinforces the view that for many people stressful life events can be growth-promoting and foster maturation," the researchers say. "Even if symptoms persist for some time," they add, "the individual can master the trauma and resume control of his/her life."

Being raped, particularly by someone she thought she could trust, shattered Anna-Marie's fragile sense of self-esteem precisely because it dredged up memories of earlier abuse by another person she thought she could trust. Her memories surfaced initially as dreams. If the early abuse had been not only physical but sexual, I suspect she would have had an even harder time reclaiming those early memories and reinterpreting them from an adult perspective.

Women who were sexually abused in childhood often seek treatment in their late twenties to mid-thirties. Sometimes, as with Anna-Marie, a specific event, like a rape or mugging, prompts the visit. Some women remember the earlier abuse. Others do not. Some find themselves floundering only when they enter relationships that involve trust and intimacy, such as marriage, starting a family, and caring for young children. They may find communication with a partner limited, sex unsatisfying, their bodies "turned off," or a conflict between sex and feelings of loving and caring. They may feel a lack of warmth toward their children, even a desire to hurt them. Some feel depressed and unworthy of love, not entitled to respect from others. They may start to think that life is not worth living. Some become unduly anxious and fearful. Some deaden the pain with addictions to drugs or alcohol.

Some also experience flashbacks during waking hours. These often, at least initially, entail just brief sensations, such as seeing a shadowy figure, hearing footsteps or doorknobs turning, or feeling a light, brief touch, soon after they get in bed. Moreover, vexing dreams may seize control of their nights.

Recurring dreams, particularly of being chased or attacked, suggest that such events really occurred. While many of us have dreams of being chased now and then, the chase in dreams of those who have experienced childhood sexual abuse often ends in an attack, even death. Also common are dreams of intruders, particularly interlopers who come into private spaces such as the bedroom or bathroom.

Many sexually abused women have dreams with physical sensations, such as being paralyzed, held down, choked, smothered, having something heavy on top of them, or gagging. The feelings associated with these dreams include fear, panic, helplessness, and sometimes depression. The dreams may take place in the part of the house where the abuse occurred, and may include a sensation of being cold, perhaps a "body memory" of being unclothed. Typical dreams include:

I am all alone in my bedroom in my nightgown. There is a cold wind blowing. I know something terrible is about to happen.

I am in the bathtub. I had tried to lock the door but the lock was broken. A stranger comes in.

I am being chased around the basement by a snowman with an improbably huge carrot nose.

Nightmares in those who have experienced childhood sexual abuse are less likely to be exact literal reenactments of the event than is the case in war veterans suffering from Post-Traumatic Stress Disorder (see Chapter 11), perhaps because the sexual abuse often occurs before language and memory skills crystallize. The memories may come back in bits and pieces. A dream may focus on only one aspect of the experience. One woman reported this dream:

I was drowning in white glue.

Another woman's dream:

All I saw were stained glass windows.

This woman had been molested at church by a priest. When she told her mother, her mother insisted it hadn't happened. Some women say that when they tried to report their experience of abuse, they were told, "That was just a bad dream."

When abuse starts early, perhaps in the first year or two of life, the time language is just beginning, women may find it hard later to put words to the experience, says social worker Doris Diamond. Most of these women have had no forum in which to talk about what had happened to them, a reason why it appears in their dreams and flashbacks, she notes. They may expend an enormous amount of energy trying to get rid of these dreams and flashbacks. The understandable tendency is to deny that the abuse ever happened or ever could have happened. They often distrust their own feelings and thoughts. They wonder, "Is this an hallucination, a flashback, a dream, a memory?"

"Often their perception of the reality of their experience was contradicted, they were told it's not happening, they're lying, someone will die or get hurt if they tell," Diamond says. "For an adult to behave inappropriately, to use a child for sexual gratification, is a terrible intrusion into the psychological and physical space of the child," she adds. "When that boundary has been crossed, even once, it does enormous damage to the child's sense of personal safety and self-identity. This injury persists into adult life in how people think about themselves, awake and in their dreams.

"They don't understand that they weren't to blame when an adult left his or her adult role and treated them as an object. They think, 'I could have told, I could have said no,' all kinds of things that were impossible in their households. It's hard for women to forgive themselves. They think they had the power to make the abuse stop. They didn't."

The term incest once was reserved for sexual intercourse between two people too closely related to marry, such as father and daughter, or brother and sister. Today, we use the term to refer to any sexual act that a parent, or someone in the parent's role, does for the adult's own pleasure, without regard for the appropriateness of the act for the child's own development. The adult may be a stepfather, mother, uncle, cousin, teacher, or pastor, anyone to whom the child is bound by love and trust. Anna-Marie had flashbacks of sexual abuse by her mother.

How pervasive childhood sexual abuse is remains a matter

of much debate. Freud initially proposed his "seduction theory" to account for problems in many of the women he saw. Later, he renounced this theory, attributing his patients' reports of their early experiences to fantasy. Some therapists today think his change of mind was a concession to the moral climate of the time and to the sensibilities of the fathers and husbands who paid their daughters' and wives' bills. Some authorities today cite evidence to suggest that one girl in three and one boy in 10 experience sexual abuse.

As Sue Blume observes in *Secret Survivors*, "Incest is possibly the most crippling experience that a child can endure. It is a violation of body, boundaries, and trust. Unless identified and dealt with, the emotional and behavioral aftereffects can stay with the victim. The very defenses that initially protect the incest survivor later lock these problems into place, interfering with adult functioning and preventing healing or change."

According to Judith Herman, author of *Father–Daughter Incest*, the abuse usually starts when a child is between the ages of six and 12. The sexual contact, she says, typically begins with fondling and gradually proceeds to masturbation and oral–genital contact. It may not involve vaginal intercourse, at least until the child reaches puberty. It may not even involve violence or threats of violence, since a daughter usually bows to her father's authority. Incest could involve watching a child undress or engage in sexual acts, showing a child pornographic pictures, and even certain mind games, such as an adult's telling a child he has x-ray vision and can see through her nightie. Sometimes a father offers positive inducements for continuing the relationship, Herman says. He may single out one daughter for special attention, privileges, or gifts, all of which can serve to alienate her from her mother and sisters and brothers.

In most cases, the sexual contact doesn't stop until the child finds the resources to escape. The child victim keeps the secret, fearing not only that no one would believe her but that telling would make her mother sick or cause the father to be sent to jail or result in being sent away herself. "These prospects," Herman notes, "are terrifying to any child."

Often, the oldest daughter is the victim. The abuser may then move on to younger sisters and brothers. Boys are abused sexually far less often than girls, and men are abusers far more often than women. Even young children who are the target of the abuse may recognize that they are protecting other children in the family. Sometimes a child may be protecting her mother. By yielding to the father or stepfather or boyfriend, she keeps the abuser from hurting or abandoning her mother. In some instances, if the abuse was not violent, it may have felt good, and it may have been the only touching, the only closeness, the child received.

"It's hard for women who have been abused to talk about their experience," Diamond says, "because talking makes it real. But once they can talk about it," she notes, "healing can begin." Diamond, who directs the Family Therapy Institute of Provident Counseling in St. Louis, works with women in groups lasting just six sessions. One requirement of participation is that the women also must be in individual therapy and committed to continuing it during their groupwork and afterward. Also, women who enter the group already have acknowledged that the abuse occurred, even if their memories remain vague.

In the group, women learn that they are not alone and, most importantly, that they were not at fault. One important activity is sharing recollections written out of class. "The writing often helps them to access the dream material and give form to their experience," Diamond says. As memories start to return, the women may feel terrible pain, then retreat to denying their experience, she notes. "They may say, 'I'm just having these weird dreams, I must be making this up.'"

The women sometimes reexperience the abuse in a dream,

no longer as a child, but rather at their present age. That makes the event harder to deny. One woman's dream:

My father was on top of me in bed. His breath stank of alcohol.

In some dreams, they may be trying to comfort their father. In such dreams, Diamond suggests, they may be trying to reassure themselves that the experience is over now and that they can get past it.

⇨ SELF-HELP: Using dreams to speed healing

The groupwork aims to enable the women to rewrite the story of their past so that they can live with it in the present. Once they confront what happened to them, they can corral their dreams. Furthermore, sometimes they can use their dreams to help the healing process. One woman frequently awakened in fright from dreams of a looming, ominous, shadowy figure at the foot of her bed. She drew on her religious education and transformed the specter into an angel, stationed at the foot of her bed to protect her. Another saw in her dreams her father raping a small, tearful child. She knew she was the child, but she also knew she now was an adult. She changed the dream so that she watched the event as a fly on the wall. She could tell herself, "That was another me, a younger me, a long time ago."

The healing process is painful and difficult. Often, women who have suffered abuse have trained themselves not to cry, not to have feelings, not to acknowledge their pain, or to inflict pain on themselves, as Anna-Marie did. These strategies, protective during childhood, diminish the quality of their lives later on. When the feelings first return, women fear that once they start sobbing they may not stop.

David Calof, clinical director of the Family Psychotherapy Practice of Seattle, works intensively with dreams in individual therapy with adult survivors of childhood abuse. One woman initially sought help for depression. She had no memory of childhood abuse, but Calof started to suspect it after she reported this recurring dream:

There was dirty laundry everywhere, on the floor, on shelves, littering my whole house.

In his office, Calof asked her to act the dream out, to walk from one imaginary pile to another, describing what she saw and felt as she did so. At first, her feeling was one of helplessness: "There's a big mess here and I have to clean it up." Using hypnosis, Calof suggested that she continue the dream and try to find out why all this laundry was in her house. During the six months she was in therapy, the woman had a series of some 20 "dirty laundry" dreams. Some of these dreams occurred while she was under hypnosis, most when she was at home asleep.

In the first of these, she found she had piles containing her own dirty laundry and her father's, mainly his briefs. She began to sort the laundry, separating her father's from her own, and to use separate laundry baskets. She started to wash her own separately. When she began to hang out the clean laundry in her dreams, she realized she didn't want her father's near her own. Eventually, she decided she didn't want to wash her father's dirty laundry any more. She told him he could come and get it if he wanted it. With this last dream, Calof reports, she felt tremendous liberation. In waking life, she had distanced herself from her father and from the past. "She came in depressed," he says. "She left six months later no longer depressed."

Another woman who sought Calof's help in overcoming her depression told him a dream that she'd had three times in the preceding week:

I was at a landfill, a garbage dump. My house was there. It was just a shanty. My husband and children were in it. Coming over a hill was a huge bulldozer that was going to roll over my house. I tried to stop it but I couldn't. I was pushing futilely against the blade as it was getting closer and closer.

Calof asked, "Who was driving the bulldozer?" The woman immediately started to cry and disclosed that she was having an affair. The driver was her lover. Because of the abuse she'd suffered in childhood, she felt overwhelmed and frightened by the sustained intimacy of marriage. Trying to dilute the intensity of her fears, she turned to another man. As the dream graphically demonstrated to her, however, the affair had the potential to wreck her home and marriage. After having this dream repeatedly, she finally acknowledged its message. She disentangled herself from the affair and began to work on improving her relationship with her husband.

As we have seen, the aftereffects of childhood abuse, particularly sexual abuse, may color all aspects of a woman's life. We now know that certain kinds of recurring dreams, particularly those involving attacks, often serve as a red flag to alert us to the possibility of early sexual abuse. We can use these dreams to help uncover the awful early secrets that we'd prefer to ignore. However, they need not be a continuing fixture in our lives. We also can change our dreams to help us master our pain, to permit us to continue our lives, no longer as victims, but as survivors.

The key steps, as for Anna-Marie, are these:

- Remember you're no longer a helpless child. Work to portray yourself as an adult in your dreams.
- Speak out in your dreams. Confront the abuser.
- Praise yourself for being active on your own behalf.

Healing Post-Traumatic Stress Disorder

S HELL SHOCK. War neurosis. Battle fatigue. These are three of the older names for what we now call Post-Traumatic Stress Disorder (PTSD). This disorder exploded into public consciousness only after the Vietnam War, but as we have seen, soldiers are not the only ones who suffer from it. Like victims of rape and long-standing sexual or other physical abuse, soldiers who have been in combat, survivors of torture, death camps, and other horrendous experiences, all may develop similar symptoms. Indeed, in the face of events that shatter our sense of personal safety and our confidence that we can cope, we all are vulnerable to PTSD.

Symptoms may surface soon after the event or not for months or years later. Disturbances of sleep and dreams are hallmark symptoms of PTSD. Indeed, these problems may make PTSD worse and keep it going. The development of sleep troubles in those who served in combat, as one example, is easy to understand: It was not safe to sleep. Those who did were likely to be taken unaware, then possibly maimed or killed.

Nor is the appearance of nightmares surprising. Many veterans describe their war experiences as a living nightmare. Nightmares in PTSD most commonly reenact specific events. One soldier dreams of firing at an unexpected movement or shadow that turns out to be a child, another of seeing a buddy's legs blown off by a land mine.

Some people suffer repeated flashbacks, daytime episodes so vivid that they think they are reliving the event or watching it unfold. These are the waking equivalent of nightmares. Closely allied with flashbacks are exaggerated startle reactions, a kind of revved up hyperalertness, the parallel of abrupt arousals during sleep. A war veteran may jump at the sound of a car backfiring or popcorn cooking on the stove or even throw himself to the ground as if to escape attack. A person who's been mugged may scan crowds for hostile-looking strangers and leap away or strike back if merely brushed against. A child who's been beaten may flinch at an adult's touch. Simple triggers can set off all the sensations associated with the original experience, such as rapid heartbeat, labored breathing, tense muscles, and a flood of anxiety, along with painful memories.

People with PTSD may find themselves overwhelmed with tears or prone to lashing out in anger, without apparent provocation or in a way that exceeds what we consider an appropriate response. This symptom is a bit harder to under-stand. It may represent a surfeit of emotion, feelings that the person may be trying to avoid but that nonetheless break through to the surface.

One of the symptoms of PTSD is emotional numbness, sometimes called emotional anesthesia. People may say they don't feel anything at all. They may lack the words to express what they feel or may choose not to talk about the experience, believing no one else can understand what they have been through. This symptom offers protection from feelings that are overwhelmingly painful. Attempts to blunt tormenting memo-ries also may lead to self-medication with alcohol and drugs.

Some people with PTSD describe themselves as "going through the motions of living," but without joy or sorrow, warmth or rage, without interest or pleasure in activities they formerly enjoyed. As a result, they may pull back from closeness with other people. They may have difficulty holding a job. They try to avoid the pain of further losses by insuring that there will be nothing more to lose. Family members understandably may feel hurt or shut out. It's hard for those who wish to provide comfort to see this symptom as an attempt at self-protection.

You've heard the expression, "Once stung, twice shy." Those who have been through some painful event may learn to avoid situations that remind them of it. For many veterans of Vietnam, the intensive television coverage of the Persian Gulf war churned up memories of their experiences, which surfaced in unusually vivid dreams; some refused to watch television or read newspapers.

A child attacked and bitten by a black dog while walking home from school may refuse to walk on the street where the attack occurred. Or she may scream and run at the sight of the same breed of dog, or any black dog, or even any dog at all. People involved in serious car accidents may avoid a particular stretch of roadway or, in extreme cases, driving or riding in a car. They attach their fear to neutral situations and thus develop phobias.

People who have lived through a disaster that others did not survive, a plane crash or tornado or battle in which others were wounded and died, for example, may feel guilty about surviving. This may happen even to those who were hurt, but not as seriously as some others. Rather than rejoicing in their good fortune and attributing it to the vagaries of fate, they may feel responsible for not doing all they might have done to avoid the tragedy or to save others.

"If only I had left home five minutes sooner, if only I had not insisted on flying that day, if only I had been standing two yards farther away ...." The list of "if onlys" is endless. Like combat veterans who witness or participate in acts that society ordinarily finds unacceptable, such as killing other people, survivors often feel intense guilt. This guilt may spiral downward into depression.

Until recently, mental health professionals thought events most likely to cause this type of long-term harm were those outside the range of ordinary human experience. However, that view is shifting. Few of us go through life without encountering catastrophes such as sudden injuries or serious accidents, physical assaults, seeing someone seriously hurt or killed, news of the sudden death or injury of someone close, house fires, or natural disasters such as tornados or earthquakes. (*See* Appendix for "Post-traumatic Stress Disorder Symptom Checklist" p. 282.)

Naomi Breslau and her colleagues at the Henry Ford Hospital surveyed a random sample of more than 1000 young adults from a large health maintenance organization in Detroit about their exposure to these and other catastrophic events. Four out of 10 of those surveyed had been involved in such events. However, only one out of 10 developed PTSD. Why that one? Studies of Vietnam War veterans provide some clues.

VIETNAM COMBAT VETERANS

The Vietnam War was an unpopular one, and one that the United States lost. Many of those who fought were only 18 or 19 years old, teenagers whose sense of self-identity had yet to solidify. They rotated in and out of units individually, not with a group of men with whom they had trained. As a result, units lacked cohesiveness and troop morale was low. There were no front lines. Troops often fought hard and suffered considerable casualties to capture territory, only to lose it and have to fight to regain it later. Many questioned the meaning of their efforts.

Returning veterans did not find the tickertape parades and flag-waving crowds that greeted veterans of previous wars. Instead, they often met revulsion and cries of "murderer" and "baby-killer." As one much-decorated survivor of fierce fighting told *Discover* magazine writer John Langone, "The best part was finding out you could do things you never thought you could do. The worst part was finding out that you did the things you never thought you would do."

Researchers have long speculated about factors that determine who will suffer long-lasting effects from terrible experiences, and who will not. In one study, John Helzer of the University of Vermont and colleagues at Washington University studied nearly 1000 enlisted men who returned from Vietnam in September 1971. The researchers interviewed all of them within the first year after coming home and more than half of them two years later.

At the first interview, one in 12 men reported loss of energy or appetite, trouble sleeping, thoughts of death, and other symptoms of depression. Two years later, two in 12 had such symptoms. About one quarter of those who were depressed had taken time off from their regular activities because of their depressive symptoms. Those who had experienced the most combat were the most likely to become depressed.

Being wounded was an even stronger predictor of becoming depressed than experiencing combat. That alone may not seem surprising. However, Helzer also found that the soldiers who were wounded were more likely to have dropped out of school, been arrested, and abused alcohol and drugs before entering the service than those who were not wounded. "Assignment by platoon leader or a company commander to a combat mission is presumably not a random event," Helzer notes. "It is not difficult to imagine that men who had behavior problems tended to get undesirable duty assignments more frequently." Perhaps those with such characteristics also took more risks during combat and were less likely to follow orders. Thus, they may have been more likely to get in harm's way. The more behavior problems the men had before their service experience, the earlier their breaking points and the more frequent their later emotional difficulties.

Of the nearly three million Americans who served in Vietnam, one million of them as combatants, a significant percentage—estimates vary wildly, but, it's generally agreed, more than in any other war—may suffer PTSD. Some 15–20 years later, those who served in Vietnam are more than twice as likely as soldiers who did not serve there to suffer from serious psychological problems, such as depression, alcohol abuse, and anxiety. They also are more likely to commit suicide and to have automobile accidents.

The customary treatment for PTSD includes psychotherapy for the individual alone, and often also with members of their family and with others who have undergone similar experiences. In individual therapy, we help our patients to reconcile the differences between the world they thought they were living in and the world into which the calamitous event thrust them. We also try to help them rebuild their self-esteem and their sense of being in charge of their own lives.

In family therapy, we work to improve communication and to enable someone who has walled off feelings to show affection again and take part in family life. In group therapy, those who have suffered similar blows can share their experiences and their feelings about them. In the process, survivors can help each other see that others acted the same way in similar circumstances. This knowledge can help relieve guilt and enable people to put the experience behind them and move on. There is a place, in all of these treatments, for dreamwork, since dreams provide a look at feelings often denied in waking.

Studies of sleep and dreams in Vietnam veterans help illuminate why some continue to have disrupted sleep and violent dreams long after returning home, and why, for yet others, these problems do not emerge until months or years later. Cincinnati psychiatrist Milton Kramer and his colleagues studied 16 Vietnam veterans in their sleep laboratory. Eight with PTSD reported at least one disturbing dream per week. The others reported fewer than two disturbing dreams per year.

Ray was one of those with PTSD. Ray suffered from nightmares the first year after he returned home. These gradually disappeared but returned about 10 years later when his marriage began to fall apart. After three stormy years, his wife of eight years told him she had found someone else. Although he hated to leave his four children, he loaded his truck, kissed the kids good-bye, and drove away. His departure occurred just two weeks before his dream study in Kramer's laboratory.

Ray was a carpenter and mechanic who described himself as an independent person. He didn't show much emotion and said he was unable to cry. Ray's father died before his first birthday, leaving his mother with seven children. He was the second-youngest and the family scapegoat. His mother and older sisters, Ray said, often blamed him for things he did not do.

One dramatic and painful instance occurred when Ray was just five years old. He was playing with a boy the same age who lived next door, whose older brother had told him that if he poured gasoline on himself and lit a match, he would not burn. Ray warned the boy not to do it, but the child didn't listen. Ray was blamed for the boy's death. That boy's mother was Ray's schoolteacher from first to fifth grades. At school, she kept Ray locked in a closet. As a result, he did not learn to read or write. He never told his mother, because he feared she would not believe him. He quit school at age 12 and wandered around doing odd jobs until he enlisted in the army at age 18.

Ray had many ghastly memories from his time in Vietnam. While driving in a jeep, he and his buddy ran over a land mine. Both were thrown out; the buddy was killed. Ray carried the body 12 miles to a camp, although he did not remember doing so. On another occasion, while walking down a street in

Saigon, he saw a group of Marines gathered around a little boy with a basket. Suddenly, there was an explosion. The next thing he saw were the Marines lying dead with their intestines falling out.

Just then Ray noticed another boy with a basket nearby. Thinking he, too, had a bomb, Ray ran over and started to choke the child. The boy's mother hit him with an umbrella, but Ray did not stop until he killed the boy. Only then did he discover that the boy's basket contained only bread. Ray's guilt was enormous. That same night, on his way back to camp, he saw women impaled on tall poles hanging by the side of the road, an image that continued to haunt him. In a fourth incident, he went to visit a Vietnamese family with whom he had become friendly and to whom he often brought food. He found that the father, mother, and two children were dead.

Here are Ray's dreams from one of his five nights in the sleep laboratory, more than 10 years after his war experiences:

Dream 1

"I was driving a truck in Vietnam and was getting ready to get blown up. I've had this dream many times. There were no other people in the dream. I got blown up and found myself in a rice paddy."

Dream 2

"I was walking down the streets of Saigon. There were six Marines on the other side of the street. A boy came up behind them selling things out of a basket. There was an explosion. The Marines were lying on the ground. A lot of people were running around. I saw another boy. I wound up killing this boy by choking him to death."

Dream 3

"There was an explosion that killed four people. A grenade was in the back seat of the truck. I threw it into some people and drove off. I was

riding with another guy and heard something tinkle in the back seat. I looked around, saw a grenade and I picked it up and threw it. It hit some people, both men and women. I just kept driving. I felt mad in the dream."

Dream 4

"I was driving a truck. There was a girl hanging upside down, slit open and her intestines were hanging down. I was thinking about going back because a guy in the village had been burned alive. Someone had poured gasoline on him. I turned around and went away from the village."

In Ray's dreams, both the recent destruction of his marriage and the violence of his Vietnam experiences blended into the guilt and death events from his early childhood. In his waking life, Ray handled his anger over his wife's infidelity passively, by retreating and leaving his children behind. He just drove away in his truck. This experience resonated with his guilty memories of both his active role in attacking the child in Vietnam and his passive role in the death of his childhood playmate, for which he received the blame nonetheless. These images occurred over and over in his dreams. We can see his alternating dream dimensions: attack/retreat, death/survival, guilt/innocence, anger/control. These he juxtaposed from dream to dream.

In the first dream, he was attacked, but he survived. In the second, he attacked and killed an innocent child. In the third, he was attacked and retaliated. He was angry, but survived by retreating. In the last, someone else was killed. He retreated and survived. The lesson he learned is that attacks may destroy the innocent. To retreat is to survive. If he does not control his anger, he may be lethal. He might rip the guts out of his wife and kill his innocent children, the "four people" he threw the grenade at as he drove off in his third dream.

"In the Vietnam veteran with PTSD, there is a breakdown in current life situations which echo and stir up similar problems from the past," Kramer notes. "Those aspects of Vietnam which are in focus currently are those which have some meaning as determined by the historical past." The Vietnam experience thus becomes a metaphor for a veteran's chronic interpersonal difficulties, current and past.

Ray's dreams on this night all contained war references. In Vietnam veterans with PTSD, perhaps 50% of all dreams involve war scenes. Veterans who do not have PTSD dream of the war far less often. Psychoanalyst Harry Wilmer studied 359 dreams collected from 103 combat veterans seven to 16 years after the men had returned from Vietnam. Many of the 359 dreams were recurrent dreams, so his study actually reflects thousands of dreams that the men had experienced. Common themes included killing or being killed, dying or seeing someone die, being wounded or seeing someone wounded, and seeing atrocities.

More than half of the dreams replayed the same images of specific experiences again and again. Some examples:

"I see a chaplain giving last rites to a head."

"My buddy and I are about two feet apart in a foxhole on top of the hill. We have to stay in the same foxhole. We can't even get out to stretch our legs because of the sniper fire. I am talking with my buddy. It is dark. He lights a cigarette and all of a sudden his head blows off. His brains come out all over me. I wake up screaming."

About one fifth of the dreams of the veterans Wilmer interviewed involved war experiences that might have happened to them but did not occur exactly as dreamed. One man, for example, reported having this recurring dream about an event he had not participated in but had witnessed:

"Just out of Chu Lai in a helicopter, a Vietnamese interpreter was try-ing to get the North Vietnam Army prisoner to talk. He told him to talk or we would throw him out. He wouldn't talk. They kicked him out of the helicopter. He hit the ground. He was literally split into four pieces."

The remainder of the dreams of veterans in Wilmer's study were like ordinary nightmares. One example:

"My weapon jams. I look to the right and see a monk in a brown habit on the side of the mountain looking down. His hood slips down, and there's a skull, and it seems like it is laughing."

With recovery from PTSD, there's a progression from dreams of actual events to ordinary nightmares, Wilmer says. The dreamer learns to understand the meaning of his experi-ence in new ways. This healing can take place spontaneously or with the aid of therapy.

Despite the unique character of significant early life events, the commonalities in the dreams of many Vietnam vet-erans with PTSD—themes of helplessness, vulnerability, and irreconcilable guilt—make group dream therapy both possible and highly successful, a Veterans Administration study shows. In a group, men loathe to reveal feelings they think will make others view them as weak discover that they are not alone, says psychiatrist Stephen Brockway of the Phoenix Veterans Administration Medical Center. In the company of others, vet-erans find it is safe to talk about atrocities committed in a moment and regretted ever since. They explore reasons for their acts, such as rage over buddies mutilated or killed in booby traps. Also, says Brockway, "the group presses for the individual to forgive himself and embrace life instead of death."

In a program developed by Brockway and his colleagues, patients record their dreams in a journal in which they also

204 / CRISIS DREAMING

keep an autobiography and daily reflective writings. About 15–20 patients meet in once-a-week sessions lasting about 90 minutes, with one to three people recounting recent dreams.

As each person relates his dream, another member of the group writes it verbatim on a blackboard. Another records it in a dream notebook, from which members may obtain photocopies of their dreams for further study. A leader and two co-therapists attend each session, but encourage patients to do most of the clarifying, translating, and interpreting of dreams. They give new members a brief orientation on how dreams work, talking about, for example, picture language and dream symbols.

After hearing each dream, the group explores it according to a three-step plan, Brockway reports. The dreamer first identifies the day residue or triggers for the dream. Then, with the group's help, he identifies feelings experienced during and after the dream. The last step consists of brainstorming possible meanings of the dream, with attention to the past, present, and future. Often, the group takes brainstorming a step further, just as we do in the RISC program, to devise possible endings that would help the dreamer master the situation.

The dreams of one of the combat veterans in the group illustrate this process. The man, whom the researchers call R.H., was 37 when he joined the group, some 15 years after his service in Vietnam. He was depressed and had attempted suicide. A veteran of two tours in the Army Infantry from 1966–1968, he'd seen heavy combat. Toward the end of his second tour, he was pinned down for three days at the Da Nau Bridge near Cambodia. As sergeant and squad leader, he was in charge of a platoon of 40 men, 14 of whom were killed during those three days. Each week he brought in a dream.

Dream 1

"I'm alone at the north end of the Da Nau Bridge. A freedom bird (a 707) lands and I board in full combat gear. The plane is loaded with

soldiers all in class A's (dress uniforms). I sit down next to a white, young lieutenant. The lieutenant starts arguing with me about the war and accuses me of killing civilians and water buffalo. The lieutenant reminds me that they are here to protect the Vietnamese people. The plane lands in San Francisco, but I am thrown off at Da Nau where I started from. I am no longer alone, but with [names of several, including his best buddy—all killed]. They said, 'You'll never leave.' They are all full of rage. I wake up screaming."

Among the triggers R.H. identified for this dream was talking the previous day with someone who had the same last name as a buddy killed in action. He identified feelings of anger, confusion, fear, helplessness, and guilt. Out of the brainstorming session came such thoughts as "stuck in Vietnam" and "Maybe I'm the only one still fighting the war. Maybe I should give it up."

Dream 2

"I'm alone at the Da Nau Bridge. A jetliner lands. I get on the plane in combat gear, and I'm alone. I think I'm home and get off the plane, but I'm back at Da Nau. The only person there is my wife. She's scared and mad at me. 'If you'd quit arguing with people, they'd let you go home.' I agree; we'll try that. We try to get on the plane but the ramp is hundreds of miles long. It goes on forever. I'm holding on to her. We continue the hard walk up the ramp."

This dream, R.H. said, was a continuation of the previous week's dream. It showed feelings of false hope, fear, desperation, and determination. R.H. acknowledged, "I have a fear of not getting back from Vietnam." While brainstorming about the dreams, he said he also realized, "My wife is faithful to me despite my problems. The bridge is between two different worlds. I haven't made it yet, but I'm on the ramp."

In the next week, R.H. had a dream that he described as "the first nonfrightening dream I've had since Vietnam."

Dream 3

"I'm on the airplane ramp running with my wife. We're throwing off combat gear. We're looking for the plane in the distance. We're in good shape and we're not getting tired. We're trying to find the airplane, but we're not worried."

Despite mild anxiety, the feelings in this dream were essentially positive. There was relief, eagerness, and no fear. "I'm in between Vietnam and home in the PTSD unit," R.H. said. "I'm moving toward healthy control of my life."

R.H.'s progress was not only obvious to him but also encouraging to other members of the group, Brockway says. In this way, group members help each other to heal. In the company of others with similar experiences, they can reexamine combat memories. "Group consensus that the only viable choice was made, with comments such as 'that's fate ... that's war ... you're alive, he's dead,' or the shouldering of part of the burden of guilt, or the reframing of a painful memory, all lead to immense relief," Brockway says. "Group dreamwork promotes trust, intimacy, and support while allowing the member to maintain needed control."

Virtually every participant in the group initially reported recurrent dreams in which they were helpless, hopeless, and terrified, Brockway and his colleagues found. The next most common theme was an inability to leave Vietnam physically or emotionally. Many dreams showed persistent rage, with themes such as blowing up VA facilities or poisoning Vietnamese people, covering a nagging guilt or fear. Veterans new to the group related apprehensive dreams showing ambivalence about entering the program and concerns about authority and trust. Only rarely did any patient dream of grandiose revenge, in the manner of a Rambo movie.

Nearly all patients gained relief from their dreams of helplessness, the researchers found when they assessed 55 dreams processed by the group in a seven-month period. The men still dreamed of Vietnam, but they transformed their experience into a positive one. One man, for example, dreamed of a reunion of patients in Vietnam with everyone wearing Hawaiian tourist shirts and carrying cameras. Says Brockway, "Nightmares, formerly viewed as enemies, become messengers, and finally, dreams become friends."

VETERANS OF WORLD WAR II

The conventional wisdom is that time heals all wounds. However, wounds that cut to the quick may fester if they don't reccive the proper attention. Atlanta psychiatrist Thomas Fulmer describes a man referred to him from the diabetes clinic, a man markedly uneasy about seeing a psychiatrist. In the first hour, he talked mainly about the stress of his illness, his fine family, and his three grown sons. Only when the hour was nearly up did the man relate that since the end of World War II, some 35 years earlier, he had dreamed—at least three nights a week and in exact detail—about an event that took place near the end of the war.

The man told Fulmer that he had landed in Europe on D-day and fought in many battles. In a small village, he and his squad intercepted a group of fleeing enemy soldiers. He took aim, fired, and killed one. When he got up to the body, he turned it over and saw that he had killed "a beautiful blond-haired blue-eyed boy not more than 14 or 15 years old."

The memory remained in his dreams, waking him in an extreme state of agitation. He was horrified by his act and flooded with feelings of sadness and remorse. He said he had never, not once, been able to return to sleep after this dream. The next day, he would feel overcome with guilt and withdraw from his family.

The man declined a return appointment but said that he would call if he decided to continue. During the next two years, he saw Fulmer only nine times at irregular intervals.

The second and third visits were much like the first. At the end of the third, Fulmer told him that he agreed that the dream described a real event; it was not an imagined experience.

At the next session, the man reported, "Doc, you broke the monster's back. I haven't dreamed as much and they haven't been as bad." The dreams did, however, continue. Over the next several sessions, Fulmer pondered how best to help the man. He recalled that the man had not mentioned his sons since the first meeting. Fulmer told him he presumed that all three were beautiful blond-haired blue-eyed boys. Sobbing, the man said, "And, Doc, would you believe that every day of their lives when I looked in their faces, I saw the face of the boy I killed."

The man arrived for his next visit even more depressed. Fulmer told him that it seemed that he had been waiting for 35 years to be forgiven, but for that to happen he would have to forgive himself. It was four months before the man returned. He said that he didn't need to talk; the dreams had stopped. He presented Fulmer with a large basket of fresh vegetables that he and his grandsons had grown. Says Fulmer, "From the way he said it, I knew he could look them in the face."

Craig Van Dyke and his colleagues at the Veterans Administration Medical Center in San Francisco report a World War II veteran who first started having nightmares 30 years after a war experience virtually identical to that of Fulmer's patient. This man and his squad had fought off a German attack. Afterward, he and a few others went out to explore the battlefield. They found that some of the dead soldiers were adolescent boys, wearing German army uniforms but "armed" only with imitation rifles.

Over the years, Van Dyke and his colleagues learned that the man occasionally dreamed about the war. He said, however, that these dreams were not frightening. A successful architect, he worked productively and raised a family. He even visited former battlefields without feeling any disturbing emotions. The nightmares began only after he became ill and had to retire earlier than he wished. What troubled him the most in his nightmares was that they often incorporated his grandchildren, aged 8 and 12. In the dreams, they appeared as adults.

The nightmares began with an accurate recapitulation of events, with his squad having to take cover as a German patrol marched toward them. Just as he was about to fire, his grandson, dressed in a German uniform, would jump up beside him and shout, "Don't shoot!" The man would awaken upset and in tears, unable to decide whose side his grandson was on and whether he should shoot or quietly let himself and his grandson be shot.

Why did these nightmares take so long to appear? When the man was well and working, Van Dyke and his colleagues suggest, he could deny or bury his terrible memories. His deteriorating health and the loss of his job rekindled memories of an earlier time when he felt helpless, when he took the "health" and promise of a future away from the young German men. In his dreams, he substituted his grandson for the adolescents who were grandsons of other men. This man's situation was similar to those Kramer found in his study of Vietnam veterans and we found in our study of people who become depressed and suffer painful recurring dreams in the process of divorce.

Van Dyke asks: "Does a person ever really get over such things? Or do they become part of him—permanently a part of his potential reactivity to renewed stress—so that when he is sick enough, or bereaved enough, or scared enough, the prior events, linked directly or by some thread of feeling or theme, come back to him explicitly?"

We answer: They stay, but they do not have to cripple. When trouble strikes, ideally even before trouble strikes, the memory connections between feelings of vulnerability and images of successful coping can be strengthened, so that the latter can help protect against the former.

HOLOCAUST SURVIVORS

When subjected to ghastly horrors—far beyond the ability of most people even to imagine—we may, with sustained and deliberate effort, wall ourselves off from them. In his book *Survival in Auschwitz,* Primo Levi describes two recurrent dreams he and other prisoners experienced. In one, they dreamed of food. In their sleep, they moved their empty mouths and ground their teeth as they consumed imaginary meals. In the other, they dreamed of returning home and trying to tell their families about their concentration camp experiences. But no one listened.

For many of those who survived concentration camps, "forgetting" became an active process, a conscious attempt to banish memories of their agony from mind. "To talk about what happened," says one survivor, "is to descend into darkness. On the surface my life is busy and full and probably looks relatively normal. I work in my garden, I take care of my home, I enjoy my grandchildren. I try to push those terrible thoughts out of my day," she adds, "but they return at night."

Therapists usually try to help their patients to recover long-buried memories and to reexamine still-painful experiences from the past in the light of later life. The general idea is to "confront and conquer." However, a recent sleep laboratory study of Holocaust survivors suggests that in some circumstances, thrusting painful memories out of sight and keeping them hidden may be more desirable than reviewing them again. Peretz Lavie and Hanna Kaminer of the Technion-Israel Institute of Technology in Haifa found that well-adjusted Holocaust survivors managed to banish memories even from their dreams.

They studied the sleep and dreams of 23 survivors, all of whom lived in Europe under Nazi occupation. Eleven survived concentration camps, while 12 spent most of the time in hideouts or on the move. The researchers compared them with 10 men and women who were Israeli-born and lived during the war in what was known then as Palestine. All participants in the study were around 60 years old. None had any major physical or mental illness.

The researchers interviewed the participants about six key areas of life adjustment: work, marital and family relationships, friendships, physical health, mental health, and general satisfaction in life. About half the survivors—five men, six women—had problems in at least three of these areas. The researchers termed them the "less-adjusted" survivors. The others—five men, seven women—reported trouble in only one area, about the same as the healthy Israelis. These were the "well-adjusted" survivors.

All of the study participants spent four nights in the sleep laboratory, where the researchers awakened them in REM sleep and asked them to report everything going on in their minds just before awakening. They then answered questions: Did they recognize the people in the dream? Did they know the places in the dream? Was the dream from the past? The present? Did they play an active or passive role? The final query aimed to tap emotions: The researchers asked, "How do you feel about the dream?"

Not surprisingly, the less-adjusted group showed more disturbed sleep. They took longer to fall asleep and slept more fitfully, getting less sleep overall. When awakened during REM sleep, they recalled dreams about half of the time. The well-adjusted Holocaust survivors remembered dreams only a third of the time, and the ones they did recall tended to be brief and unimaginative. By contrast, the healthy Israelis remembered dreams at eight out of 10 awakenings, as is normal.

The less-adjusted subjects saw other people in their dreams

as dangerous, bad, strange, or sick, and they dreamed more about people from their remote past. The well-adjusted survivors and the healthy Israelis dreamed more about people from their present lives. Half of the dreams in the less-adjusted survivors focused on actual danger to the person's life, on being attacked, or on the need to escape to avoid death. Their dreams often took them right back to the concentration camps.

One man reported:

"I saw some Germans, many Germans. They were making selections. It was in Auschwitz. I was there, they dragged me out of the train. Nobody knew where to go. Then I felt great fear since they started sorting us. We still didn't know anything. They told me where to stand, but as that was the side of the gas chambers, I ran to the other side. But they told me the same thing and I ran back again. A German soldier caught me, beat me, and took me back there. He had a big dog. I was very afraid. I can see the dog.... And then you woke me up."

Another member of the less-adjusted group told this dream:

"I got a blow in my teeth ... and my whole jaw fell apart. Metal fragments fell out of my teeth and then the teeth themselves fell out. I was all swollen. Many people came, physicians, too. But I did not have money to pay."

And another:

"People are beaten up and you just stand by. Little children—really little ...."

It's no surprise that some apparently choose not to remember. The well-adjusted survivors, Lavie and Kaminer say, did not appear to have "paid" for their low rate of dream recall in any noticeable way. All enjoyed a full and healthy life and some achieved considerable professional success. Interestingly, in waking life, some shut out the past so effectively that their close relatives did not know about their experiences during the war.

It's possible, of course, that those who are well-adjusted now, more than 40 years later, may have done their productive crisis dreaming during the intervening years. They may have come to terms with this experience as best they could and progressed beyond the need to strive for further mastery. Furthermore, it will be interesting to see if events common in late life, such as illness, retirement, or the death of a loved one, will trigger a resurgence of dreaming about the Holocaust. The experience of combat veterans suggests that may happen.

⇨ **SELF-HELP: Battling the war within**

As horrible as war experiences are, not all veterans, even those who witnessed or participated in the worst atrocities, developed PTSD. Those who proved most susceptible were those who'd had experiences earlier in life that resonated emotionally with their war experiences. The war, in turn, heightened their sensitivity to later traumas. Experiences even many years after returning home, such as the failure of a marriage or loss of a job, fell on fertile soil.

Those who had the most trouble recovering from Vietnam combat had the same characteristics as those in our divorce study who developed depression. Those whose prewar experiences included few friendships that built self-esteem, little family support, and parents with psychiatric problems developed PTSD more often than other combat veterans. World War II veterans and others whose war experiences triggered PTSD also may have been those predisposed to this response by events of early life. Such events, while unchangeable, can be reinterpreted from a later life perspective.

People who have experienced the trauma of war often benefit from sharing their feelings with others who understand first-hand the bad times they have had. A dream-sharing group is wonderful for this purpose. While those still haunted by the horrors of war often are told, "Forget it; it's over," dreams do not forget.

History books may say a war has ended. However, for some who have been through it, particularly those who grew up without building strong fortifications in early childhood, it may erupt again on a different front. Without help, without dreams that provide self-images of successful coping, the war within may never end.

12

Little Kids, Big Problems

O N A SWELTERING July afternoon in 1976, three masked gunmen hijacked a busload of children on their way home from daycamp in Chowchilla, California. Taking the bus to a remote spot, the trio ordered the 25 children and their driver off the bus. They crammed their victims into two vans with blackened windows, then drove around for 11 hours. They gave the terrified youngsters—the oldest 14 years of age, the youngest, only five—no food or water. They made no bathroom stops.

It was 3 A.M. before the vans halted. The sweaty, weary children were pulled out one by one. A masked man with a flashlight under his chin questioned them, while another pointed a gun directly at them. The men then stripped each child of some personal possession, a toy, a T-shirt, shoes. They ordered each child to "Get down into that hole," a descent into blackness. Once the children and their driver were inside their prison, the carcass of an old trailer truck buried in an abandoned quarry, the men sealed the entrance with a metal plate and shoveled dirt and rocks over the opening.

Inside the buried truck, the children found old mattresses, soggy potato chips, cans of musty water, and a few flashlights. Conserving the flashlight batteries, they spent two fearful days in the dark. When the ceiling began to collapse, two of the older boys led a valiant effort to tunnel through to the surface. The children scooped out a tunnel, one handful of dirt at a time, and escaped.

A hundred miles from home, they were not yet at the end of their ordeal. The bus driver walked some distance before finding a phone. Sheriff's deputies arrived quickly, but it already was dusk. The children, particularly the youngest, balked at boarding another bus. Some tried to run away. Finally, they were taken to the nearest place with room for them to eat and sleep—the local jail. Doctors examined them, police questioned them, and when they arrived at home the next morning they found not only parents but FBI agents, police, and reporters with microphones and television cameras.

The perpetrators, one the son of the quarry's owner, were found, arrested, and jailed. They did not speak at their trial. No motive for the kidnapping ever was established.

None of the children died. None sustained physical injuries. However, contrary to initial proclamations of doctors and others, the children were not "all right."

Every child suffered emotional aftereffects, Lenore Terr, a University of California child psychiatrist, found. Terr volunteered to see the children after learning from a newspaper article a few months later that many of them suffered fears and terrible nightmares. In the first year after the kidnapping, she talked with all 23 of the children who still lived in Chowchilla, as well as one who had been let off the bus a few minutes before the kidnapping occurred. She talked with them again, four to five years later, and she continues to follow them today to assess long-lasting effects. Hers is the first study to examine the reactions of a single group of children of different ages and stages of development to the same horrifying event.

During the first year, the children saw literal playbacks of the kidnapping in their dreams. Some dreamed of being in the hole or bouncing around in the dark. "I dreamed we went to the cemetery where my grandma is buried," one reported. Four years later, most still had repetitive nightmares. Although these bad dreams occurred less often, with the events more disguised, their intensity remained high.

"When I asked if they still dreamed about the kidnapping, they said, 'No,'" Terr reports. "But if I said, 'Tell me any dream,' they reported dreams bearing the stamp of the trauma. The night after a fight with his father, one boy, for example, dreamed that his father was kidnapped by three men resembling the schoolbus kidnappers. In the dream, the men put his father in a sack, hung him up and killed him."

The way these dreams stick in memory shows their impact, Terr says. "Why else," she asks, "when I ask them to tell me any dream, would they tell me a trauma dream?"

Some of the children reported waking from terror dreams without being able to recall the contents. Such youngsters, particularly if they were very young at the time of the kidnapping or simply were not good at putting feelings into words, often expressed their anxiety at night by crying out or walking in their sleep.

HOW CHILDREN DREAM

Dreams in children, like those in adults, provide an open window on the mind at work. Babies still in the womb experience REM sleep. Newborns spend as much as 50% of their time asleep in REM sleep. This bombardment of internal excitation may prepare the infant's brain to receive the sights and sounds of the outside world, an important task for the first few months of life. By six months of age, the amount of REM sleep drops to 20–25%. It stays at that rate well into old age.

Once we can process our impressions of the world and store them in memory, we are ready to begin to dream. It is hard to know at precisely what age dreaming begins, since telling a dream to someone else requires the ability to translate from visual to verbal terms, a task that is somewhat like describing a carnival to a blind person. Sometimes the first evidence that a child dreams comes when a dream prompts action. At age three, my daughter Carolyn woke up and socked her sleeping older sister, "because," she told me, "Chrissy was being so mean to me."

Sleep researcher William Dement reports an incident involving his own daughter before she had her second birthday. One morning he went into her room before she awoke and saw her eyes moving. The child suddenly said, "Pick me! Pick me!" "I woke her," Dement recalls, "and she immediately said, 'Oh Daddy, I was a flower.'"

Young children often do not distinguish between dreams and reality, as parents discover when called on to comfort a tearful child awakened from a bad dream. After checking for wet diapers and providing some cuddling, all many people know to do is to turn on the light to show the child the difference between the real safe world and that of the nightmare. We attempt to comfort, saying, "See? There is nothing there." A more lasting form of reassurance is provided by teaching a child to recognize a dream as a product of his or her own creation.

Age has a potent impact on the kinds of dreams children have. Dreams, in turn, tell us about the child's development. The skills needed to produce good dreams take years to mature.

Sissy, age three, reported this dream:

A monster with big wings was coming after me.

Her sister Wendy, who is eight years old, told this dream:

My mom, my sisters, and I were all goats. We lived happily. One day I got mad at them and I killed them. My mom was a goddess. I was on earth, starving, for I was still a baby and needed milk. My mom felt sorry for me and made it rain warm milk so I wouldn't starve.

Wendy's dream is not only longer but far more complex in imagery and narrative. Her ability to communicate it in words is better, too. Wendy's little sister fears monsters that fly at night. Wendy fears the consequences of her own impulses to hurt her mother and sister.

Psychologist David Foulkes of the Georgia Mental Health Institute has spent many years studying dreams in children. His early research at the University of Wyoming shows that children's dreams follow a regular sequence of stages over the years. The changes reflect more than the increasing ability to use language to describe dreams. They represent real developmental steps in the dreams themselves. "Proficiency in dreaming," Foulkes says, "evolves hand-in-hand with waking cognitive ability."

Some of the children began coming to his laboratory for periodic "sleepovers" when they were as young as three or four. In these early years, the children had few dreams. Most of their laboratory awakenings yielded nothing. "Empty-REMpty" Foulkes called them. When children this age tell a dream, it usually is short, typically only a single image. The main character is often an animal, such as a fish swimming or a dog barking. The animals seem to stand for the child himself or herself and express simple feelings, such as fatigue or hunger. Three- and four-year-olds lack the self-knowledge to build a good internal image of themselves to use as a dream character. Their dreams are more literal than imaginative.

By age five, dreams become longer and more storylike. They involve more interactions among the characters, including family members, but still lack self-representation. Some children continue to have animal dreams, which often express problems the child may be having in controlling his or her impulses; Wendy's goat dream is a good example. Animals may become more fanciful. Machines appear.

Witches, ghosts, monsters, and menacing machines populate the bad dreams of five- and six-year-olds. Some children keep bad dreams to themselves because they believe that telling a dream will make it come true. Indeed, this notion sometimes persists into adulthood.

However, telling bad dreams, often a comfort to adults because it diffuses anxiety, may help children, too. A parent needs to listen attentively and not dismiss the fears with a comment like "It's just a dream." A parent who values dreams can instill the same feeling in a child by saying, "That's an interesting story you were telling yourself." This observation helps children to recognize that they write the scripts of their own dreams. Going on to ask, "I wonder why you told yourself this story?" replaces fright with curiosity and prompts introspection.

Children remain passive observers of dream action until about age eight. At this age, Foulkes finds, they report dreams after most REM sleep awakenings, just as adults do. A real self-character emerges in their dreams. Statements such as "I was thinking" or "I was feeling" become part of the dream story. On most nights, the feelings in the dreams of most middle-class children eight years old and younger are good ones.

Feelings of guilt, fear, and anger begin to show up in dreams between ages nine and 13. Brian, a nine-year-old boy, told me this dream:

I was playing by the edge of a lake when a sea monster rose up its long neck suddenly and wanted to play with me. My mother was frightened. She shouted at it and came running, and the sea monster sank back, and I was sad. I tried to tell my mother that it was a good monster, but she didn't believe me.

Something that Brian has discovered feels good, playing with his erect penis, upset his mother. Brian replayed the experience to reevaluate his feelings. He was confused. How should he feel about himself? He was sad about his mother's reaction but decided he knew best: It was a good monster. Brian handled the problem in his dream by detaching the offending element from his own body. He made the monster sink out of sight when Mother showed up. By denying this part of himself, he temporarily gained peace. However, he will need to re-own his sexual feelings later or he will run into problems.

At about age 13, dreams become more imaginative. Teenagers think more abstractly both when awake and in their dreams. They struggle with issues revolving around control of self, others, and the environment. Driving or riding in cars and sexual interactions are popular topics. Teenagers have come a long way from the empty REM periods of the three-year-olds.

The changes that take place during childhood and adolescence show that humans learn to dream. In that process it is most important that we learn to see ourselves in relation to others in our world—a complex and abstract idea that we generalize from direct interactions with others and our perception of how they respond to us. Such learning takes time.

Our self-image forms the bedrock of the life story we strive to maintain in our dreams. Dreams indicate the state of our self-knowledge and our emotional development. Dreams reflect our ability to represent ourselves and our experiences and to juggle and reassign some features of these experiences to other persons, objects, or imaginary creatures. A good dream is a skilled production, a creative recombination of images stored in memory.

WHEN DREAMS ARE DISTURBED

Although we create dream images from social experiences, dreams are not themselves social acts. No one corrects our misperceptions of meanings in dreams as they do when we are learning spoken language. Foulkes concludes from his work that the potential for us to create dream narratives is wired into our brains as surely as our ability to develop spoken language, and both go through an orderly developmental pattern. The single-image, literal dreams of early childhood form the basic alphabet we use later to construct more complex narratives.

Traumatic events that occur in childhood threaten this orderly process. Four years after their kidnapping, 14 of the Chowchilla children still dreamed of their own death. In these invariably horrifying dreams, the children sometimes continued to see themselves or others after they had "died." Or, they told Terr, the dream blacked out entirely at that instant. They thought the death dreams predicted that they would die soon.

Some of the children became unusually fearful of mundane things, such as darkness, strangers, or white vans. Four years later, their memories of the traumatic event remained intact and detailed. The abduction left 23 of the 25 children pessimistic about the future and their place in it. They expect to die at an early age or to encounter additional disasters. Many cannot envision marriage, children, or a career.

For comparison purposes while she conducted her four- to five-year follow-up of the Chowchilla children, Terr interviewed two other groups of children, with particular emphasis on their predictions for the world's future, their own futures, and their dreams. One group included 25 age-matched, healthy children from two towns near Chowchilla, children not known to have experienced trauma. The other group consisted of 25 children of about the same ages whom she saw for psychiatric evaluations not related to trauma. Eight of the 25 healthy children and six of Terr's young patients without trauma histories also reported that they had dreams of their own deaths. When she asked these children, "Tell me the worst, the scariest thing, you can remember," most related highly distressing events. Nearly all, Terr found, had suffered severe, unexpected fright or sudden bouts of unconsciousness.

One girl, for instance, had been hospitalized for pneumonia. Later, she was in a minor car accident. Though not physically hurt, she was quite scared. In her dream, she was injured in a car crash and taken to a hospital where she died. For others, the trauma consisted of having had high fevers or of having fainted from heatstroke. These experiences also prompted dreams of dying. The loss of consciousness, Terr suggests, is close to the actual experience of death, at least in the child's mind. It takes away the childhood sense of invincibility.

When a child who suffers a common event such as an illness or accident lives in a general context of love and support, the impact of a one-time trauma has some cushioning. However, such events—even for children who are loved and supported, even if the events are sudden and brief, even in children as young as two, even if not talked about—seldom are forgotten. They leave behind unmistakable memory traces that show up in fears, games, or play activities in which the child reenacts the terrible event. And they show up in dreams.

"Childhood trauma," Terr writes in her book *Too Scared To Cry*, "sets horrible images, once and for all, into the mind's circuitry. These horrid pictures will 'run' by day, unconsciously impelling silent musings, fantasies, physical discomforts, actions and play. But the pictures will also 'run' by night (in the R- and X-rated versions), propelling the kind of dreams that, as Macbeth says, 'murder sleep.'"

Having these highly charged images in the memory bank means that new experiences, even minor ones, that evoke feelings of fear and powerlessness will produce echoes of these earlier images for a long, long time to come, perhaps even for a lifetime. The adult view of childhood as a time of innocence and freedom from worldly cares is nostalgic, shaped more by wishful thinking than by reality.

Bad things happen in the lives of many, perhaps most, children. Parents are struck down, cars crash, pets die, lightning strikes, children are physically abused.

What happens to children whose daily lives are tinged by violence, who must learn early on to be wary of untended packages in public places, who lose friends or relatives to random bombings of buses or churches, who return from school to find their homes destroyed by missiles, who are dragged from bed by air raid sirens and strapped into gas masks by frightened parents, who are on their school playground when a deranged man splays bullets into the crowd?

One clue comes from studies of their dreams. Yoram Bilu of the Hebrew University of Jerusalem studied more than 2000 dream reports from 11- to 13-year-old Jewish and Arab children living in towns, villages, refugee camps, and other settings in Israel and the West Bank. He found an overabundance of aggression and violence and a paucity of friendliness. Nearly every other Arab child and every fifth Jewish child reported at least one dream of an encounter with the other side.

In more than 200 such dreams, the children typically perceived themselves as victims of aggression, usually initiated against them by adults. The aggression usually involved high levels of violence, with assailants, both initiators and retaliators, seeking to inflict physical injury and death on their adversaries. The typical encounter dream of Jewish children, for example, involved an Arab terrorist attack. The Arab children dreamed of themselves as victims of terror and violence, mainly instigated by Israeli soldiers. For both groups of children, the dream attacks often took place in locations normally deemed safe, such as the child's home, neighborhood, or school, without the protective presence of the child's parents or other adults. Both Jews and Arabs were depicted in each other's dreams in stereotyped fashion, stripped of both individuality and humanness. "Since today's preadolescent dreamers are the politicians and soldiers of the coming decades, these firm, well-established schemes and images, if taken seriously," Bilu writes, "bode ill for the stability and persistence of the conflict."

External events are horrific enough. When the attack on personal integrity or survival comes from someone close, like a parent or teacher, or when it defines the child as basically bad, unlovable, or a nonperson, the child's sense of self-esteem is compromised so severely that the dream program of the self may be seriously damaged.

San Francisco psychologist Patricia Garfield asked 13 girls, aged 13–20, to describe their "worst dreams." All were victims of severe sexual abuse at the hands of their fathers or other male adults taking the father's place. Not surprisingly, the most common dream theme was that of being attacked, and the most common emotions in dreams were helplessness and terror. One child, abused by both her stepfather and her mother's ex-boyfriend, reported this dream:

"After X molests me, he gets my mom and my brother and me and takes us outside to this big shoe. It has a cannon in it and he takes my mother and puts her in the cannon and shoots her out. And I have to watch him KILL my mother. The same with my brother and then he does it to me."

After her stepfather molested her, another child had asked to live with her biological father. She dreamed:

"I am back home with my mom and stepfather, and my real father came to the house to talk with them. After a while he comes out and tells me I can't come down because he doesn't want me. My stepfather just laughs."

The child's dream, Garfield says, reflected her fear that telling would expose her to ridicule and rejection.

Several of the girls found ways to cope with their nightmare demons. One, when she dreamed of being knifed in the armpit, saw herself being rushed to a hospital. In her dream, she reported:

"I almost died, but I hung on for my boyfriend and my sister."

Another girl, with recurrent dreams about being chased by a huge, wild cat, finally dreamed the beast hugged her, promised to protect her, and then turned into her mother.

Abused children, Garfield points out, need guidance to find the positive signs of strength in their dreams. She asked one girl how she could improve a dream of falling, breaking her back, and dying. The girl replied, "I could just break my back and not die." This type of answer, Garfield says, is in stark contrast to those of nonabused children, who invent rescuing helicopters or Superman saviors.

WHEN CHILDHOOD DREAMS LAST INTO ADULTHOOD

Bad dreams may "go underground" as we grow older, but they often resurface in times of trouble. Patti, an attractive and talented woman in her late twenties, a professional singer, came to see me seeking relief from her lifelong nightmares. Patti reported that she moaned, screamed, or awakened crying at least four times a week, often more than once a night. Pert and athletic, Patti looked as healthy and happy as a breakfast food ad. But all was not well with her emotionally.

Patti remembered having nightmares when she was a child. They scared her so much that she would run to her parents' bedroom and crawl into their bed. The nightmares continued throughout her brief, unhappy marriage, driving her husband to sleep on the couch. Patti now was sharing an apartment with another woman. Patti had a boyfriend but was afraid to sleep with him for fear her nighttime noises would frighten him and drive him away.

As a singer, Patti had an unpredictable work schedule and traveled frequently. People in hotel rooms near hers sometimes called the management to report sounds of a woman being attacked, a frequent theme of Patti's nightmares. Often she awakened whimpering, drenched in sweat, with her heart pounding. These were some recent dreams Patti remembered:

My dog was shot.

Someone was being suffocated in the next room.

A dog was biting off my hands.

I was being held captive in a small room, like a closet, being made to perform acts of prostitution and told if I got pregnant I would have to perform my own abortion.

I'm a soldier. I lost my rifle. We were supposed to pull out, but I didn't want to go without my rifle. The rest of the troops left. I never found it, and now I'm accused of treason for having deserted my troops.

The dimensions in Patti's dreams—male/female, danger/safety, guilt/innocence, helpless/capable—come up on the disturbing side. They reflect her confusion over her sexual identity, concerns about being attacked, and feelings of shame and powerlessness. Where do such dreams come from in such a pleasant, seemingly normal woman?

Patti was an adopted child. Her own mother and father never married. Patti did not know her father's name. Patti's mother had lived with her brother and his wife during her pregnancy. She left town soon after Patti was born, prematurely and weighing only three pounds. Patti's aunt and uncle, who already had an adopted son, adopted her. Later, they had a child of their own, another girl.

Patti learned to call her biologic mother "aunt" and her

adoptive parents, "mother" and "father." No one ever spoke to Patti about the circumstances of her birth, but conversations that stopped when she entered the room, mysterious glances between adults, and other hints convinced her quite early in childhood that something having to do with her was wrong. By the time she was in grade school, she had pieced the story together herself, although she knew that she was not supposed to talk about it. It was the first secret burden she assumed.

Patti's mother later married and had other children. So Patti had half-sisters and half-brothers who viewed her as a more distant relative. No wonder she had some identity confusion. Patti regarded herself as a child of sin, a view that damaged her self-esteem in a basic way early in her life.

In her adoptive family, Patti was the middle child. The family was working-class. Both her father and brother were alcohol and drug abusers. Patti's role in the family was that of the good child, her mother's pet.

"I am the only one to attend college. I put myself through and made something of myself," Patti said. However, she saw this role as a burden, one that meant she must succeed. Her brief early marriage was a disaster. She was a big disappointment to her husband who told her she was "stupid" and "not sexy enough." According to Patti, he wanted a garter-belted seductress who would dance on the tabletop. What he got was Doris Day.

Patti's self-confidence was so damaged in this marriage that she had an affair with a married man. She felt she had to prove to herself that she was a sexually attractive woman. She had never told her husband about the affair and still felt guilty about it. She was afraid she would lose her boyfriend, Frank, should he find out—another guilty secret about herself.

Patti spent two nights in our sleep laboratory. We didn't disturb her during the first night, but she showed a typical picture of dream anxiety with many awakenings interrupting each of her REM periods.

The second night we taped a switch to Patti's palm. We asked her to make a fist when she was having a bad dream. When she pressed the switch, it made a mark on her recording chart, alerting us to awaken her to report what had been going through her mind. That night, she had two bad dreams.

Dream 1

I met an older man in a bar, a heavyset guy. He wanted to dance. I thought one dance won't hurt, but then I couldn't get away. He followed me to my room, came in, and started to beat me.

Dream 2

This involved my dog Toto, a great dog, a great companion, I've had him for five years. He was being attacked by giant bugs in armor, and huge tarantulas and scorpions. I was scared, I was panicked, but I knew that if I could not control my panic, I would not be able to save Toto. It would be my fault if he died.

In reflecting on the first dream the next morning, Patti observed, "I'm always getting myself in bad situations. I have to learn how to say 'No' at the beginning." In examining the second, she said that she was deathly afraid of bees, particularly their "stingers." Her dream suggested that she feared that male sexuality would rob her of her "safe" substitute love—her dog.

After this night, Patti and I agreed that she should begin RISC therapy. She would bring in her notes of any remembered nightmares or dreams once a week, and we would try to uncover their meaning and deal with the problems they represented to her.

The first week Patti arrived with 10 dreams to discuss. In three, she was being attacked by a man and trying unsuccessfully to escape. In the others, she also focused on her own ineptitude or guilt about "messing up." In one, for example, she was about to be married, but there was something wrong with everything, including her dress. In another, she and Frank were having his parents over for dinner, but the house was a disaster and their dinner a real mess. Her dreams showed she couldn't trust men or herself to carry out marital roles successfully.

Perhaps the most revealing dream of this first week was this one:

My ex-husband and another man were threatening to go through all my belongings looking for information. I had hidden a paper in my hand and was trying to keep it from them. I woke up feeling I should tell my boyfriend about my affair. The other man in the dream was my brother.

Her guilt about her affair, her fears of "messing up" in her new relationship, helplessness in the face of male intrusion into her life space, sexuality coupled with aggression, and the presence of her brother in the last dream, all combined to suggest the type of help Patti needed with her dreams.

Behind each dream is its historical background, the memories of previous unsuccessful attempts at solving crises that undermined Patti's sense of security and self-esteem. These memories and the feelings connected with them were the roots of Patti's nightmares. Every dream showed failed attempts to solve problems. Patti's first dream dimensions centered around these issues: guilty/innocent, attacking/attacked, helpless/helping, masculine/feminine, hidden/exposed.

Patti's second therapy session was less productive. She brought in fewer dreams to discuss, and these dreams frightened her less. Why? During the week between her first and second sessions, she took some direct action on her own. She told Frank about her affair. He accepted it with understanding, relieving her of one of her dark secrets. But that was only the beginning. After that immediate relief, she had two terrible nights and awakened crying one time with what she called an incest dream.

My brother was threatening me about never seeing my family again. He was going to blackmail me with something that was in a letter that I had written that revealed incest.

Once the guilt about her real adult affair abated, a third guilty secret had surfaced, one she had worked hard to keep secret even from herself. Why was her brother threatening to cut her off from the family? Patti thought that this dream related to an event, maybe a dream, maybe something real, that happened when she was small. She remembered feeling her brother's hand inside her pajama panties. She believed he came into her room while she slept, knelt beside the bed, and felt her under the covers. She told her mother at the time, but still was not sure if it was a true experience. In her dream, she linked this early incest memory to letters that exposed her recent sexual guilt. These referred to the letters she had sent to, and had received from, the married man with whom she had an affair. She had been so afraid that her husband would find them that she had shredded them.

I suspected the childhood "incest" experience may have been only a sexually stimulated dream, a fantasy, perhaps through identification with her birth mother. It permitted her to escape having to acknowledge her sexual impulses by shifting them to her brother. Now, in adulthood, she still projected her sexual feelings onto dirty old men who chased her. Until she could accept herself and her own impulses, how could she ever have a normal sexual love relationship?

Patti's early identification of herself as a child of sin and the refusal of her adoptive parents to disclose the facts of her birth were the likely sources of her early childhood nightmares. Her parents allowed her to sleep with them when she had nightmares, possibly heightening the forbidden sexual stimulation and leaving her further confused and conflicted about her sexual identity. No wonder she saw herself as forced to be a prostitute or as a soldier who has lost her rifle—a man without a penis—guilty of treason to her own sex.

As we worked on her dreams, Patti came to these conclusions on her own. Our work together went smoothly and quickly. The negative dimensions in her dreams gave way to positive ones. The nightmares subsided. After only eight weeks of RISC therapy, ordinary dreams began to take their place. One report:

I dreamed I was watching myself dancing a ballet and receiving flowers and applause for a good performance.

This is a successful dream in which her sex role is clearly feminine and okay.

I dreamed I went back to my old house to see if my ex-husband had another girl living with him.

Patti said she hoped this dream would come true. It would relieve her of feeling further responsibility for disappointing her husband sexually if he now had a new partner.

Patti hoped Frank would propose marriage. She wanted children of her own before it was too late. Frank was several years younger than she, which made him safer for her. She felt more mature and in charge, but he was in less of a hurry than she. She told me if he didn't propose soon, she would.

Patti never managed to stop a dream of being attacked and helpless while the dream was in progress. She began to dream, however, that she could be a competent helper rather than a victim. She successfully activated images of having a more desirable role. One example:

I dreamed about some girls running down the road noticing a car accident and a man lying on the side of the road bleeding. I gave orders and yelled for help. I gave him CPR. Blood was all over the place. I held his hand and wouldn't let him look in the mirror.

In her dream, she saw that men, too, may be vulnerable. She could be the strong one.

None of these dreams evoked moaning or woke her in terror. In all of them she behaved competently and carried through successfully what she wanted to do. After this session, we had a break for a month of vacation time. She and Frank spent the time together. When she returned, we had two more sessions. Frank had proposed. He and Patti set a wedding date. Patti was calmer, less fidgety. Her only remaining uncomfortable dreams were those in which her former husband came to reclaim her. She felt she could cope with her feelings about him, however. She had settled many issues from the past and looked forward to the future. She had accepted herself as a feminine, sexual, good person with happy dreams and peaceful nights.

Could Patti have accomplished all this by herself? Probably not. She needed to work with someone because her problems had started so very early in her childhood. Yet she changed a lot in only 10 sessions. Patti's success was possible because she also had many strengths. She had good coping skills. She had put herself through college, worked at a job she liked, had a close relationship with her adoptive mother, made friends easily, and kept them. Her nightmares focused on one problem: her self-esteem rested on being "good" and thus precluded sexuality. We concentrated our work on reshaping her self-image around this issue, helping her to see that it was all right for her to feel and be a sexual woman.

Beth, another woman who came to our sleep center seeking relief from bad dreams, also suffered a childhood trauma that undermined her sense of competence and self-esteem. At 39, Beth felt she had never been able to live up to her own potential. She had been a star pupil but held back from achieving all that she was capable of doing. She had never completed her graduate studies.

"I feel like I'm on a side track, that I've been 'blowing it' and will die unfulfilled," she told me. She could not settle on a direction or even identify the problem. She lived alone, never married, and recently had started to drink heavily. "No one will ever love me," she said. "Something is wrong with me." Why did she sell herself short?

Beth told me about her early years. Her parents were never happy, she said, but waited to divorce for her sake until she was 24. She was her father's girl and was never close to her mother. Once the divorce was final, her mother left the state and her father quickly remarried. She lost them both. What she saw as her father's desertion hurt the most.

In her first treatment session, Beth related a classic dream of helpless passivity.

I was off on a wrong road. Trying to turn, I got stuck in the mud. I had to go in another direction, but the road was impassable and I couldn't see how to get back.

I asked her to record her dreams for us to work on together and told her how to look for their dimensions. She brought two dreams to our second session:

Dream 1

I visited my mother in a nursing home. I pulled back the curtain, and she was excited to see me. I told her I came a long way to see her. She couldn't hear me. I shouted to her, but still she was deaf to what I was saying. It was frustrating. I couldn't get through to her.

Dream 2

I was in church. It was my responsibility to read the scripture, but I was in the wrong position to be heard. I was at the back of the church without a microphone. I paused to figure out what to do. The priest didn't realize I wasn't through and went on with the service, leaving me frustrated.

These two dreams unlocked a host of memories for Beth. Her father was a church pastor. One day when she was about 10 years old, her mother told her they were going to drive around to find Beth's father. Beth recognized that something was terribly wrong. She begged her mother to tell her what was happening. The mother made her promise never, never, to tell, to keep the secret to her grave: Her father was having an affair. They were going to track him down. Beth was very upset.

When Beth and her mother returned home, Beth ran to her room and cried and cried. Just before her father came home, her mother told her she must stop crying immediately and never let him know she knew about the affair. She must never talk to him about it or show her feelings of betrayal to him. From that time on, Beth froze into silence and immobility. She became unable to communicate, to feel, to dare to be herself.

"What could you do to change these dreams, to make them come out better?" I asked her. For the nursing home dream, she settled on using a nonverbal way to get through to her mother. She would hug her and give her a little pinch. That would get her attention!

For the church dream, she decided that she would walk down the aisle toward the front, reading as she went. Then the priest would see her and hear her. This decision melted the ice with which Beth had surrounded her emotions when her mother had insisted she deny her feelings. Tears poured from Beth in every session.

As Beth planned more assertive action in her dreams, she began to apply the lessons to the rest of her life. She left her deadend job and went back to school to start a new doctoral degree. She felt sure that this time she could express herself freely and enjoy being herself. Her dream dimensions—being silent/speaking up, being betrayed/being supported, feeling frozen/feeling free—were now all on the positive side.

Both Patti and Beth grew up with images of themselves as bad in ways they couldn't fix. Patti moaned at night as she pictured men attacking her. Her illegitimate birth made her feel ashamed and vulnerable to sexual abuse. She was so inhibited sexually that her husband divorced her, leaving her with a sense of failure and worsening her already low self-esteem. Understanding her dreams helped her to acknowledge that her sexuality was an acceptable part of her life and to act on this new self-image with a new partner.

Beth saw that acting on feelings could be dangerous. Her father's action upset her mother and threatened the marriage. Her mother's injunction against talking crippled Beth's initiative. Better not to act at all than take a chance on saying or doing the wrong thing.

Changing the self-image in dreams frees the mind to imagine better ways to be; it gives permission for positive action and the communication of feelings. Patti learned to see herself as a helper to others in her dreams, and Beth learned to speak up. The changes they made in working with their dreams increased their confidence and empowered them to act in new ways in their waking lives. A little dream success made a lot of difference for both of these young women.

⇨ SELF-HELP: Helping children to learn from their dreams

The dreams that we remember are those that stir up strong feelings. These dreams often involve a real sense of threat to the self. This threat may be an internal one, like Brian's that his sexual feelings were not acceptable. In the earliest dreams we remember, the threat usually is external.

When children first learn that not all adults are benign or that even parents can become hostile at times, they create monsters, giants, and witches to give form to their fears. They may dream of being chased, trapped, or attacked, while remaining powerless to help themselves. In such dreams, they are dealing with their sense of vulnerability, which for children, because they are smaller and weaker than adults, is a real issue. Some people keep these early images in their active dream repertoire and replay them in various forms later in life whenever they feel helpless.

In book after book, writer/illustrator Maurice Sendak brings us face to face with creatures who roam through dreamland. "The night Max wore his wolf suit and made mischief of one kind and another," Sendak tells us in *Where The Wild Things Are*, he was sent to bed without his supper. In his dream, Max journeys through night and day to join toothy, large-clawed monsters in a wild, wordless rumpus. He discovers that he is the most wild thing of all. Sendak's *In the Night Kitchen* follows Mickey, a young boy who tumbles out of bed and into the clutches of three hefty Oliver Hardy-lookalike bakers who mix him into their batter. The irrepressible Mickey fashions an airplane out of bread dough and makes his escape.

Common problems we all face in growing up—learning to protect ourselves from physical injury, coping with hostility, learning to live with our own upsetting feelings—fuel the creation of our early dream images. We cannot shield all children from accidents, from injuries, from pain, from war, but we can be alert to the dreams that traumatic events leave behind, the sad self-stories that need better endings.

We can encourage our children to share their dreams, and especially their nightmares. We can familiarize ourselves with how they handle the common problems that we expect to show up in the dreams. If they are falling, we can help them learn to fly or build haystacks to blunt the impact of a fall. If monsters chase them, we can teach ways to tame the savage beasts. Sendak's Max tames the wild things with the magic trick "of staring into all their yellow eyes without blinking once."

Some children relate their dreams better by acting them out or drawing them than they do by using words. In her book *Nightmare Help*, Anne Wiseman suggests using drawings to help your child master the conflicts the dream expresses. Once the monster is down on paper, you can encourage the child to draw a cage around it, for example, or add helpers to the picture. Children need to know they don't have to face their troubles all alone. Asking, "What can you do to make this dream come out better?" can help your child develop positive coping strategies.

Wiseman reports that her own son had bad dreams about their house burning down. Her husband suggested to the boy that next time he had one of these dreams, he put the fire out. One morning the boy came to breakfast full of excitement. He did it. He put the fire out! When his parents asked him how, he said proudly, "I peed on it." They may have traded one nighttime problem for another!

One of my patients told me she had repeated nightmares of being trapped in a burning building from age three on. These dreams started after a real incident. She and a small friend were playing with a doll and arguing about who should get to hold the toy. Her father, who was raking leaves and burning them nearby, became irritated with the children's wrangling. He grabbed the doll and threw it on the fire. Only in adulthood, after suffering from this nightmare for decades, did this woman find a solution. She learned to levitate in her dreams, to escape the fire by floating away.

As Terr's studies show, being young and vulnerable when

trouble strikes can damage one's sense of security that all is well. For children wounded by trauma, there are few good nights and sweet dreams. They need to talk about their nightmares, to express their fears, and to learn to counteract them with images of successful coping.

Prevention is far better than treatment. Dreams are a wonderful resource for parents to use to assist their children to build a firm identity. Children need to feel their dreams are interesting and understandable and that if their dreams are frightening, they can share them and get the help they need to handle the feelings the dreams express. Regular dream checkups, much like medical and dental checkups, can help children stay well. Try this family activity: Make dream sharing part of a weekend morning breakfast. Have a scariest dream day, a happiest dream day, a best-ever dream day, and enjoy sharing the stories dreams have to tell.

While it is possible to repair a damaged self-image later in life, to activate alternate scenarios that represent the positive sides of a person's dream dimensions, and to strengthen the likelihood of using these new images to create new dreams with healthier responses to future crises, the task takes longer and is tougher than creating a strong self-image in childhood.

13

When Dreams Don't Work
the Way They Should

OH MY GOD, I think I just killed two people," Kenneth
James Parks told Toronto police officers. He had stum-
bled into their station, with blood dripping from multiple
deep wounds in his hands, just before 5 a.m., on May 24, 1987.
Police found his mother-in-law stabbed to death, and his
father-in-law, bleeding profusely, alive but unconscious, in
their home a block away.

Parks' hands were so severely cut that police had to stop
taking his statement and drive him to a hospital when his confused state cleared enough for him to begin to feel the pain.
The surgeon who repaired the wounds called them "defen-
sive." Police deduced that Parks had grappled with his mother-
in-law for control of the kitchen knife he had used to kill her.

At his trial, Parks claimed that he had gone to sleep in his
own home, 14 miles away, and awakened only after the murder.
He had no memory of driving to his in-laws' home or of the
event itself. I was one of two sleep specialists who interviewed
Parks and helped prepare his defense. We concluded that he
had been sleepwalking and in a confused state at the time. We
thought it was the only reasonable diagnosis. There was no

other medically acceptable explanation. The jury judged him not guilty by reason of sleepwalking and acquitted him.

Parks' case is an extreme example of what happens when the dream system fails. The line between sleeping and waking blurs. The sleeper is propelled from bed—pulled, it seems, by some strong sense of being threatened. He is partly awake, partly asleep. He often acts violently and without conscious thought. So far, we have explored bad dreams that follow bad experiences and sometimes disrupt sleep for many years; now we look at the far end of the spectrum, the equivalent of volcanic eruptions on the surface of sleep. Our appreciation for how dreams serve to maintain emotional equilibrium in our lives comes in part from seeing what happens when dreams don't work the way they should.

Parks was the first person in Canada to win acquittal for murder with a sleepwalking defense. The case is not over, however. As this book was being written, prosecutors were appealing the case before the Supreme Court of Canada.

Parks' case, while exceptionally rare, is not unique. The medical literature contains reports of more than 30 similar cases, dating back to 1859 when Esther Griggs threw her baby out the window. Dazed with sleep, she thought that her house was on fire. She was trying to save her child's life. A passing constable who was an eye witness gave a convincing account of her behavior to a grand jury.

SLEEPWALKING

While sleepwalkers only rarely display violence toward others, they frequently harm themselves, by crashing into furniture, for example, or falling out of windows. Along the way, they acquire bruises, cuts, and broken bones. Young sleepwalkers usually show poor coordination and clumsiness, but as adults, they sometimes accomplish feats that require considerable dexterity, such as knotting a tie or driving a car. Often they engage in automatic behaviors, such as opening and closing a drawer or turning a faucet on and off over and over.

These acts are idiosyncratic, but sleepwalkers tend to repeat themselves on future occasions. Sleepwalkers who eat when they make their rounds often make their way back to the refrigerator, for example. And they often eat ordinarily unpalatable foods, such as raw bacon or packaged cookie mix. Some eat strange combinations of foods. Sleep specialist Neil Kavey of Columbia University has a patient who makes sandwiches by putting candy bars between two pieces of bread. Many of the night eaters are people who are dieting during the day. They can't understand why they are not losing weight and profess surprise over finding a mess in the kitchen or food wrappings in the bedroom.

Sleepwalkers are not acting out their dreams. Indeed, sleepwalking occurs during a partial arousal from the deepest stage of NREM sleep, usually about an hour after the start of sleep, before REM sleep begins. Sleep specialist Roger Broughton of Ottawa General Hospital, who played a key role in Parks' defense, first described this phenomenon in 1968. Recent studies show that brain activity during sleep can be quite complex. In fact, rapid shifts to and from sleeping, waking, and dreaming, may account for many of the bizarre behaviors described here.

Despite the complicated acts some people perform while sleepwalking, the ability to control what one does in this state is severely limited, Broughton says. "It is impossible, for instance, that a person could formulate a plan before falling asleep and then carry it out while sleepwalking," he said in testimony at Parks' trial.

SLEEP TERRORS

Sleepwalking, along with behavior such as sitting up or mumbling a word or two, represents the mild end of a spectrum of abnormal arousals that may disrupt sleep. At the more severe end are sleep terrors, sudden arousals with blood-curdling screams or crying, often accompanied by signs of intense fear. Both sleepwalking and sleep terrors are quite common in preadolescent children, so common in fact that doctors consider them within the range of normal. About 15% of all three- to nine-year-olds walk or cry out in their sleep, typically only once every few weeks but sometimes as often as several times a week. Most episodes of sleepwalking last less than 15 minutes. By contrast, parents report that episodes of sleep terrors often last much longer, sometimes more than an hour.

Sleepwalkers usually are quiet. Occasionally, sleep terrors cause a child to scream first and then run or flail about, as if trying to avoid some terrible threat. Such episodes are most likely to occur when a child is overtired, has a fever, or is taking medication that affects the central nervous system.

During sleep terrors, an agitated, screaming child may be difficult, if not impossible, to console. He or she may misperceive a parent's attempts to provide comfort, becoming even more distraught, even hysterical. The child's eyes may be open, but the child stares glassy-eyed rather than focusing. A sleepwalking child may stumble about, trying to find the bathroom, and sometimes mistake a waste basket or a closet for the toilet. If awakened, the child may be confused and disoriented. Since children do not remember these episodes at all the next day, they have a hard time believing the stories others tell about them.

Both activities run in families. With no specific treatment, most children gradually outgrow these behaviors by the time they are teenagers. There are no lasting consequences, although these episodes may disrupt the rest of the family's sleep and increase stress in the home. If frequent, they also may interfere with sleeping at a friend's house, attending overnight camp, or going on family trips.

Parents brought their 12-year-old son to our sleep center

because the boy had walked to a friend's house in his pajamas, with bare feet, in the winter at midnight. He knocked on the door and asked the astonished parents if his friend could come out and play. The boy's memory started only when his friend's parents asked him if he knew what time it was.

Perhaps one or two of every 100 adults still sleepwalks occasionally, once or twice a year. A smaller number starts to sleepwalk or to experience sleep terror attacks in adulthood. Sometimes, severe psychological stress serves as the trigger. One has only to think of Lady Macbeth. However, the cause usually is a subtle one.

One of my adult patients, Ben, fractured his spine and punctured a lung in a fall from a second-story window. He was sleeping alone on a hot summer night without pajamas. He said he "woke up" to feel dampness under him. He was yelling, "Help! Someone help me." His neighbors were calling out of their windows to ask, "What happened?" and "Are you all right?"

Ben found he was lying naked on his back in a pool of blood, with no idea of how he came to be outside on the ground. He got up and went inside the building, walked upstairs, and found the door to his apartment locked. When his roommate did not respond to his knocking, he rang his neighbor's door bell to ask him to phone his roommate. All of these events took place before he began to feel pain. Ben remembers that it was 12:03 A.M. on his digital clock when he went to bed, and it was 12:36 A.M. when paramedics arrived to take him to the hospital, where he stayed many weeks recovering. Whatever led to his accident happened within the first half hour of sleep before dreaming began.

Ben told me that he had yelled in his sleep since his late teens. In these earlier episodes, he often had an image of being locked in a supermarket freezer with the walls coming in on him.

Why did he get out of bed that night? In the sleep laboratory, brainwave recordings show that both sleepwalkers and those who have sleep terrors have trouble shifting from the first long, deep NREM sleep period into the active sleep of REM. Outside noises, such as a door slamming or a car alarm going off suddenly, may trigger abrupt, but only partial, arousals from deep sleep. So can an internal stimulus such as an overfull bladder. Both children and adults who experience sleep terrors or who walk in their sleep often are late bedwetters.

Activities that intensify the first deep-sleep episode of the night may further promote these arousals. These include a day of heavy exercise or a few nights of sleep loss. Extra deep sleep at the beginning of the night seems to heighten the pool of feelings being prepared for expression in dreaming. In the same circumstances, the ordinary sleeper may have a nightmare in the first REM period. However, those who have difficulty shifting into REM sleep may wet the bed or embark on some bizarre activity. There are plenty of cases of sleepwalkers jumping out of a window to escape some threat, fighting someone they imagine is attacking them, or trying to rescue someone they believe to be in danger.

One of my patients, a 24-year-old man, lifted his waterbed, a huge dead weight, believing that his nephew was trapped underneath. Another time, the same man ripped the wooden framework off his windows to free his sister and brother-in-law whom he believed to be buried in the wainscotting. His strange nocturnal activity began some eight years earlier, after he and a friend saved two children from drowning. During this life-and-death crisis, he, too, was badly frightened. He continued to repeat his act of rescue in his sleep, but he didn't dream it; he acted it out. Another of my patients dragged his wife out of bed to save her from an illusory fire.

In explaining their nocturnal performances, such people often say that they have to take some extreme action to avoid being crushed or smothered. They typically describe themselves as deep sleepers. Their effort to break out of a deeper than normal sleep gives rise to the imagery of a weight that is holding them down. This effort may trigger acts of violence. Most of them have smashed objects, often injuring themselves severely enough to require surgery. Many have hurt others, often those they loved most dearly.

Kenneth Parks was too upset to sleep the night before he murdered his mother-in-law. He had been gambling on horse races and losing money, as his wife discovered when he forged her name to a check. In an attempt to cover his debts, he embezzled $32,000 from his employer and lost that at the track, too. His employer discovered the theft and fired him, adding to his woes. Although he had promised to make restitution, he had no clear idea of how he was going to do it.

Parks had not yet told his in-laws about his troubles, but he knew his wife had spoken to them. He and his wife had planned to visit her parents the next day, to talk about the situation, announce his commitment to seeking treatment with Gamblers Anonymous, and reassure the in-laws that he would work hard to settle his debts. We can imagine his confusion over how to proceed, his guilt about his behavior, and his fears of being humiliated when he confessed his misdeeds.

As Parks' gambling debts mounted, he became more and more secretive and withdrawn, more and more depressed. He didn't share his wretched feelings with his wife. He hadn't slept well in months, and the little sleep he did get was fitful, light, and short. His wife often went to bed without him, while he stayed downstairs watching television long after midnight.

There was one more factor: The day preceding the murder, Parks played rugby for the first time in many months. Because he was out of shape, this workout left him physically exhausted. The last thing that he remembers clearly from the night of the murder was seeing the end of *Saturday Night Live*. He finally fell asleep on the living room couch.

We suspect that on the night Parks killed his mother-in-law, he fell into a long, deep sleep, longer and deeper than his normal pattern, a kind of catch-up sleep. He was in panic about his debts and in turmoil over having to go and face his in-laws next day with no certain plan of how to make good. The strength of these feelings, and perhaps some outside noise, even from a television show, must have broken through the restraints of sleep and roused him...but only partially.

He had fallen asleep wearing the jogging pants and T-shirt he intended to wear to bed. He had on no socks or underwear. In his strange half-way state, he pulled on a windbreaker, picked up car keys, and left his house without locking the door. When he walked into the police station, his shoes were still untied. He cannot remember driving to his in-laws' house, a route he traveled frequently, or how he got in.

We assume that since he was not fully aware of what he was doing or why, he must have made enough noise upon entering to awaken the couple who were sleeping in a first-floor bedroom. Who or what he imagined them to be, he has no idea. He had no motive for killing them. Indeed, he was quite fond of them, and they of him. The in-laws were people of modest means. There was no money to be had from their deaths. They had no life insurance.

According to the scenario that the police reconstructed, the couple probably did not recognize their son-in-law in the dark. Or perhaps Parks rang the doorbell and roused his mother-in-law, who let him in. He then hit her with a tire iron. She ran to the kitchen and grabbed a knife to protect herself. Meanwhile, Parks moved on to the bedroom. His father-in-law awakened to find hands around his throat. Parks choked the man until he was unconscious.

Presumably Parks and the older woman struggled for possession of the knife, with him grabbing it by the blade and slicing his hands to the bone. In the process, he killed her. He then returned to the bedroom and stabbed his father-in-law. Parks, 23 at the time of the murder, was six foot five and weighed 280 pounds. Ordinarily, he was soft spoken and sweet-natured. Ironically, his mother-in-law had nicknamed him "The Gentle Giant."

That night, Parks' wife was asleep upstairs. She did not hear him leave the house. Parks has no memory of the events of that night from the time he fell asleep at home to the time he began to "wake up," 14 miles away in his in-laws' home, when he looked down at the face of a woman whom he saw as "needing help."

He heard the couple's younger children upstairs crying. Frightened awake by the noises of the attack, they had barricaded themselves in a bedroom. Parks walked up the stairs, leaving a trail of bloody handprints. He remembers calling, "Kids, kids," thinking he could reassure them. The children reported they heard only someone making grunting "animal noises." They escaped through a window and ran to a neighbor's house. Parks tried to use the phone to call the police, but his hands were too badly cut to manage it. He then drove around the corner to the local police station to get help.

Parks was devastated by the experience. When I met him in his jail cell nine months later, he still could not own up to the act. He kept trying to explain it to himself as being the work of some other person, an unknown intruder who preceded him to his in-laws' house. He knew there was evidence that he was the culprit, and he stared at his scarred hands as proof. Yet he had no way to explain any of the night's events to me or to himself.

Over and over as I interviewed him, he asked with real bewilderment, "Why would I do that, when I had everything to lose and nothing to gain?" Parks asked me tentatively if I could help him to get back the memory of this night. I asked him gently, "Would you want to?" He thought it over and said, "Only if you could take it away again."

Parks refused bail and waited in jail more than a year for his trial, because, he explained to me, he felt it was not safe for him to sleep at home with his wife and small child. "If I could do that once," he said, "I might do it again." Others who have acted violently while sleepwalking often express the same anguish. On calling to make an appointment soon after a violent sleepwalking episode, one man told me he had been drinking 17 cups of coffee at night to keep from falling into a deep sleep.

Several of Parks' cellmates and others in the same cell block confirmed that his sleep behavior was strange. He would sit up abruptly and shout out in sleep. The others often tried to rouse him by banging on the metal pipes, making enough noise to awaken others, but not Parks. Sleep specialist Broughton recorded Parks' sleep for two nights in a makeshift sleep laboratory at the jail while Parks awaited trial. These recordings show the typical pattern of the sleepwalker: An abnormally prolonged first deep-sleep cycle punctuated by abrupt arousals, instead of the normal smooth ascent from deep sleep through light sleep into REM sleep.

Many other experts also examined Parks. Psychologists, psychiatrists, and neurologists gave him multiple tests to try to discover some explanation for his bizarre act. None found any evidence of a mental disorder, a seizure disorder, or any other neurological problem. Only his family history offered pertinent clues, a strong line of relatives who were bedwetters or sleepwalkers.

Plato, writing in *The Republic* in the fourth century B.C., said, "In all of us, even in good men, there is a lawless wild-beast nature which peers out in sleep." Sigmund Freud saw dreams as a safety valve that relieved the tensions generated by our unacceptable, unconscious wishes, allowing us to stay asleep. Sometimes, Freud acknowledged, this process fails, "when the unconscious jars upon the preconscious so violently that it is unable to continue sleeping."

While Freud did not deal with the sleep terror experience, he spoke of bad dreams as attempts to master events we are unable to master in reality. Sleep terrors show us a breakdown of the usual order of sleep and dreams: Normally a day thought or experience related to an on-going concern stays active as we fall asleep. The feelings associated with the thought cue the network that holds memories related to these feelings. This network becomes active when we enter REM sleep.

If this sequence is interrupted before REM sleep occurs, we do not have the protective safety of muscle paralysis. If the raw feeling is overwhelming, it bypasses reason and goes straight to action. Terror attacks, which take place before dreams begin, help us see what is happening in the transition between waking and dreaming. The bridge between the two is feeling, often intense feeling stirred up by some crisis. Kenneth Parks had gambled away his own money and that of his employer. He had been fired. He had mortgaged his home. He was on the brink of losing his freedom and perhaps his wife, family, and home.

Sam, a man dying of an inoperable cancer, whom we met briefly in Chapter 9, jumped out of bed one night soon after falling asleep. Noise made by his son, who had come home late, must have aroused him, but he did not awaken fully. He thought his son was a giant, seven feet tall, who wanted to kill him. Sam ran to another room, grabbed his World War II souvenir Samurai sword and chased his son around the house. His wife kept shouting to him, "It's only a dream, Sam, only a dream." Luckily, she finally got through to him, and he awakened completely. Shocked at what he had done, he and his son embraced in tears.

Sam's spirits had plunged as his illness progressed. He had seriously considered suicide to resolve his feelings of guilt at "putting everyone through this hell." He felt out of touch with everyone, even himself. He described himself as feeling "a violent rage" inside. In his terror attack, this rage erupted from the safe confines of sleep.

Why did he see his beloved son as an enemy? Possibly only

because the boy was there and had made a noise that had disturbed his sleep. Perhaps also because the boy was young and healthy, while Sam was neither. In his hallucinatory state, Sam's feelings overwhelmed him, and, like Parks, he fought because he felt his life was in danger.

Sam was neither awake nor dreaming when this episode occurred. We deduce this from several facts: Sam could move;in fact, he ran. While dreaming, we have a profound loss of the ability to move the big muscles that we need for action. Another sleep disorder, known as REM Sleep Behavior Disorder, is an important exception to this generalization. Timing, however, remains an important distinction between that disorder, in which people act out their nightmares, and the confused actions that occur during sleep terrors.

Sleep terrors take place early in the night, soon after sleep starts. Attacks of REM Sleep Behavior Disorder occur later in sleep. Sam did not recognize his son and did not hear his wife for several minutes. His lack of responsiveness is characteristic of someone in deep sleep. People who are dreaming usually can be aroused fully just by calling their name. Finally, unlike the horror-filled tales of those acting out their nightmares, Sam's experience had no narrative. He had only the image of the giant, coupled with a strong feeling of panic and of the need to defend himself. Ken Parks said he had no images at all.

Freud suggests that our daytime preoccupations, like Sam's concern with his impending death, stir up a normal basic wish, in this case, to live longer. On the night of Sam's terror episode, the noise of his son returning home interrupted his sleep before he had a chance to dream about his feelings with safety. This noise startled him and propelled him out of bed as if to meet an emergency. The combination of the overwhelming feeling that he was going to die, plus the external noise, caused him to perceive mistakenly that his life was in immediate danger. It was pure feeling that drove Sam to attack. His dreamwork had no chance to design a way to cope with his fears of dying.

How often this kind of dangerous aborted dreaming occurs is hard to estimate. I personally have treated more than a dozen cases in the past few years. All were pleasant young men, in their twenties to early thirties, clean-cut and polite. Indeed, they often were overly polite. What they had in common usually is considered a virtue: trouble expressing their negative feelings. Not only did they not blow their tops, swear, slam doors, or get miserably unhappy during the day, they did not spend much time thinking about themselves, at least in ways they could communicate easily. They were, in a word, overcontrolled. They were doers, not thinkers. They all worked hard at ordinary jobs. They did what other people expected them to do, without complaints about their lives. Most were unusually large men, tall and well-developed, capable of forceful action, perhaps a reflection of exposure to elevated levels of growth hormone during adolescence. All had more than the usual amounts of deep sleep, the time when growth hormone is produced.

Most were under some unusual pressure when their sleep-walking or sleep terror episodes occurred. All of them came to our attention because one or more of these episodes got them into serious trouble. None had any recollection of what he had done. Only a few could tell me anything about what they believed to be happening that led them to behave in an extraordinary way. Here again, they reported perceiving that some extreme danger threatened themselves or a loved one. All had abnormally low amounts of REM sleep.

Richard Viano pleaded self-defense in the 1983 murder of his wife. He recounted the events of the evening to me this way: His wife came home late, about 11:30 P.M., from a club meeting. He was already asleep. He did not expect her to join him in bed because she had a bad cold and had slept in another room for the previous few nights.

"She jumped on me, I guess to surprise me," he said. "She always was a joker. The room was in complete darkness at the time. I startled up. I was not fully awake and did not recognize her." Viano, a big man, an archer with immensely strong arms, reacted as if his life were in danger. "I thought I was being attacked by an intruder," he said. "I grabbed her in a choke hold and threw her off the bed. I killed her."

His first thought was for his children's safety. He ran to their room to see if they were all right. Only then did he turn on his bedroom light and uncover the body tangled in the bed clothes. When he found that it was his wife, he sat bewildered on the edge of the bed and cried.

Viano said he'd been a deep sleeper his whole life. If suddenly aroused, he was confused. At his trial, his friends testified that once he was asleep, he was nearly impossible to awaken. When they camped out together for hunting or fishing trips, they tried yelling at him or pounding on him, usually to no avail. If they managed to rouse him, he was incoherent.

He spent four nights in our laboratory. We could not prove that he was an unusually deep sleeper, however. Being charged with murder may be enough to create the kind of anxiety that lightens anyone's sleep.

Was Richard Viano, like Sam and Kenneth Parks, in a crisis state? Yes, he was. Moreover, his predicament undermined the credibility of his defense: He had been having an extramarital affair. The woman involved testified that she had ended their sexual relationship some months before. Friends and family testified that they knew he had confessed the affair to his wife and that she had forgiven him, that indeed, the couple was planning to have another child. However, the jury refused to accept his plea of "accidental death." It convicted him of murder.

He was guilty of adultery, but murder? His psychological tests showed him to be a person with little insight or understanding of himself, a naive, "nice" young man, very much like Kenneth Parks. The killing occurred about an hour after he fell asleep, the usual time for the first deep sleep period. Those who are disoriented when suddenly aroused, or who respond with violence, suffer what sleep specialists sometimes call "sleep drunkenness." Unlike Parks, Viano had no history of sleepwalking, sleep terrors, or bedwetting.

Parks' acquittal frightened many people, including Parks himself. He asked me many times, "Will I do it again?" Fortunately, violence during sleep is rare. There are no recorded cases of anyone's committing a second murder while sleepwalking. What does he need to get over this crisis? We return to our four familiar factors: good friends, good genes, a good self-image, and good dreams. Except for his genes, which gave him a legacy of sleepwalking, Parks can work to overcome what he lacks. The specific advice that I gave him has worked well for him and can help others who arouse from sleep in confusion. The self-help section at the end of this chapter includes this advice.

REM SLEEP BEHAVIOR DISORDER

We've looked at individuals whose violence erupts during deep sleep, when there is no paralysis of the big muscles, those that control the arms and legs. Now let's turn to those who literally act out their dreams. It's important to keep in mind that muscles other than those needed for breathing and those that move the eyes normally are virtually paralyzed during REM sleep. You've probably seen a sleeping dog or cat make small twitches during sleep. Humans do that, too. Paralysis of the big muscles presumably is part of nature's grand design. It keeps us safely in bed. However, as we mentioned earlier, a few people are exceptions to this rule. They retain all or part of normal muscle tone even in REM sleep, sometimes with drastic consequences.

In his dream, one man trapped a deer that ran into his barn. He seized its head and started to break its neck. The "deer" turned out to be his wife, whose screams fortunately roused him. Another dreamed he was a football player, wearing a uniform and shoulder pads. Thinking he was charging an opponent, he lunged into the dresser in his bedroom and severely gashed his forehead. These are among the nearly 300 people with REM Sleep Behavior Disorder seen by University of Minnesota researchers Carlos Schenck and Mark Mahowald, who identified the problem in 1986.

People with REM Sleep Behavior Disorder often seriously injure themselves or others. A teenaged boy kicked his way through glass patio doors, reaping injuries that required two hours of surgery and nearly 200 stitches. One man, while in a hospital intensive-care unit for injuries sustained on a previous night, leapt out of bed and fractured a vertebra in his neck, narrowly escaping permanent paralysis. In desperation, another man ties himself to his bed every night. Others zip themselves into, and frequently tear their way out of, sleeping bags.

Curiously, people with this disorder often have similar dreams that involve being attacked or saving loved ones from attacks. While dreaming he was rescuing his drowning wife, one man dragged her around the bedroom by her hair. One man dreamed he dived off a sinking ship. He broke his nose on the bedside table.

In their waking lives, most of these people are not in crises. They are mentally healthy, easygoing, nonaggressive people. Their personalities are much like those of people who suffer sleep terrors in adulthood. Their nighttime behavior is out of keeping with their daytime actions. Although REM Sleep Behavior Disorder may occur even in young children, most of those who develop it are aged 50 and older. Perhaps a third have neurologic problems resulting from strokes and other degenerative diseases that cause loss of the protective control of muscle paralysis ordinarily occurring in REM sleep. Some also have life-long histories of abnormal sleep behavior, including yelling or flailing about. Clonazepam (brand name: Klonopin), a prescription medication that helps muscle relaxation, often is used to treat sleep terrors and violent behavior associated with sleepwalking. It keeps people safely in bed.

Confusional arousal may have played a role in yet another murder case, a controversial one that puzzled the minds of several judges and juries. It began October 4, 1980, when police found the nude body of Karen Anne Phillips, aged 24, in her Oak Park, Illinois, apartment. She had been raped and bludgeoned to death. Police determined that the murder had occurred between 1 and 3 A.M. the night before. They canvassed the area, telling neighbors that if they remembered anything unusual, "no matter how silly it might seem," to let them know.

Two days later, at the urging of his wife and friends, a man who lived two doors away from Phillips called police to report a horror-filled dream he'd had the night of the murder. Steven Paul Linscott told them he had dreamed of a young woman being beaten to death by a young man. A 27-year-old Bible college student, Linscott lived and worked as a counselor at a halfway house for ex-convicts. He said he thought his description of the man in his dream might help identify and catch the murderer.

Linscott met with detectives over the next several days, providing more than six hours of tape-recorded statements about his two-part dream. In the first part, a young woman opens her door to talk with a young blond man, who looks like a salesman. The man enters the apartment, holding something behind his back. They are standing in a living room with a couch and maybe a stereo. Suddenly, the man's expression turns "evil."

At this point in the dream, Linscott told the police, he awakened in distress. He got up and walked around his own apartment. Noting that it was 1:30 A.M., he then returned to sleep, where he "witnessed" the conclusion of the dream. Part of the story was missing, almost as if he left the room for a few minutes while the video of the dream kept going. His view, he said, now was over the shoulder of the murderer. He saw the man repeatedly raise his arm and strike the woman on the head with a blunt object. He counted 23 blows. She fell to her knees. There was a lot of blood.

The police said that Linscott's dream revealed how the crime most probably was committed, even to the number of blows. They prepared a sketch of the murderer, based on Linscott's description of the salesman in his dream. The sketch resembled Linscott himself, turning his dream into a living nightmare. Police said the dream included details only the killer could have known. They viewed it as a veiled confession. They arrested him and charged him with the murder.

Evidence presented at the trial included Linscott's dream report, expert testimony that Linscott's hair matched hair found in Phillips' apartment and on her body, and results of blood tests that did not exclude Linscott as a suspect. A jury found him guilty. He was sentenced to 40 years in prison.

No evidence was presented of any motive for the murder. In fact, there was no evidence that Linscott even knew the woman. He said he had no memory of leaving the apartment that night, and no one saw him on the street. There was no blood on any of his clothing. Fingerprints taken at the scene did not belong to him. However, there were no other suspects.

Linscott was freed on bail in 1985 pending the outcome of his appeal. In 1991, the Illinois Supreme Court ordered a new trial, ruling that prosecutors misrepresented the key physical evidence against him in their arguments to the jury. At issue were statements that Linscott's hairs "matched" those found at the crime scene and that results of the blood tests suggested a relatively small pool of suspects. The court said prosecutors implied this evidence was conclusive when it suggested only that Linscott could not be excluded as a suspect.

Did he really do it? Could he have walked out of his building and into another one, gained entrance to the apartment of a stranger late at night, brutally attacked her, and returned home without any awareness of what he had done? When I reviewed the case for the district attorney's office, I concluded that it was possible that he could have committed this crime in a confused state of consciousness, for which he had no memory.

Linscott was under a lot of pressure at the time. His grades were slipping in school, and he had financial problems at home and two young children to feed. He had taken up part-time door-to-door sales work to help make ends meet. Like Ken Parks, Linscott had been sleeping restlessly and having violent dreams, his wife reported. He got up so frequently at night that she had stopped taking note of this behavior. She could not tell the police whether or not he was in bed at the time of the murder.

Linscott's friends and fellow students rallied to his support, claiming that he is not the sort of person who could rape and murder. Certainly not when he is awake. However, unusual emotional states can prompt unusual nighttime acts and leave no memory behind. How else can we explain the dream? Coincidence? Clairvoyance?

These cases we've just reviewed show how much we need to have a regular cycle of dreams working across the night. When we don't dream, the monster feelings within us can get out and cause us to commit extreme acts. While the conscious mind lies asleep, our primitive instincts of flight or fight may put us or someone else in danger. Dreams cannot do their work if we get up and abort them.

⇨ SELF-HELP: Helping those with abnormal sleep-related behaviors

When abnormal sleep-related behaviors pose a danger to the sleeper or to others, it's wise to seek evaluation by a sleep specialist. You may obtain a list of specialists in your area by writing the American Sleep Disorders Association, 1610 14th Street N.W., Suite 300, Rochester, Minnesota 55901. If violence is included, sleep specialists commonly advise their patients and their patients' families to:

- Make the sleeper's bedroom safe. Remove potentially dangerous objects, secure balcony doors and windows, and install protective gates on stairways or use an electric eye to trigger an alarm. Aim to protect the person but not to block a fast exit in case of fire.
- Try not to awaken someone who is sleepwalking or in the throes of a sleep terror attack. If possible, gently guide the person back to bed, and stay nearby to be sure of their safety.
- Help the patient to avoid getting overtired. Encourage both children and adults to keep a regular sleep/wake schedule, with no exercise in the evening and no all-nighters. Avoiding fatigue will help minimize the odds of having an extra-long first deep-sleep cycle.
- Ask the doctor about medication. People with sleep terror attacks and REM Sleep Behavior Disorder may benefit from taking a muscle-relaxing medication, such as clonazepam (brand name: Klonopin), before sleep. This drug, which requires a prescription, lightens the first deep-sleep cycle and prevents the abnormal abrupt arousal before REM sleep. If a person progresses normally into REM sleep, then dreams will have more chance to do their work.

To these tips I add another:

- People with sleep terror attacks need to work with a good psychotherapist to learn to handle daytime tensions as they occur, to develop coping skills to work things out when awake, to share feelings with those close to them, and to discover what their dreams have to say. Those who find their dreams disturbing can use the RISC method to understand what's wrong and to make their dreams work out better.

14

Expanding Your
Dream Appreciation

*I*T'S BEEN NEARLY 100 YEARS since Freud told us to look through the window of dreams to see our inner lives. We've learned much about dreams since then, but most people still do not know how to integrate fully their sleeping and waking selves nor how to use their dreams for help in times of crisis: as a resource to illuminate the link between their most pressing current emotional concerns and all that has happened to them before.

For the first half of this century, the exploration of dreams was the province of specialists. Psychoanalysts used dream interpretation to help patients discover the motivation for their troubling behavior. In the 1950s, dreams moved from the privacy of the analyst's office to the more public arena of the sleep laboratory. Scientists began a rigorous study of when, where, and why dreams occur. This work yielded a road map through the night's mental landscape. Research showed that dreams are both regular and plentiful; we all dream three, four, or even five times a night, every night.

These sleep laboratory discoveries caught the fancy of the general public. On learning that their internal, all-night, free cinema provided a new film every 90 minutes, many people began to wonder how they could catch more of the shows. They wanted to know if missing out on remembering dreams robbed them of something of value for their everyday lives. Their interest prompted mental health professionals to develop guidelines to help people capture their dreams and understand what their dreams meant. The self-help revolution of the past two decades further heightened interest in using dreams to foster self-awareness and personal growth.

DREAM GROUPS

New York psychiatrist Montague Ullman was among the first to assert that working on dreams with a small group of other people can help us to understand ourselves better. While dreaming, Ullman says, we examine ourselves through a clear lens. However, when awake, we may look at the same situation through rose-colored glasses. Moreover, we're seldom aware that our vision is colored. The perspectives that others offer may help us to see our own dreams in a new way.

In their book *Working with Dreams*, Ullman and Nan Zimmerman show just how valuable group dreamwork can be. In one illustration of the group process, they start with this dream from Lillian, a young woman who recently returned from a skiing vacation:

"I was at a ski lodge. I was in one room and decided to go into the room next-door. It was a very large room. This room was very nice. It had lots of people in it who were having a good time. There were lots of goodies around and it was a big party. I thought to myself, 'Why didn't I get to this room before?' I walked out the back door and decided to ski. There was a mountain right behind me. I was by myself."

Following Ullman's procedure, a dreamer shares her dream, while the other members of the group listen and take notes. The dreamer then remains silent, listening carefully while other members of the group try to make the dream their own. They tell their feelings about what the dream would signify in their own lives if they had dreamed it. This practice often illuminates feelings that the dreamer has but has not yet recognized. Letting the group work on the dream's meaning before the dreamer does so, Ullman says, provides many more paths of investigation than would be likely if the dreamer shared her thoughts first.

Lillian's dream prompted numerous different feelings in the members of her group. Among them:

"I felt as if I were going off on my own and it took courage."

"I felt frightened about going into that large room."

"I wanted to be with the others but pulled away."

"I had a feeling of disappointment and envy as if it were too late."

Next, group members begin to work with the images in the dream, again treating them as if they were from a dream of their own. Ullman suggests people look at the images, not as literal statements, but as metaphors for some aspect of their lives. There is no right or wrong way to see these images, he stresses. We all use symbols in our own unique fashion. Moreover, even an idea that is way off target may help a dreamer to define more precisely what an image is not and thus get closer to figuring out what it is. In the case of Lillian's dream, these were among the various responses:

"The mountain suggests both struggle and accomplishment."

"Skiing is a lovely sport. I feel alone."

"The picture that comes to my mind is that of a sad waif,

pressing her nose against a store window and looking sadly at all the goodies beyond her reach."
"Someone got there first and spoiled it, as if I have an older sibling who got there first. I felt left out."

After hearing these thoughts, Lillian burst into tears. When she regained her composure, she shared with the group the feelings that the others' experience of her dream had evoked in her.

"When we started I had no idea what the dream was about, other than its connection to my recent ski vacation," she told them. "When you began talking about sadness, deprivation, and then mentioned sibling rivalry, everything suddenly fell into place and this terrible sadness came over me.

"My brother was with us on this vacation. He is 10 years older and he did get all the goodies. For the first time I felt the sadness of it all and the sense of loss.

"The other day a friend of mine who had just met my brother sized him up as a vulnerable guy. This shocked me," she continued. "I had always idolized him. My reactions to this led to the dream. I began to realize my friend was right and if I had only known this before it would have saved me a lot of pain. That big room in the dream was his room. I could see only the goodies.

"It was too threatening to me to see the vulnerability," she observed. "I had to walk away and embark upon my own lonely struggle. It's scary to go down the mountain alone."

In this last step in which the dreamer shares his or her feelings with the group, just as with RISC therapy, the dreamer is the final authority on what the dream means. The dreamer always is in control of how much to share and what to accept from others. The dreamer can stop work on the dream at any time. Often, the group work will provide the dreamer less with explanations than with ideas for further reflection. As a final step to a dream-sharing experience, members of the group will ask the dreamer questions, such as: "What did you feel like when ... ? Can you tell us more about ... ?" These questions also aim to prompt further exploration and to bridge the images in the dream with the waking events that stimulated them.

The group work stops when the dreamer is ready to stop. If successful, Ullman says, group members function as midwives. They bring the dream into the world. Once their job is over, the work of the one who gave birth to the dream begins in earnest. Group members, as well as the dreamer, benefit from the process, he says, and not simply in terms of learning to decode their own dreams better. The process of working on someone else's dream helps group members to see their own biases more clearly.

Some of the techniques developed for group dreamwork translate well to working on dreams on your own. If a dream's meaning proves elusive, for example, tell it to yourself in the third person. That will give you a little more distance and objectivity. It even may be useful to imagine your dream as someone else's dream and to think about the significance of that dream for this other person.

My concept of dream dimensions also would be a useful addition to group dreamwork. If working with Lillian on her dream, for example, I might ask her, "What's the opposite of 'large,' then 'nice,' 'good time,' 'goodies,' 'big,' and finally, 'delayed?'" Lillian's answers might help her to identify feelings of deprivation she developed as a younger sister who envied the privileges and possessions given to her older brother. I also might ask Lillian to pursue the opposites of "back," "alone," and "behind." She might then begin to think about her tendency to withdraw rather than to confront her jealousy and remorse.

I would sum up Lillian's dream this way: "I was small and late in coming to a place where I saw others having it better than I did, where they seemed to be enjoying themselves. But I backed out to go it alone." If Lillian arrived at this interpretation herself and found it distressing, she could apply the RISC method. The next step would be for her to devise ways to make the dream come out better and to try to incorporate them the next time she had a similarly disturbing dream.

Once you decide you're interested in working on your dreams with other like-minded people, the first challenge is to get started. Getting four to seven interested people together at the same time every week is not easy. Psychologist Gayle Delaney, who has led dream-study groups for 17 years, offers a step-by-step guide to her method of group dreamwork in her book *Breakthrough Dreaming*.

Her method differs somewhat from Ullman's, but the goal is the same: to enhance the dreamer's self-understanding and foster personal growth. In Delaney's groups, dreamers bring a written report of a dream to a group session and distribute it to the other members. After the dreamer tells a dream, with feeling, group members take turns at interviewing that person. Using a series of structured questions, they ask about the emotions, settings, people, objects, and action.

Delaney urges interviewers to pretend to come from another planet. Thus, the interviewer tries to set aside preconceived knowledge or opinions about the events in the dream, and the dreamer works hard to define and describe images as if talking to someone who has never heard of them before. As one example, a person who dreamed of George Bush would be asked, "Who is George, and what is he like?"

For one dreamer, Delaney explains, George might be a trustworthy and solid, if undramatic, man who is uncommonly prepared for his job. His appearance in a dream may call the dreamer's attention to someone in her waking life with similar qualities she otherwise may not have appreciated. Another dreamer might describe George as one of the "old boys" who has utterly failed to understand or improve the lot of women in this country. This dreamer might say these traits epitomize her father, her husband, or her boss.

To wrap up the approximately two-and-a-half-hour session following Delaney's method, the dreamer or another member of the group takes a few minutes to summarize the interview. The group then concludes by eliciting the dreamer's reaction to their work together.

As you work to decode your dreams and apply their lessons, you will gain in both skill and confidence. You will find that your grasp of a dream's meaning comes more quickly once you become familiar with the opposing principles you used to build them—your dream dimensions. Because all of us have our blind spots, you may benefit from working on your dreams with another person, a spouse or friend, or with a group of other dreamworkers. Indeed, sharing a dream may be, by itself, enough to trigger new insight. If you are willing to share a dream, you also may be more open to new ideas about it. For a list of dream-sharing groups in your community, write: The Association for the Study of Dreams, Box 1600, Vienna, Virginia 22180.

WHEN YOU NEED OUTSIDE HELP

Group dreamwork, it is important to recognize, is not the same as group psychotherapy. Although dreamwork in the company of others may well be therapeutic—that is, healing— for both the dreamer and other group members, the focus of such work is on understanding the dream, not on helping the dreamer to overcome interpersonal problems. Participating in a dream group is no substitute for psychotherapy when that is indicated.

How far anyone wants to go in pursuit of dream health is a matter of choice, much like choices made about waking health. We can improve our diet on our own and create our own exercise program, or we can see a diet counselor, join a fitness center, and get other professional help. We usually can treat a sprained ankle at home; however, if we suspect a broken bone, we need to see a physician.

The recognition that we have the emotional equivalent of a broken bone often dawns gradually. Many seemingly sudden crises represent years of accumulated griefs. While the crisis builds, we may not stop to reflect on how dreams continue to sabotage our efforts to move on. Once the crisis strikes, we may be too preoccupied to explore how we can use our dreams to help make things better. That's where making it a habit to keep both a dream diary and a waking journal pays off. You'll have early warning signs of an urgent need for dream repair. Some important clues:

◆ Repeating the same bad dream over and over, particularly a dream in which you are powerless, a victim.
◆ Dreaming frequently of the past, particularly of early childhood.
◆ Moaning out loud or waking during the night feeling scared, anxious, angry, or despairing.
◆ Feeling exhausted in the morning, worn out from too much dreaming.
◆ Injuring yourself or others during sleep.
◆ Being stuck on the negative side of your habitual dream dimensions.

If you decide to seek professional help, ask your primary care physician or a friend for a referral. Your local hospital, mental health association, medical society, and associations of mental health professionals also have referral services. When you call a prospective therapist for an appointment or at your first visit, ask about his or her interest in using dreams. The therapist's answer may help influence your feelings about whether this is a person with whom you feel comfortable, someone with whom you want to work.

You or your therapist may feel you could benefit from collecting a whole night's dreams in a sleep laboratory at a local hospital. Before scheduling an appointment, call the laboratory to see if a technician can be assigned to wake you during REM periods, prompt you for dream recall, and tape record your answers. Also, ask if the laboratory will supply you with a transcript of the recordings. Because the procedure involved in recording REM sleep is less complex than that needed to evaluate a clinical sleep disorder, the cost should be less than half of that for a typical night in a sleep laboratory, which may run as high as $1000. Your health insurance may cover your night in the laboratory for dream collection, but it would be wise to check first. Also, be aware that only a small number of sleep laboratories currently offer this service; however, it should become more widely available as patient and therapist demand for it increases. Soon, too, home dream recording equipment will be available for you to use at your bedside.

THE FUTURE OF DREAMWORK

Recovery from crisis takes time. We may replay memories of guilt, anger, inadequacy, and rejection for years afterward. Those with good friends, good genes, a good self-image, and good dreams at the outset, and who form new supportive relationships come through best. Those with basic problems in their underlying self-image must revise the ways they see themselves. The task is difficult, but we can speed the recovery process by learning to heed the inner voices of our dreams and then to direct them to speak in stronger, more confident tones.

I hope that the description of many different types of crises and the ways in which they give rise to dreams has helped you reach a better understanding of both your own dreams and those that others may share with you. You now have some new tools for further self-exploration and study.

Perhaps you will try the RISC method to recognize, identify, stop, and change any dream that troubles you.

My work in crisis dreaming strengthens my belief that dreams offer far more than nighttime entertainment. Rather, they tell us about aspects of our daily lives that we unwittingly may overlook or even choose not to think about when awake, particularly in times of crisis. We can learn from our dreams when things are not right in our bodies, our minds, or our relationships with other people before we are likely to recognize these facts when awake.

Thus, dreams may be at the core of our ability to assimilate major changes in our lives, good and bad, successes and failures. At such times, dreams review the experiences that give rise to strong feelings and match them to related images from the past. They enable us to revise our pictures of our present selves and to rehearse our responses to future challenges. In times of trouble, when we suffer a loss of self-esteem or have our belief in our competence knocked out from under us, dreams help repair our damaged sense of self. Through our dreams, we review, revise, rehearse, and repair. We don't study these four R's in school. However, understanding what our dreams have to tell us may be the most important lesson we will ever learn.

Notes

CHAPTER 1. How Dreams Work

(p. 2) Breger, Louis, Hunter, Ian, and Lane, Ron. The effect of stress on dreams. *Psychological Issues, Monograph 27.* New York: International University Press, 1971;7(3).

(p. 3) Terr, Lenore. *Too Scared To Cry.* New York: Harper & Row, 1990.

(p. 10) Hobson, J. Allan, and McCarley, Robert. The brain as a dream state generator: An activation-synthesis hypothesis of the dream process. *American Journal of Psychiatry,* 1977; 134:1335–1348.

(p. 10) Hobson, Allan. *The Dreaming Brain.* New York: Basic Books, 1989.

(p. 11) Crick, Francis, and Mitchison, Graeme. The function of dream sleep. *Nature,* 1983;304:111–114.

CHAPTER 2. How Our Dreams Can Work for Us

(p. 17) Kramer, Milton, et al. The mood-regulating function of sleep. In *Sleep,* W.P. Koella and P. Levin, eds. Basel: S. Karger AG, 1973, pp. 563–571.

CHAPTER 3. A New Dream Therapy

(p. 36) Webb, Wilse B. A historical perspective of dreams. In *Handbook of Dreams: Research, Theories and Applications,* Benjamin B. Wolman, ed. New York: Van Nostrand Reinhold, 1979, pp. 13–19.

(p. 36) Freud, Sigmund. *The Interpretation of Dreams*. (First published, 1900.) New York: Avon Books, 1965.

(p. 38) McGinn, Paul R. The mind's eye: The art of Sigmund Freud. *Medicine on the Midway*, 1990;Summer:9–12.

(p. 41) Erikson, Erik. The dream specimen of psychoanalysis. *Psychoanalytic Psychiatry and Psychology*. R. Knight and C. Friedman, eds. New York: International Universities Press, 1954, pp. 131–170.

(p. 42) Levi-Strauss, Claude. *The Naked Man*. London: Jonathan Cope, 1981.

(p. 47) Kelly, George. *The Psychology of Personal Constructs*. New York: W. W. Norton & Co., 1955.

CHAPTER 4. Chasing Dreams

(p. 52) Aserinsky, E., and Kleitman, N. Regularly occurring periods of eye motility, and concomitant phenomena during sleep. *Science*, 1953;118:273–274.

(p. 52) Dement, William C. *The Sleepwatchers*. Stanford, CA: Stanford Alumni Association, 1992.

(p. 53) Dement, William, and Kleitman, Nathaniel. The relation of eye movements during sleep to dream activity: An objective method for the study of dreaming. *Journal of Experimental Psychology*, 1957;43:339–346.

(p. 53) Dement, William. *Some Must Watch While Some Must Sleep*. Stanford, CA: Stanford Alumni Association, 1972.

(p. 53) Cartwright, Rosalind. Dreams and their meaning. In *Principles and Practice of Sleep Medicine*. Meir H. Kryger, Thomas Roth, and William Dement, eds. Philadelphia: W. B. Saunders Co., 1989, pp. 173–183.

(p. 54) Snyder, Frederick. The phenomenology of dreaming. In *The Psychodynamic Implications of the Physiological Studies on Dreams*. L. Madow and L. Snow, eds. Springfield, IL: Charles C. Thomas, 1970, pp. 124–151.

(p. 58) Cartwright, Rosalind, and Kaszniak, Alfred. The social psychology of dream reporting. In *The Mind in Sleep*. Steven J. Ellman and John S. Antrobus, eds. New York: John Wiley & Sons, 1991, pp. 251–264.

(p. 58) Kramer, Milton. Liars dream but dreams don't lie. In *Sleep and Cognition.* Eds. Richard Bootzin, John Kihlstrom, and Daniel Schacter. Arlington: American Psychological Association, 1990.

(p. 60) Greenberg, Ramon, and Pearlman, Chester. The private language of the dream. In *The Dream in Clinical Practice.* J. Natterson, ed. New York: Jason Aronson, 1980, pp. 85–96.

(p. 63) Waldenberg, Patrick. *Surrealism.* New York: Oxford University Press, 1965, p. 70.

(p. 71) Bonime, Walter, with Bonime, Florence. *The Clinical Use of Dreams.* New York: Basic Books, 1962. (New York: Da Capo Press, 1982).

CHAPTER 5. Common Dreams and Normal Nightmares

(p. 72) Cartwright, Rosalind. The nature and function of repetitive dreams: A survey and speculation. *Psychiatry,* 1979; 42:131–137.

(p. 73) Bonime, Walter, with Bonime, Florence. *The Clinical Use of Dreams.* New York: Basic Books, 1962. (New York: Da Capo Press, 1982.)

(p. 74) Ullman, Montague, and Zimmerman, Nan. *Working with Dreams.* New York: Delacorte Press, 1979.

(p. 75) Adler, Alfred. *The Individual Psychology of Alfred Adler.* Heinz L. Ansbacher and Rowena R. Ansbacher, eds. New York: Basic Books, 1956.

(p. 75) Myers, Wayne. An athletic example of the typical examination dream. *Psychoanalytic Quarterly,* 1983,42:594–598.

(p. 75) Denzin, Norman. Alcoholic dreams. *Alcoholism Treatment Quarterly,* 1988;5(1–2):133–139.

(p. 77) Auden, W. H. Thanksgiving for a habitat. In *A Certain World: A Commonplace Book.* London: Faber & Faber, Ltd., 1970.

(p. 81) Hall, Calvin, and Van de Castle, Robert. *The Content Analysis of Dreams.* New York: Appleton-Century-Crofts, 1966.

(p. 82) Hall, Calvin, et al. The dreams of college men and women in 1950 and 1980: A comparison of dream contents and sex differences. *Sleep,* 1982, 5(2):188–194

(p. 82) Kramer, Milton. A city dreams: A survey approach to normative dream content. *American Journal of Psychiatry,* 1971; 127:1350–1356.

(p. 83) McGinley, Lauri. A flight attendant, DC-10 crash survivor, struggles to come back. *Wall Street Journal,* January 18, 1990, p. 1 A.

(p. 83) Rynearson, Edward. Psychological adjustment to unnatural dying. In *Biopsychosocial Aspects of Bereavement.* S. Zisook, ed. Washington, DC: American Psychiatric Press, 1987, pp. 77–93.

(p. 85) Wood, James, and Bootzin, Richard. The prevalence of nightmares and their independence from anxiety. *Journal of Abnormal Psychology,* 1990;99(1):64–68.

(p. 85) Hartmann, Ernest. *The Nightmare,* New York: Basic Books, 1984.

(p. 87) Gerne, Margarete. Problem-solving in dreams: References to the process of mourning. *Association for the Study of Dreams Newsletter,* 1989;6(2):3–4.

(p. 88) National Academy of Sciences. *Bereavement: Reactions, consequences and care.* Washington, DC: National Academy of Sciences, 1984.

(p. 89) Rynearson, Edward. Bereavement after homicide: A descriptive study. *American Journal of Psychiatry,* 1984; 141:1452–1454.

(p. 90) Shneidman, ES., quoted in Ness, David, and Pfeffer, Cynthia. Sequelae of bereavement resulting from suicide. *American Journal of Psychiatry,* 1990;147:279–285.

(p. 91) Ness, David, and Pfeffer, Cynthia. Sequelae of bereavement resulting from suicide. *American Journal of Psychiatry,* 1990:147:279–285.

(p. 91) Kilpatrick, James. A most imperfect rule. *Washington Post,* January 10, 1985.

(p. 91) Ochberg, Frank. Post-traumatic therapy and victims of violence. In *Post-traumatic Therapy and Victims of Violence.* Frank Ochberg, ed. New York: Brunner/Mazel, Inc., 1988, pp. 3–19.

(p. 93) Alverez, Rafael. On the East Coast, trouble getting word. *Baltimore Sun,* October 19, 1989, p. 12A.

CHAPTER 6. From Everyday Dreams to Crisis Dreams

(p. 96) Shukla, G.D. et al. Phantom limb: A phenomenological study. *British Journal of Psychiatry,* 1982;141:54–58.

(p. 96) Comarr, Estin, et al. Sleep dreams of sex among traumatic paraplegics and quadriplegics. *Sexuality and Disability*, 1983 Spring, 6(1):25–29.

(p. 97) Kerr, Nancy, et al. The structure of laboratory dream reports in blind and sighted subjects. *Journal of Nervous and Mental Disease*, 1982;170:286–293.

(p. 109) Cartwright, Rosalind, et al. Focusing on dreams: A preparation program for psychotherapy. *Archives of General Psychiatry*, 1980;37:275–277.

(p. 110) Fried, Risto, et al. The dream laboratory as a potentially helpful intervention in problematic psychotherapies. *Psychologica*, 1985;2:83–86.

CHAPTER 7. Facing the Crisis of Divorce

(p. 114) National Center for Health Statistics. Advance report of final divorce statistics, 1987. *Monthly Vital Statistics Report.* Hyattsville, MD: United States Public Health Service, 1990;38(12), Supplement 2.

(p. 115) Wallerstein, Judith S., and Blakeslee, Sandra. *Second Chances: Men, women & children a decade after divorce, who wins, who loses—and why.* New York: Ticknor & Fields, 1989.

CHAPTER 8. When a Crisis Leads to Depression

(p. 138) Kupfer, David. REM latency: A psychobiologic marker for primary depressive disease. *Biological Psychiatry*, 1976;11:159–174.

(pp. 139, 281) American Psychiatric Association. *Diagnostic and Statistical Manual of Mental Disorders*, Third Edition, Revised. Washington, DC: American Psychiatric Association, 1987, p. 224.

(p. 139) Cartwright, Rosalind. Dreams that work: The relation of dream incorporation to adaptation to stressful events. *Dreaming*, 1991;1(1):3–9.

(p. 141) Beck, Aron, and Ward, Clyde. Dreams of depressed patients: Characteristic themes in manifest content. *Archives of General Psychiatry*, 1961; 5:462-467.

(p. 141) Hauri, Peter. Dreams in patients remitted from reactive depression. *Journal of Abnormal Psychology*, 1976;85:1–10.

(p. 155) Cartwright, Rosalind, et al. REM latency and recovery from depression: getting over divorce. *American Journal of Psychiatry*, 1991;148:1530–1535.

CHAPTER 9. Crises of Health

(p. 157) Van de Castle, Robert. Interview with Lynne Lamberg, June, 1985.

(p. 157) Zayas, Luis. Thematic features in the manifest dreams of expectant fathers. *Clinical Social Work Journal*, 1988; 16(3):282–296.

(p. 158) Siegel, Alan. *Dreams That Can Change Your Life*. Los Angeles: Jeremy P. Tarcher, Inc., 1991.

(p. 158) Stukane, Ellen. *The Dream Worlds of Pregnancy*. New York: Quill, 1985.

(p. 160) Winget, Carolyn, and Kapp, Frederic. The relationship of the manifest content of dreams to duration of childbirth in primiparae. *Psychosomatic Medicine*, 1972:34:313–20.

(p. 161) Jung, Carl. *Collected Works*. London: Routledge and Kegan Paul, 1960.

(p. 162) Haskell, Robert. Dreaming, cognition and physical illness. Parts I and II. *Journal of Medical Humanities and Bioethics*, 1985;6:46–56 and 109–122.

(p. 162) Hilgard, E.R. *Divided consciousness: Multiple controls in human thought and action*. New York: Wiley Interscience, 1977.

(p. 162) Siegel, Bernie. *Peace, Love & Healing*. New York: Harper & Row, 1989.

(p. 163) Siegel, Bernie. *Love, Medicine & Miracles*. New York: Harper & Row, 1986.

(p. 163) Sabini, Meredith. Dreams as an aid in determining diagnosis, prognosis, and attitude towards treatment. *Psychotherapy and Psychosomatics*, 1981;36:24–36.

(p. 164) Gordon, Jennifer, and Shontz, Franklin. Living with the AIDS virus: A representative case. *Journal of Counseling & Development*, 1990;68:287–292.

(p. 164) Renshaw, Domeena. Sexual Anorexia Nervosa? *Sexual Medicine Today*, 1982;November:27–28.

(p. 164) Smith, Robert. Evaluating dream function: Emphasizing the study of patients with organic disease. Special issue: Cognition and dream research, *Journal of Mind and Behavior*, 1986; Spring–Summer, 7(2–3):397–410.

(p. 164) Smith, Robert. Do dreams reflect a biological state? *Journal of Nervous and Mental Disease*, 1987;175(4):201–207.

(p. 165) Levitan, Harold. Stressful dreams may cause asthmatic attacks. Presentation at American Psychiatric Association annual meeting, June, 1982.

(p. 166) Meany, John, et al. Psychological treatment of an asthmatic patient in crisis. *Journal of Asthma*, 1988; 25:141–151.

(p. 167) Breger, Louis; Hunter, Ian, and Lane, Ron. The effect of stress on dreams. *Psychological Issues, Monograph 27*. New York: International University Press, 1971;7(3):1–214.

(p. 175) Von Franz, Marie-Louise. Archetypes surrounding death. *In Dreams Are Wiser than Men*. Richard Russo, ed. Berkeley: North Atlantic Books, 1987.

(p. 176) Grotjahn, Martin. Being sick and facing eighty: Observations of an aging therapist. In *The Race Against Time: Psychotherapy and psychoanalysis in the second half of life*. Robert Nemiroff and Calvin Colarusso, eds. New York: Plenum Press, 1985, pp. 293–302.

(p. 176) Greenberg, Harvey, and Blank, Robert. Dreams of a dying patient. *British Journal of Medical Psychology*, 1970;43:355–362.

CHAPTER 10. Rape and Incest: From Victim to Survivor

(p. 184) Nadelson, Carol, et al. A follow-up study of rape victims. *American Journal of Psychiatry*, 1982;139:1266–1270.

(p. 186) Diamond, Doris. Interview with Lynne Lamberg, September, 1989.

(p. 188) Blume, E. Sue. *Secret Survivors: Uncovering incest and its aftereffects in women*. New York: John Wiley and Sons, 1990.

(p. 188) Herman, Judith. *Father-Daughter Incest*. Cambridge: Harvard University Press, 1981.

(p. 189) Herman, Judith. Father-daughter incest. In *Post-traumatic Therapy and Victims of Violence*. Frank Ochberg, ed. New York: Brunner/Mazel, Inc., 1988, pp. 175–195.

(p. 190) Calof, David. Interview with Lynne Lamberg, April, 1991.

CHAPTER 11. Healing Post-Traumatic Stress Disorder

(pp. 196, 282) American Psychiatric Association. *Diagnostic and Statistical Manual of Mental Disorders,* Third Edition, Revised. Washington, DC: American Psychiatric Association, 1987, pp. 250–251.

(p. 196) Breslau, Naomi, et al. Traumatic events and posttraumatic stress disorder in an urban population of young adults. *Archives of General Psychiatry,* 1991;48:216–222.

(p. 197) Langone, John. The war that has no ending. *Discover,* 1985;June:44–55.

(p. 197) Helzer, John. Methodological issues in the interpretation of the consequences of extreme situations. In *Stressful life events and their contexts.* Barbara Dohrenwend and Bruce Dohrenwend, eds. New York: Prodist, 1981, pp. 108–129.

(p. 199) Kramer, Milton, et al. Nightmares in Vietnam veterans. *Journal of the American Academy of Psychoanalysis,* 1987;15(1):67–81.

(p. 202) Wilmer, Harry. Combat nightmares: Toward a therapy of violence. In *Archetypal Psychology and Jungian Thought.* Dallas: Spring Publications, 1986, pp. 120–137.

(p. 203) Brockway, Stephen. Group treatment of combat nightmares in post-traumatic stress disorder. *Journal of Contemporary Psychotherapy,* 1987;17(4):270–284.

(p. 207) Fulmer, Thomas I. Nightmares and the blue-eyed boys. *Journal of the American Medical Association,* 1984;251:897.

(p. 208) Van Dyke, Craig, et al. Post-Traumatic Stress Disorder: A thirty-year delay in a World War II veteran. *American Journal of Psychiatry,* 1985, 142:1070–1073.

(p. 210) Levi, Primo. *Survival in Auschwitz.* New York: Macmillan, 1988.

(p. 210) Lavie, Peretz, and Kaminer, Hanna. Dreams that poison sleep: Dreaming in Holocaust survivors. *Dreaming,* 1991; 1:11–21.

CHAPTER 12. Little Kids, Big Problems

(p. 216) Terr, Lenore. Chowchilla Revisited: The effects of psychic trauma four years after a school-bus kidnapping. *American Journal of Psychiatry,* 1983;140:1543–1550.

(p. 218) Dement, William. *Some Must Watch While Some Must Sleep.* Stanford: Stanford Alumni Association, 1972, p. 53. (New York: W.W. Norton, 1978).

(p. 219) Foulkes, David, et al. REM dreaming and cognitive skills at ages 5–8: A cross-sectional study. *International Journal of Behavioral Development,* 1990;13(4):447–465.

(p. 222) Terr, Lenore. Nightmares in children. In *Sleep and Its Disorders in Children.* Christian Guilleminault, ed. New York: Raven Press, 1987, pp. 231–242.

(p. 223) Terr, Lenore. *Too Scared To Cry.* New York: Harper & Row, 1990.

(p. 224) Bilu, Yoam. The other as a nightmare: The Israeli-Arab encounter as reflected in children's dreams in Israel and the West Bank. *Political Psychology,* 1989 10(3):365–389.

(p. 225) Garfield, Patricia. Nightmares in the sexually abused female teenager. Association for the Study of Dreams: International Dream Conference III, Ottawa, Canada, 1986.

(p. 237) Sendak, Maurice. *Where the Wild Things Are.* New York: Harper & Row, 1963.

(p. 237) Sendak, Maurice. *In the Night Kitchen.* New York: Harper & Row, 1970.

(p. 238) Wiseman, Anne. *Nightmare Help.* Berkeley, CA: Ten Speed Press, 1986.

CHAPTER 13. When Dreams Don't Work the Way They Should

(p. 241) Callwood, June. *The Sleepwalker: The trial that made Canadian legal history.* Toronto: Lester & Orpen Dennys Limited, 1990.

(p. 241) Howard, Christopher, and D'Orban, P. T. Violence in sleep: Medico-legal issues and two case reports. *Psychological Medicine,* 1987;17:915–925.

(p. 242) Kavey, Neil. Somnambulistic bulimia. *Sleep Research,* 1988;17:268.

(p. 242) Broughton, Roger. Sleep disorders: Disorders of arousal? *Science,* 1968,159:1070–1078.

(p. 255) Mahowald, Mark, and Schenck, Carlos. REM Sleep Behavior Disorder. In *Principles and Practice of Sleep Medicine.* Meir H. Kryger, Thomas Roth, and William Dement, eds.

Philadelphia: W.B. Saunders, 1989, pp. 289–301.

(p. 255) Mahowald, Mark, et al. Sleep violence—forensic science implications: Polygraphic and video documentation. *Journal of Forensic Sciences*, 1990;35(2):413–432.

(p. 256) Kelley, Jack, and Green, Michelle. A vision of murder. *People Weekly*, May 15, 1987;27:30+

CHAPTER 14. **Expanding Your Dream Appreciation**

(p. 261) Ullman, Montague, and Zimmerman, Nan. *Working with Dreams*. New York: Delacorte Press, 1979.

(p. 265) Delaney, Gayle. *Breakthrough Dreaming: How to tap the power of your 24-hour mind*. New York: Bantam Books, 1991.

Appendix

DEPRESSION SYMPTOM CHECKLIST

Below are the criteria health professionals use to diagnose major depression. The diagnosis requires that a person has at least five of these symptoms for at least two weeks and that the symptoms interfere with daily living.

1. Loss of interest or pleasure in all or almost all activities.
2. Lack of response to people or things that used to bring pleasure.
3. A prevailing mood of sadness that is regularly worse in the morning.
4. Insomnia; waking up at least two hours before usual time of awakening, or sleeping excessively nearly every day.
5. Energy loss; slowed down activity, or agitation.
6. Loss of appetite and/or rapid weight loss when not dieting.
7. Previous episodes of depression that were followed by complete or nearly complete recovery.
8. Feelings of excessive or inappropriate guilt and pessimism.
9. Diminished ability to think or concentrate, or indecisiveness.
10. Recurrent thoughts of death; suicidal thoughts.

(Adapted from the *Diagnostic and Statistical Manual of Mental Disorders*, Third Edition, Revised. Washington, DC: American Psychiatric Association, 1987.)

POST-TRAUMATIC STRESS
DISORDER SYMPTOM CHECKLIST

Health professionals use the criteria below to diagnose PTSD:

A. *Having a stressful experience that would cause distress in almost everyone*

B. *Re-experiencing that event in at least one of the following ways:*

1. Recurrent, intrusive memories of the event
2. Recurrent, distressing dreams of the event
3. Sudden acting or feeling as if the event were happening again
4. Intense distress at exposure to events that recall the experience, such as anniversaries

C. *Numbing of general responsiveness in ways that include:*

1. Efforts to avoid thoughts or feelings associated with the event
2. Efforts to avoid activities or situations that arouse recollections of the event
3. Inability to recall an important aspect of the event
4. Lowered interest in significant activities
5. Feelings of detachment or estrangement from others
6. Restricted range of feelings
7. Sense of a foreshortened future

D. *Persistent symptoms of increased arousal that include at least two of the following:*

1. Difficulty falling or staying asleep
2. Irritability or outbursts of anger
3. Difficulty concentrating
4. Hypervigilance
5. Exaggerated startle response to noise or touch
6. Physical symptoms, such as sweating, on exposure to events that recall the experience

E. *Persistence of the symptoms in B, C, and D of at least one month.*

(Adapted from the *Diagnostic and Statistical Manual of Mental Disorders*, Third Edition, Revised. Washington, DC: American Psychiatric Association, 1987.)

Index